DETAILED CONTENTS

KU-015-167

Applications of
Case Study
Research

EDITION

To Karen, With My Enduring Love

Applications of
Case Study
Research

EDITION

Robert K. Yin

Los Angeles | London | New Delhi
Singapore | Washington DC

Los Angeles | London | New Delhi
Singapore | Washington DC

FOR INFORMATION:

SAGE Publications, Inc.
2455 Teller Road
Thousand Oaks, California 91320
E-mail: order@sagepub.com

SAGE Publications Ltd.
1 Oliver's Yard
55 City Road
London EC1Y 1SP
United Kingdom

SAGE Publications India Pvt. Ltd.
B 1/I 1 Mohan Cooperative Industrial Area
Mathura Road, New Delhi 110 044
India

SAGE Publications Asia-Pacific Pte. Ltd.
33 Pekin Street #02-01
Far East Square
Singapore 048763

Acquisitions Editor: Vicki Knight
Associate Editor: Lauren Habib
Editorial Assistant: Kalie Koscielak
Production Editor: Astrid Virding
Copy Editor: Megan Speer
Typesetter: C&M Digitals (P) Ltd.
Proofreader: Ellen Brink
Indexer: Molly Hall
Cover Designer: Candice Harman
Marketing Manager: Helen Salmon
Permissions Editor: Adele Hutchinson

Copyright © 2012 by SAGE Publications, Inc.

Printed in the United States of America

Library of Congress Cataloging-in-Publication Data

Yin, Robert K.
Applications of case study research/Robert K. Yin.—3rd ed.
p. cm.
Includes bibliographical references and index
ISBN 978-1-4129-8916-9 (pbk.)

1. Social sciences—Methodology.
2. Case method. I. Title.

H61.Y56 2012
300.72'2—dc22   2011005041

This book is printed on acid-free paper.

11 12 13 14 15 10 9 8 7 6 5 4 3 2 1

BRIEF CONTENTS

LIST OF TABLES, FIGURES, AND EXHIBITS

Tables

Figures

Exhibits

LIST OF BOXES

PREFACE

Case study research continues to be an essential form of social science inquiry. The method should be one of several that a social scientist or team of social scientists would consider using. Other methods include surveys, experiments, quasi-experiments, quantitative modeling to analyze archival data, histories, and qualitative research (e.g., ethnography). Depending on the situation, case study research may be conducted alone or in combination with these other research methods. All have complementary strengths and weaknesses. However, none of the uses of case study *research* pertains to using case studies as a *teaching tool*, which is not the subject of this book.

WIDESPREAD USE OF CASE STUDY RESEARCH BUT LITTLE METHODOLOGICAL GUIDANCE

Case study research has covered a broad variety of subjects, such as community studies, education, public health, businesses and industry, public policy and public administration, and social and societal problems and controversies. In addition, case study research has a long and important role in clinical and biographical research, including research on infants, children, youths, and families.

Within evaluation research, case studies of specific programs, projects, and initiatives also have been conducted with some frequency. In these evaluative situations, the case studies commonly have been used to document and analyze implementation processes. Case studies, therefore, traditionally have been associated with *process* evaluations. However, as demonstrated by some of the applications in this book, the method also has been and can be used to document and analyze the *outcomes* of interventions. The cases may cover programs sponsored by federal agencies or initiatives supported by private foundations.

Despite its widespread use, case study research has received perhaps the least attention and guidance among nearly all social science research methods. The methodological literature covers the topic in little depth. Methods courses in universities tend to embed case study research within another topic—qualitative research—which in fact may be considered a different method (e.g., Yin, 2011b). Similarly, although research case studies do appear with (surprising) frequency in the mainstream journals of the various academic disciplines and professions, no cross-disciplinary or cross-profession journal focuses exclusively or even heavily on case study research methods.

Moreover, the most common textbooks on social science methods in general, and on evaluation research methods in particular, still give only secondary attention to the case study method. You should beware that when such discussions are too brief, they also may be misleading—typically confusing case study research with the less desirable quasi-experimental designs. Suffice it to say that, distinct from any quasi-experimental design, case study research has its own method and rationale (e.g., Cook & Campbell, 1979, p. 96; Yin, 2011a).

PURPOSE AND SCOPE OF THIS BOOK

This book, *Applications of Case Study Research*, tries to fill a little of the void. This single volume offers a variety of practical and contemporary applications of case study research and evaluation. For guidance purposes, the book points to methodological issues or features while presenting individual applications as concrete examples.

The book contains 21 applications, with 18 of them (all but the applications in Chapters 7 and 10) coming from studies that I have designed or conducted. By having access to all the applications, experienced investigators and students alike may be better able to emulate case study research techniques and principles in their own research. Most of the applications appear as separate chapters, but Chapter 3 has five applications, Chapter 8 has three, and Chapter 10 has two.

A companion textbook, *Case Study Research: Design and Methods*—now in its fourth edition (Yin, 2009a), with its first edition appearing in 1984—fully discusses the principles and procedures integral to the case study method, citing a large number of well-known if not famous case studies that are available in journals and books. However, the companion text does not contain full applications or actual case studies as does this book on *Applications of Case Study Research.*

At the same time, the inherent nature of applications or illustrative examples is that they are specific. As a result, any given reader is likely to have differing interests in any given application. Some applications will be directly relevant to a research project at hand or being contemplated, but other applications may seem to be part of some alien world with an unfriendly technical vocabulary.

Given this circumstance, two strategies were used in designing this book to make it as attractive and useful to as broad a research audience as possible. First, the book contains applications on a diverse array of topics, in the hope that every reader will find at least one application directly relevant to her or his ongoing case study research interests. Second, the applications have been organized to cover different methodological issues that can suggest solutions to problems commonly encountered when doing case studies. Let's talk about the diversity first.

DIVERSITY OF APPLICATIONS IN THIS BOOK

First and foremost, the applications cover life in local communities and their public services. Such subjects have been a frequent topic of field-based research (e.g., Marwell, 2004; Small, 2006; Walker & McCarthy, 2010). Reflecting these topics, the applications in this book cover community organizing (Chapters 5 and 6), fire protection services and local law enforcement (Chapters 2 and 14), and the peculiar problem of understanding how local service innovations become routinized or sustained over long periods of time (one of the five applications in Chapter 3).

Second, the applications cover particular sectors, such as education and public health. In education, the applications range from K–12 settings (Chapter 4 and one of the five applications in Chapter 3) to university settings (Chapters 7 and 11). In public health, the applications have mainly been devoted to prevention services, whether dealing with substance-abuse prevention (Chapter 13 and the three applications in Chapter 8) or HIV/AIDS prevention (Chapter 15).

Third, several applications address the workings of business firms as well as economic development issues more generally. The applications are directed at small businesses (Chapters 9 and 12), local economic development partnerships, and high-tech firms and their research parks (two of the five applications in Chapter 3). The effects of a military base closure on a local economy, as well as the demise of an extremely large firm, also are the subjects of separate applications (the two applications in Chapter 10). In addition, there is an application (one of the five applications in Chapter 3) on a common but poorly understood commercialization process—how sound research-based ideas (in this case, innovative ideas produced by natural hazards research) are eventually put into commercial practice (in this case, to protect communities from disasters).

The book gives less emphasis to another common brand of case studies: research on individual persons. This type of case study research is represented by the clinical literature (e.g., clinical psychology, psychiatry, and social work), by biographies and oral histories of famous people, by related fields such as criminology and its case studies of archetypal criminal offenders, and by studies that have called attention to "everyday" persons—such as school principals and single-parent heads of households—who have nonetheless done remarkable things with their lives. Only Chapter 4 of this book approaches a case study of an individual. Instead, the dominant genre of cases represented in this book involves institutions or organizations, because the greater challenge over the years seems to have been in using case study research and evaluation to investigate these more multifaceted phenomena.

METHODOLOGICAL TOPICS

Aside from the diversity of applications, the book uses a second strategy to make it useful: The selected applications deliberately cover important and different methodological situations encountered in doing case study research. You will find these situations covered in three ways: the organization of the book into five parts, a series of 26 Boxes, and a series of 12 Inside Stories.

The Book's Five Parts

First, the book has 15 chapters organized into five parts. Each part covers a major methodological situation for doing case study research:

- *Part I:* Starting points (Chapters 1–3): a brief introduction to the case study method, a sample of field notes, and the role of theory in doing case studies (illustrating the use of theory in exploratory, explanatory, and descriptive case studies)
- *Part II:* Descriptive case studies (Chapters 4–6)
- *Part III:* Explanatory case studies (Chapters 7–10)
- *Part IV:* Cross-case syntheses (Chapters 11 and 12)
- *Part V:* Case study evaluations (Chapters 13–15)

The five parts are intended to direct your attention to the commonly occurring situations relevant for doing case study research.

Of these five parts, Part I contains a refresher to the entire case study method (Chapter 1) and also a snatch of the field-based notes that might come from an initial fieldwork experience (Chapter 2). Part I's final chapter (Chapter 3) describes the role of theory in doing case studies—which may be your single most important aid in doing case study research. Theory is not only helpful in designing a case study but also can become the vehicle for generalizing a case study's results. This critical role of theory has been integral to the development of sound case studies, whether consisting of a single case or multiple cases. As a result, Chapter 3 has five applications showing how to integrate theoretical concerns in five different situations. If you derive no other benefit from this book, an understanding of the use of theory and an appreciation for the five applications in Chapter 3 can go a long way in helping you design implementable, useful, and generalizable case studies.

The remaining four parts all deal with different case study situations. If your aim is to do a case study to portray what happened in a particular case, you are likely to be aiming for a *descriptive* case study (Part II). If you want to address *how* and *why* events might have happened as they did—including a consideration of alternative "hows" and "whys" (*rival explanations*)—the relevant type is likely to be an *explanatory* case study (Part III). Alternatively, you might have been able to examine multiple cases as part of the same case study, leading to your needing to know how to conduct *cross-case syntheses* (Part IV). Finally, you might be using the case study method to *evaluate* some kind of initiative (Part V).

In addition to the methodological support derived from the five parts, the book engages in two other ways of covering the methodological issues as mentioned earlier, represented by a series of Boxes and a series of Inside Stories. These two series are discussed below, but as a preview, Exhibit 1 arrays all the Boxes and Inside Stories according to their methodological topics, ranging from designing case studies to presenting case study reports. Each item in the exhibit then has a cross-reference to the chapter in which the item can be found.

Exhibit 1   Boxes and Inside Stories, Arrayed by Methods Topics

Methods Topic	Title of Box	Box No.	Chap.	Title of Inside Story	Chap.
Using the case study method:					
• Research questions				Posing Initial Research Questions	2
• Case study situations	Qualitative and Quantitative Research	23	13	Studying Innovations	14
	Guidelines for Case Study Evaluations	21	13		
	Exploratory Case Studies	3	3		
Designing case studies:					
• Unit of analysis	The "Case" as the Unit of Analysis	25	15		
• Single or multiple cases	Importance of Multiple-Case Studies	16	11	Implementing Exemplary Case Designs	12
	Exemplary Case Designs	12	9		
• Use of theory	Using Theory in Case Study Research	2	3		
	Theories for Descriptive Case Studies	8	6		
	Generalizing From a Case Study	22	13		
• Replication designs	Replication, Not Sampling, for Multiple-Case Studies	26	15		
	Direct and Theoretical Replications	18	12		
• Mixed methods	Case Studies as Part of a Mixed Methods Study	6	5		

(Continued)

(Continued)

Methods Topic	Title of Box	Box No.	Chap.	Title of Inside Story	Chap.
Collecting case study data:					
• Preparation for collecting data	Common Preparation and Training When Doing a Multiple-Case Study	19	12	Being the Subject of Questions, Not the Questioner	6
	Case Study Protocols: Aimed at the Investigator, Not Interviewees	5	4	Personal Security When Doing Fieldwork	5
	Screening Candidate Cases	4	3		
• Multiple sources of evidence	Multiple Sources of Evidence	24	14		
	Triangulation	11	9		
• Individual sources	Direct Observations in Field Settings	1	2	Media Reports as Evidence	13
	Open-Ended Interviews	7	5	Elite Interviews	4
	Archival Sources of Data	14	10	Self-Reported Data	7
				Collecting Data From Social Networks	15
Analyzing case study data:					
• Case study database	Case Study Databases	9	6		
• Analysis strategies	Logic Models	10	8		
	Explanation Building	15	10		
	Process and Outcome Evaluations	17	11		
	Cross-Case Syntheses	20	12		
	Rival Explanations	13	10		
Presenting case study reports:					
• Communicating				Chronologies	9
				Shortened Case Studies	8
• Pointing onward				Posing Questions for Further Research	11

Boxes Calling Attention to 26 Different Methodological Situations

Each of the 26 Boxes highlights a particular methodological procedure or principle, and each Box appears in a chapter whose application illustrates that procedure or principle. Each Box also concludes with a brief reference to the counterpart text (Yin, 2009a) where you can find a fuller rendition of the relevant procedure or principle.

Readers of previous editions of this book have considered the Boxes to function in an apprenticeship role, helping point to pertinent methodological issues at the same time that an application presents a case study on a particular topic. Though not claiming to be a comprehensive collection, as a group the Boxes cover nearly the entire waterfront of the case study method.

Inside Stories and Classroom Exercises

The third way of presenting methodological issues is represented by a series of Inside Stories, which follow 12 of the 15 chapters (all but Chapters 1, 3, and 10).[1] The Inside Stories are new to this edition of the book, based on feedback from the users of earlier editions.

The Inside Stories raise methodological challenges (and even dilemmas) that the author encountered in actually doing the case study presented in the pertinent chapter—or a case study similar to the one that is presented. These are common challenges that you, too, may face in doing a case study, ranging from fieldwork and interview situations to the use of archival and documentary data to the presentation of case studies (such as their length and the use of chronologies).

Connected to each Inside Story is then a *classroom exercise* that can help you either practice or preview the challenging situation yourself. The exercises also are new to this edition of the book and are intended to provide a preparatory experience before you might have to do an actual case study. The exercises, therefore, give this book an additional practical twist.

NEW MATERIAL IN THIS THIRD EDITION

This third edition expands and strengthens the material in the two previous editions. The enhancements already have been discussed and may be summarized as follows:

- An expanded text that has gone from 10 to 15 chapters, four to five parts, 16 to 21 individual applications, and 21 to 26 Boxes
- A new section of the book (Part V) on *case study evaluations*, including an entirely new chapter on the principles of case study evaluations along with a specific and new application

- Six entirely new chapters, all emphasizing single-case and simpler and more readily understood applications, including a strong introductory chapter that serves as a refresher on the case study method
- A totally new feature, called *Inside Stories*, linked to suggested *classroom exercises*

My own comments about the organization of this book have been moved from the introductory chapter in the earlier editions to the preface in this third edition. In addition, besides adding new applications, all the earlier ones have been re-edited and refined to make the entire collection more coherent.

Of special note, the previous two editions of this book did not contain the refresher to the case study method found in Chapter 1. However, reviewers of the second edition kindly suggested that the book needed to start with a short overview. Even though this book has been deliberately paired with a companion book that has the full rendition of the case study method (Yin, 2009a)—and in spite of the multiple citations to that book throughout this one—the reviewers valued having a brief refresher. They felt that it would add to the convenience of using this book as well as lay a firmer basis for understanding the applications in the subsequent chapters.

The reviewers' suggestion seemed like an excellent idea. Moreover, after the second edition had been written, I had put together three other summaries of the case study method, each aimed at a slightly different audience:

- Education (Yin, 2006—a chapter appearing in the *Handbook of Complementary Methods in Education Research*)
- Applied social science (Yin, 2009b—a chapter in the *SAGE Handbook of Applied Social Research Methods*)
- Psychology (Yin, 2011a—a chapter in the *APA Handbook of Research Methods in Psychology*)

Chapter 1 draws from all three of these previous works but is not limited to any particular academic discipline or professional area. Therefore, the chapter will hopefully help people working in many different fields.

CONCLUDING REMARKS

Overall, this third edition presents a collection of 21 individual applications of the case study method. To increase their communicability and usefulness, most of the applications have been deliberately shortened from their original length, with some having been rewritten expressly for this edition on the basis of some earlier and lengthier case study (the refresher in Chapter 1 also was written expressly for this edition). Following additional feedback from users of earlier editions of this book, the applications include a wide array of single-case studies that are well within the capabilities of solo investigators—compared to the multiple-case studies that can call for multi-investigator teams.

The applications demonstrate how case study research has been successfully conducted while calling attention to key methodological procedures. The objective, whether you are a budding social scientist or a seasoned investigator, is to enable you to strengthen your own case study research. You also might become a better critic and consumer of the case study research done by others. Case study methods need continual strengthening and reinforcement, and you are an integral part of that process.

NOTE

1. The three chapters without Inside Stories are a result of different circumstances: The refresher in Chapter 1 does not have any specific applications, the theory orientation in Chapter 3 has five applications whose challenges are similar to those covered by the applications in other chapters, and the two case studies summarized in Chapter 10 were not originally conducted by the present author.

ACKNOWLEDGMENTS

By way of acknowledgment, the work in this book reflects the stimulation and continued encouragement and support of many key persons. Professor Leonard Bickman and Dr. Debra Rog—who edited the Sage Publications series on **Applied Social Research Methods** in which the first two editions of this book appeared—have been strong supporters from the very beginning and to this day. They deserve thanks for their understanding of the place of case study research in the broader array of social science methods and for their incessant demands for more and better manuscripts on the topic. In addition, federal agencies and their project officers who have sponsored and continue to support a stream of projects using case studies (many cited in the chapters of this book) should be acknowledged and thanked.

Research colleagues also have stimulated the development of new ideas. Earlier, the collegial relationships were related to the teaching of courses at the Massachusetts Institute of Technology (MIT) and the American University (Washington, D.C.) or to summer institutes organized by the Aarhus School of Business (University of Aarhus) in Denmark.

In a complementary manner, many research colleagues from a variety of universities and research organizations have participated in case study workshops as part of the projects undertaken at COSMOS Corporation. Whether posed at these workshops or in related e-mails, the continued questions about how to use case studies to clarify specific research issues or about the particular implications of the method for the research topics being investigated often led serendipitously to new insights about case study research.

Similarly, staff and consultants at COSMOS have struggled with numerous case studies and case study research projects, creating an exciting learning environment that seems to evolve endlessly and reach continually into as yet unexplored vistas, despite the passage of more than three decades. Among COSMOS's staff, Drs. Darnella Davis and Angela Ware have been the most active in recent years, and I thank them both for their stimulating questions and contributions to applied research processes.

The learning environment also has included collaborations outside of COSMOS. Among the most recent has been work with Dr. Sukai Prom-Jackson and her colleagues in doing evaluations of the United Nations Development Programme, Professor Iben Nathan and doctoral students at the University of Copenhagen, and Professor Nanette Levinson and the students and faculty at the American University's School of International Service. I thank you all for continuing to place case study research in such a variety of contemporary settings.

Specifically in preparation of this book's third edition, I am grateful to many people who have offered helpful advice. Most important among them has been Vicki Knight, senior acquisitions editor at Sage, who prompted me to embark on the project, offered many suggestions for making the edition more usable to readers, and provided feedback on early drafts of the work. In a similar vein, many reviewers troubled to give extensive written comments on the book's second edition as a basis for the new edition:

Carolyne V. Ashton, *evaluation and research consultant*

Mette Baran, *Cardinal Stritch University*

Mark Henderson, *Mills College*

Kathryn Herr, *Montclair State University*

Robert Shick, *Rutgers University, Newark, School of Public Affairs and Administration*

Catherine Dunn Shiffman, *Shenandoah University*

Notwithstanding all these suggestions, the content of the third edition remains my responsibility alone.

Finally, the book is dedicated as before to Karen, my spouse, friend, and mother of our son, Andrew. She has continually nurtured great expectations for both of us, and her love has endured the many hours absorbed by the research and writing associated with the ideas in this book.

ABOUT THE AUTHOR

Robert K. Yin is president of COSMOS Corporation, an applied research and social science firm. Over the years, COSMOS has successfully completed hundreds of projects for federal agencies, state and local agencies, and private foundations, and most of this book's applications come from these projects.

Outside of COSMOS, Dr. Yin has assisted numerous other research groups, helping to train their field teams or design research studies. A recent engagement has been with the United Nations Development Programme, and another assignment has been to provide guidance to doctoral students at the University of Copenhagen. Currently, Dr. Yin holds the position of distinguished scholar-in-residence at American University's School of International Service (Washington, DC). Earlier, he served as Visiting Scholar at the U.S. Government Accountability Office's research methodology division and as Visiting Associate Professor at the Department of Urban Studies and Planning, MIT.

Dr. Yin has authored over 100 journal articles and books. His first book on the case study method, *Case Study Research: Design and Methods* (2009a), is in its fourth edition. He has edited two case study anthologies (Yin, 2004, 2005) and has most recently authored a new text on qualitative research methods (Yin, 2011). Dr. Yin received his B.A. in history from Harvard College (magna cum laude) and his Ph.D. in brain and cognitive sciences from MIT.

PART I

STARTING POINTS

Starting a new case study can involve much uncertainty and trepidation. The three chapters in Part I try to alleviate such stress in several ways.

First, Chapter 1 contains a brief refresher on the case study method. The refresher is based on a much longer text (Yin, 2009a) and acts as a starting point by presenting an overview of the method. The refresher also can be useful in another way. It can help you decide whether you want to use the case study method in the first place—or whether you may want to consider some alternative method and return to case study research at some later date.

Second, because case studies typically involve the collection of field-based data, Chapter 2 includes a sample of field notes. The selected notes deliberately come from the start-up phase of a new case study. They demonstrate the level of detail that might be captured from a day in the field (an urban neighborhood) but prior to having fully defined the research questions for the ensuing case study. Such a "fieldwork-first" situation may arise as a starting point in your own research.

Aside from illustrating the starting point, the notes represent the kind of notes you should be prepared to compile when doing your own fieldwork. Over the course of a single case study, the notes will become voluminous. Putting them together routinely, as well as properly filing and storing them, will become an integral part of managing your case study data collection process.

Third, Chapter 3 contains five different case study applications. Each represents starting points that paradoxically can occur throughout the conduct of a case study, not just at its beginning. The first two applications cover potentially important tasks at the actual start-up of a new case study. One application shows how an *exploratory case study* was conducted as a prelude to a full-blown case study. The other application (from a different case study) shows how the cases to be studied were identified as a result of a formal *selection and screening procedure*. Both applications try to show the benefit to be derived when some theory—usually taking the form of specifying an explicit rationale for making your key methodological choices—may then lead to your clarifying the choices and making them easier. (Note, as with the applications, that in this sense, the term *theory* refers to your thinking and struggling about concepts central to your case study rather than any formally articulated academic theory.)

Chapter 3 then proceeds to reinforce the usefulness of having some theory when you arrive at the starting points for the later stages of doing case studies. The chapter's remaining three applications, therefore, go beyond the literal start-up for a new case study. They cover the conduct of a *descriptive* case study and two variants of *explanatory* case studies. The applications show how you might call on theory to analyze the data for these kinds of case studies—the analysis phase being another common stumbling block when doing case studies. In this way, the overall purpose of Chapter 3 is to suggest the usefulness of theory—that is, logical thinking as might be couched in relation to previous research studies—as a starting point for doing case study research.

One important alert about the five applications in Chapter 3 is that all of them happen to come from *multiple-case studies.* However, the concern over the relevance of theory as helping you deal with the various starting points in doing case studies still pertains directly to single-case studies (see Chapter 1 for the distinction between multiple- and single-case studies). At the same time, you may want to satisfy your curiosity about single-case studies by briefly previewing Parts II and III of this book, all of whose applications represent single-case studies.

1

A (VERY) BRIEF REFRESHER ON THE CASE STUDY METHOD

The case study method embraces the full set of procedures needed to do case study research. These tasks include designing a case study, collecting the study's data, analyzing the data, and presenting and reporting the results. (None of the tasks, nor the rest of this book, deals with the development of *teaching case studies*—frequently also referred to as the "case study method"—the pedagogical goals of which may differ entirely from doing research studies.)

The present chapter introduces and describes these procedures, but only in the most modest manner. The chapter's goal is to serve as a brief refresher to the case study method. As a refresher, the chapter does not fully cover all the options or nuances that you might encounter when customizing your own case study (refer to Yin, 2009a, to obtain a full rendition of the entire method).

Besides discussing case study design, data collection, and analysis, the refresher addresses several key features of case study research. First, an abbreviated definition of a "case study" will help identify the circumstances when you might choose to use the case study method instead of (or as a complement to) some other research method.

Second, other features cover the choices you are likely to encounter in doing your own case study. Thus, the refresher discusses the

- definition of the "case" in case study research,
- benefits of developing a theoretical perspective in conjunction with your design and analysis tasks,
- importance of triangulating among data sources,
- desired vigor in entertaining rival explanations during data collection, and
- challenge of generalizing from case studies.

AUTHOR'S NOTE: This chapter was written expressly for this book but draws from three previous summaries of the case study method (Yin, 2006, 2009b, and 2011a).

To maintain its brevity, the refresher gives less attention to the reporting phase of case studies, although a few words of advice are still offered with regard to presenting case study evidence.

The refresher concludes by discussing the positioning of the case study method among other social science methods, such as experiments, quasi-experiments, surveys, histories, and statistical analyses of archival data. The conclusion suggests the possibility that case study research is not merely a variant of any of these other social science methods, such as quasi-experiments or qualitative research, as has been implied by other scholars. Rather, case study research follows its own complete method (see Yin, 2009a).

A. CASE STUDIES AS A RESEARCH (NOT TEACHING) METHOD

An Abbreviated Definition

All case study research starts from the same compelling feature: the desire to derive a(n) (up-)close or otherwise in-depth understanding of a single or small number of "cases," set in their real-world contexts (e.g., Bromley, 1986, p. 1). The closeness aims to produce an invaluable and deep understanding—that is, an insightful appreciation of the "case(s)"—hopefully resulting in new learning about real-world behavior and its meaning. The distinctiveness of the case study, therefore, also serves as its abbreviated definition:

> *An empirical inquiry about a contemporary phenomenon (e.g., a "case"), set within its real-worldcontext—especially when the boundaries between phenomenon and context are not clearly evident* (Yin, 2009a, p. 18).

Thus, among other features, case study research assumes that examining the context and other complex conditions related to the case(s) being studied are integral to understanding the case(s).

The in-depth focus on the case(s), as well as the desire to cover a broader range of contextual and other complex conditions, produce a wide range of topics to be covered by any given case study. In this sense, case study research goes beyond the study of isolated variables. As a by-product, and as a final feature in appreciating case study research, the relevant case study data are likely to come from multiple and not singular sources of evidence.

When to Use the Case Study Method

At least three situations create relevant opportunities for applying the case study method as a research method. First and most important, the choices among different research methods, including the case study method, can be determined by the kind of research question that a study is trying to address (e.g., Shavelson & Towne, 2002, pp. 99–106). Accordingly, case studies are pertinent when your research addresses either a *descriptive* question—"What is happening or has happened?"—or an *explanatory* question—"How or why did something happen?" As contrasting examples, alternative research methods are more appropriate when addressing two other types of questions: an initiative's effectiveness in producing a particular outcome (experiments and quasi-experiments address this question) and how often something has happened (surveys address this question). However, the other methods are not likely to provide the rich descriptions or the insightful explanations that might arise from doing a case study.

Second, by emphasizing the study of a phenomenon within its real-world context, the case study method favors the collection of data in natural settings, compared with relying on "derived" data (Bromley, 1986, p. 23)—for example, responses to a researcher's instruments in an experiment or responses to questionnaires in a survey. For instance, education audiences may want to know about the following:

- How and why a high school principal had done an especially good job
- The dynamics of a successful (or unsuccessful) collective bargaining negotiation with severe consequences (e.g., a teachers' strike)
- Everyday life in a special residential school

You could use a questionnaire or other instrument to study these situations, but doing some original fieldwork, as part of a case study, might go further in helping you best understand them.

Third, the case study method is now commonly used in conducting evaluations. Authoritative sources such as the U.S. Government Accountability Office (1990) and others (e.g., Yin, 1992, 1994, 1997) have documented the many evaluation applications of the case study method.

Caveats and Concerns in Doing Case Study Research

Despite its apparent applicability in studying many relevant real-world situations and addressing important research questions, case study research nevertheless has not achieved widespread recognition as a method of choice. Some people actually think of it as a method of last resort. Why is this?

Part of the notoriety comes from thinking that case study research is the *exploratory* phase for using other social science methods (i.e., to collect some data to determine whether a topic is indeed worthy of further investigation). In this mode, case study research appears to serve only as a prelude. As a result, it may not be considered as involving a serious, much less rigorous, inquiry. However, such a traditional and sequential (if not hierarchical) view of social science methods is entirely outdated. Experiments and surveys have their own exploratory modes, and case study research goes well beyond exploratory functions. In other words, all the methods can cover the entire range of situations, from initial exploration to the completion of full and final authoritative studies, without calling on any other methods.

A second part of the notoriety comes from a lack of trust in the credibility of a case study researcher's procedures. They may not seem to protect sufficiently against such biases as a researcher seeming to find what she or he had set out to find. They also may suffer from a perceived inability to generalize the case study's findings to any broader level.

Indeed, when case study research is done poorly, these and other challenges can come together in a negative way, potentially re-creating conventional prejudices against the case study method. In contrast, contemporary case study research calls for meeting these challenges by using more systematic procedures. As briefly introduced in this chapter, case study research involves systematic data collection and analysis procedures, and case study findings can be generalized to other situations through analytic (not statistical) generalization.

At the same time, the limited length of this chapter precludes a full rendition of how to deal with all the methodological challenges—such as addressing concerns regarding *construct validity, internal validity, external validity,* and *reliability* in doing case study research. You should consult the companion text for a fuller discussion of how the case study method handles these concerns (see Yin, 2009a, pp. 40–45).

B. THREE STEPS IN DESIGNING CASE STUDIES

Explicitly attending to the design of your case study serves as the first important way of using more systematic procedures when doing case study research. The needed design work contrasts sharply with the way that many people may have stumbled into doing case studies in an earlier era. When doing contemporary case studies, three steps provide a helpful framework for the minimal design work.

1. Defining a "Case"

The first step is to define the "case" that you are studying. Arriving at even a tentative definition helps enormously in organizing your case study. Generally, you should stick with your initial definition because you might have reviewed literature or developed research questions specific to this definition. However, a virtue of the case study method is the ability to redefine the "case" after collecting some early data. Such shifts should not be suppressed. However, beware when this happens— you may then have to backtrack, reviewing a slightly different literature and possibly revising the original research questions.

A "case" is generally a bounded entity (a person, organization, behavioral condition, event, or other social phenomenon), but the boundary between the case and its contextual conditions—in both spatial and temporal dimensions—may be blurred, as previously noted. The case serves as the main *unit of analysis* in a case study. At the same time, case studies also can have nested units within the main unit (see "embedded subcases" in the next section).

In undertaking the definitional task, you should set a high bar: Think of the possibility that your case study may be one of the few that you ever complete. You might, therefore, like to put your efforts into as important, interesting, or significant a case as possible.

What makes a case special? One possibility arises if your case covers some distinctive if not *extreme, unique,* or *revelatory* event or subject, such as

- the revival or renewal of a major organization,
- the creation and confirmed efficacy of a new medical procedure,
- the discovery of a new way of reducing gang violence,
- a critical political election,
- some dramatic neighborhood change, or even
- the occurrence and aftermath of a natural disaster.

By definition, these are likely to be remarkable events. To do a good case study of them may produce an exemplary piece of research.

If no such distinctive or unique event is available for you to study, you may want to do a case study about a *common* or *everyday* phenomenon. Under these circumstances, you need to define some compelling theoretical framework for selecting your case. The more compelling the framework, the more your case study can contribute to the research literature. In this sense, you will have conducted a "special" case study. One popular theme is to choose an otherwise ordinary case that has nevertheless been associated with some unusually successful outcome.

2. Selecting One of Four Types of Case Study Designs

A second step calls for deciding whether your case study will consist of a single or multiple cases—what then might be labeled as a *single-* or a *multiple-case study.*[1] Whether single or multiple, you also can choose to keep your case *holistic* or to have *embedded* subcases within an overall holistic case. The resulting two-by-two matrix leads to four different case study designs. These, together with the dashed lines representing the blurred boundary between a case and its context, are illustrated in Figure 1.1.

For example, your holistic case might be about how and why an organization implemented certain staff promotion policies (holistic level), but the study also might include data collected about a group of employees—whether from a sample survey, from an analysis of the employees' records, or from some other source (the embedded level).[2] If you were limited to a single organization, you would have an embedded, single-case study. If you studied two or more organizations in the same manner, you would have an embedded, multiple-case study.

The multiple-case design is usually more difficult to implement than a single-case design, but the ensuing data can provide greater confidence in your findings. The selection of the multiple cases should be considered akin to the way that you

Figure 1.1   Basic Types of Designs for Case Studies

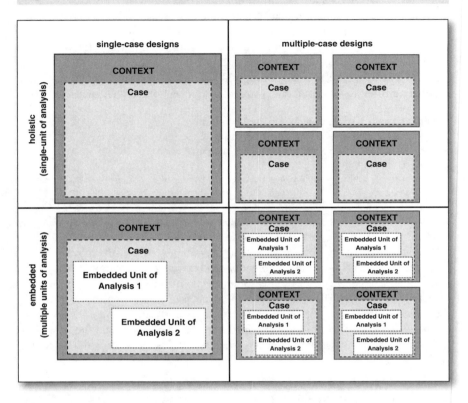

SOURCE: COSMOS Corporation.

would define a set of multiple experiments—each case (or experiment) aiming to examine a complementary facet of the main research question. Thus, a common multiple-case design might call for two or more cases that deliberately tried to test the conditions under which the same findings might be *replicated*. Alternatively, the multiple cases might include deliberately contrasting cases.

As an important note, the use of the term *replication* in relation to multiple-case designs intentionally mimics the same principle used in multiple experiments (e.g., Hersen & Barlow, 1976). In other words, the cases in a multiple-case study, as in the experiments in a multiple-experiment study, might have been selected either to predict similar results (*direct replications*) or to predict contrasting results but for anticipatable reasons (*theoretical replications*).

An adjunct of the replication parallelism is the response to an age-old question: "How many cases should be included in a multiple-case study?" The question continues to plague the field to this day (e.g., Small, 2009). Students and scholars appear to assume the existence of a formulaic solution, as in conducting a *power analysis* to determine the needed sample size in an experiment or survey. For case studies (again, as with multiple experiments) no such formula exists. Instead, analogous to the parallel question of "how many experiments need to be conducted to arrive at an unqualified result," the response is still a judgmental one: the more cases (or experiments), the greater confidence or certainty in a study's findings; and the fewer the cases (or experiments), the less confidence or certainty.

More important, in neither the case study nor the experimental situation would a tallying of the cases (or the experiments) provide a useful way for deciding whether the group of cases (or experiments) supported an initial proposition or not. Thus, some investigators of multiple-case studies might think that a cross-case analysis would largely consist of a simple tally (e.g., "Five cases supported the proposition, but two did not") as the way of arriving at a cross-case conclusion. However, the numbers in any such tally are likely to be too small and undistinguished to support such a conclusion with any confidence.

3. Using Theory in Design Work

A third step involves deciding whether or not to use *theory* to help complete your essential methodological steps, such as developing your research question(s), selecting your case(s), refining your case study design, or defining the relevant data to be collected. (The use of theory also can help organize your initial data analysis strategies and generalize the findings from your case study—discussed later in this chapter.)

For example, an initial theoretical perspective about school principals might claim that successful principals are those who perform as "instructional leaders." A lot of literature (which you would cite as part of your case study) supports this perspective. Your case study could attempt to build, extend, or challenge this perspective, possibly even emulating a hypothesis-testing approach. However, such a theoretical perspective also could limit your ability to make discoveries (i.e., to discover from scratch just how and why a successful principal had been successful). Therefore, in doing this and other kinds of case studies, you would need to work with your original perspective but also be prepared to discard it after initial data collection.

Nevertheless, a case study that starts with some theoretical propositions or *theory* will be easier to implement than one having no propositions. The theoretical propositions should by no means be considered with the formality of grand theory in social science but mainly need to suggest a simple set of relationships such as "a [hypothetical] story about why acts, events, structures, and thoughts occur" (Sutton & Staw, 1995, p. 378). More elaborate theories will (desirably) point to more intricate patterns. They (paradoxically) will add precision to the later analysis, yielding a benefit similar to that of having more complex theoretical propositions when doing quasi-experimental research (e.g., Rosenbaum, 2002, pp. 5–6, 277–279). As an example, in case study evaluations, the use of *logic models* represents a theory about how an intervention is supposed to work.

This desired role of theory sometimes serves as one point of difference between case study research and related qualitative methods such as *ethnography* (e.g., Van Maanen, 1988) and *grounded theory* (e.g., Corbin & Strauss, 2007). For instance, qualitative research may not necessarily focus on any "case," may not be concerned with a unit of analysis, and may not engage in formal design work, much less encompass any theoretical perspective.

In general, the less experience you have had in doing case study research, the more you might want to adopt some theoretical perspectives. Without them, and without adequate prior experience, you might risk false starts and lost time in doing your research. You also might have trouble convincing others that your case study has produced findings of much value to the field. At the same time, the opposite tactic of deliberately avoiding any theoretical perspective, though risky, can be highly rewarding—because you might then be able to produce a "break-the-mold" case study.

C. CASE STUDY DATA COLLECTION

Varieties of Sources of Case Study Data

Case study research is not limited to a single source of data, as in the use of questionnaires for carrying out a survey. In fact, good case studies benefit from having *multiple sources of evidence.* Exhibit 1.1 lists six common sources of evidence. You may use these six in any combination, as well as related sources such as focus groups (a variant of interviews), depending on what is available and relevant for studying your case(s). Regardless of its source, case study evidence

Exhibit 1.1   Six Common Sources of Evidence in Doing Case Studies

1. Direct observations (e.g., human actions or a physical environment)

2. Interviews (e.g., open-ended conversations with key participants)

3. Archival records (e.g., student records)

4. Documents (e.g., newspaper articles, letters and e-mails, reports)

5. Participant-observation (e.g., being identified as a researcher but also filling a real-life role in the scene being studied)

6. Physical artifacts (e.g., computer downloads of employees' work)

can include both *qualitative* and *quantitative data.* Qualitative data may be considered non-numeric data—for instance, categorical information that can be systematically collected and presented in narrative form, such as *word tables.* Quantitative data can be considered numeric data—for instance, information based on the use of ordinal if not interval or ratio measures.

Again, you will have to consult other references to cover all these sources comprehensively (e.g., Yin, 2009a, pp. 98–125). However, a quick review of three of the most common sources will give you an idea of the data collection process.

Direct Observations: Two Examples

Let's start with one of the most common methods: making *direct observations* in a field setting. Such observations can focus on human actions, physical environments, or real-world events. If nothing else, the opportunity to make such observations is one of the most distinctive features in doing case studies.

As an initial example, the conventional manner of collecting observational data takes the form of using your own five senses, taking field notes, and ultimately creating a narrative based on what you might have seen, heard, or otherwise sensed. (The application in Chapter 2 provides an example of such a narrative.) Mechanical devices such as audiotape recorders or audio-video cameras also can help.

Based on these observations, the composing of the narrative must overcome the caveat discussed earlier by presenting the observational evidence along with a careful note: whether the presentation represents your trying to be as neutral and factual as possible, whether it represents the view of (one or more of) the field participants in your case study, or whether it represents your own deliberate interpretation of what has been observed. Any of the three is acceptable, depending on the goal of your data collection, but you must explicitly clarify which of the three is being presented and avoid confusing them inadvertently. Once properly labeled, you even may present information from two different points of view, again depending on the goal of your data collection and case study.

Besides this traditional observational procedure, a second way of making direct observations comes from using a formal observational instrument and then noting, rating, or otherwise reporting the observational evidence under the categories specified by the instrument. Use of a formal workplace instrument, aimed at defining the frequency and nature of supervisor-employee interactions, is a commonplace practice in doing management research. Such an instrument allows the observational evidence to be reported in both narrative and tabular forms (e.g., tables showing the frequency of certain observations). In a similar manner, a formal instrument can be used to define and code other observed interactions, such as in a study of the two-way dialogue between a doctor and a patient or between a teacher and a class. In any of these situations, the interactions may have been observed directly or recorded with an audio-visual device.

Open-Ended Interviews

A second common source of evidence for case studies comes from *open-ended interviews,* also called "nonstructured interviews." These interviews can offer richer and more extensive material than data from surveys or even the open-ended portions of survey instruments. On the surface, the open-ended portions of surveys may resemble open-ended interviews, but the latter are generally less structured and can assume a lengthy conversational mode not usually found in surveys. For instance, the open-ended interviews in case studies can consume two or more hours on more than a single occasion. Alternatively, the conversations can occur over the course of an entire day, with a researcher and one or more participants accompanying one another to view or participate in different events.

The flexible format permits open-ended interviews, if properly done, to reveal how case study participants construct reality and think about situations, not just to provide the answers to a researcher's specific questions and own implicit construction of reality. For some case studies, the participants' construction of reality provides important insights into the case. The insights gain even further value if the participants are key persons in the organizations, communities, or small groups being studied, not just the average member of such groups. For a case study of a public agency or private firm, for instance, a key person would be the head of the agency or firm. For schools, the principal or a department head would carry the same status. Because by definition only one or a few persons will fill such roles, their interviews also have been called "elite" interviews.

Archival Records

In addition to direct observations and open-ended interviews, a third common source consists of archival data—information stored in existing channels such as electronic records, libraries, and old-fashioned (paper) files. Newspapers, television, and the mass media are but one type of channel. Records maintained by public agencies, such as public health or law enforcement or court records, serve as another. The resulting archival data can be quantitative or qualitative (or both).

From a research perspective, the archival data can be subject to their own biases or shortcomings. For instance, researchers have long known that police records of *reported crime* do not reflect the actual amount of crime that might have occurred. Similarly, school systems' reports of their enrollment, attendance, and dropout rates may be subject to systematic under- or overcounting. Even the U.S. Census struggles with the completeness of its population counts and the potential problems posed because people residing in certain kinds of locales (rural and urban) may be undercounted.

Likewise, the editorial leanings of different mass media are suspected to affect their choice of stories to be covered (or not covered), questions to be asked (or not asked), and textual detail (or lack of detail). All these editorial choices can collectively produce a systematic bias in what would otherwise appear to be a full and factual account of some important event.

Case studies relying heavily on archival data need to be sensitive to these possible biases and take steps to counteract them, if possible. With mass media, a helpful procedure is to select two different media that are believed, if not known, to have opposing orientations (e.g., Jacobs, 1996). A more balanced picture may then emerge. Finding and using additional sources bearing on the same topic would help even more.

Triangulating Evidence From Multiple Sources

The availability of data from the preceding as well as the three other common sources in Exhibit 1.1 creates an important opportunity during case study data collection: You should constantly check and recheck the consistency of the findings from different as well as the same sources (e.g., Duneier, 1999, pp. 345–347). In so doing, you will be *triangulating*—or establishing converging lines of evidence—which will make your findings as robust as possible.

How might this *triangulation* work? The most desired convergence occurs when three (or more) independent sources all point to the same set of events, facts, or interpretations. For example, what might have taken place at a group meeting might have been reported to you (independently) by two or more attendees at the meeting, and the meeting also might have been followed by some documented outcome (e.g., issuance of a new policy that was the presumed topic of the meeting). You might not have been able to attend the meeting yourself, but having these different sources would give you more confidence about concluding what had transpired than had you relied on a single source alone.

Triangulating is not always as easy as the preceding example. Sometimes, as when you interview different participants, all appear to be giving corroborating evidence about how their organization works—for example, how counselors treat residents in a drug treatment facility. But in fact, they all may be echoing the same institutional "mantra," developed over time for speaking with outsiders (such as researchers or media representatives), and the collective "mantra" may not necessarily coincide with the organization's actual practices.

Reviewing the literature may help you anticipate this type of situation, and making your own direct observations also may be extremely helpful. However, when relying on direct observations, note that another problem can arise. Because you may have prescheduled your presence in a field setting, the participant(s) may have had the opportunity to customize their routines just for you. So, getting at the actual practices in the organization or among a group of people may not be as easy as you might think. Nevertheless, you always will be better off using multiple rather than single sources of evidence.

Using a Case Study Protocol

In collecting your data, and regardless of your sources of evidence, you will find the development and use of a *case study protocol* to be extremely helpful, if not essential. The typical protocol consists of a set of questions to be addressed while collecting the case study data (whether actually taking place at a field setting or at your own desk when extracting information from an archival source).

Importantly, the questions in the protocol are directed at the researcher, *not* at any field participant. In this sense, the protocol differs entirely from any instrument used in a conventional interview or survey. The protocol's questions in effect serve as a mental framework, not unlike similar frameworks held by detectives investigating crimes, by journalists chasing a story, or by clinicians considering different diagnoses based on a patient's symptoms. In those situations, a detective, journalist, or clinician may privately entertain one or more lines of inquiry (including rival hypotheses), but the specific questions posed to any participant are tuned to each specific interview situation. Thus, the questions as actually verbalized in an interview derive from the line of inquiry (e.g., mental framework) but do not come from a verbatim script (e.g., questionnaire).

Collecting Data About Rival Explanations

A final data collection topic stresses the role of seeking data to examine *rival explanations.* The desired rival thinking should draw from a continual sense of *skepticism* as a case study proceeds. During data collection, the skepticism should involve worrying about whether events and actions are as they appear to be and whether participants are giving candid responses. Having a truly skeptical attitude will result in collecting more data than if rivals were not a concern. For instance, data collection should involve a deliberate and vigorous search for "discrepant evidence," as if you were trying to establish the potency of the plausible rival rather than seeking to discredit it (Patton, 2002, p. 276; Rosenbaum, 2002, pp. 8–10). Finding no such evidence despite a diligent search again increases confidence about your case study's later descriptions, explanations, and interpretations.

Rival explanations are not merely alternative interpretations. True *rivals* compete directly with each other and cannot coexist. In other words, research interpretations may be likened to a combatant who can be challenged by one or more rivals. Rivals that turn out to be more plausible than an original interpretation need to be rejected, not just footnoted.

Case study research demands the seeking of rival explanations throughout the research process. Interestingly, the methodological literature offers little inkling of the kinds of substantive rivals that might be considered by researchers, either in doing case study research or other kinds of social science research. The only rivals to be found are methodological but not substantive ones—for instance, involving the null hypothesis, experimenter effects, or other potential artifacts created by the research procedures.[3] In contrast, in detective work, a substantive rival would be an alternative explanation of how a crime had occurred, compared with the explanation that might originally have been entertained.

Presenting Case Study Evidence

Properly dealing with case study evidence requires a final but essential practice: You need to present the evidence in your case study with sufficient clarity (e.g., in separate texts, tables, and exhibits) to allow readers to judge independently your later interpretation of the data. Ideally, such evidence will come from a formal *case study database* that you compile for your files after completing your data collection.

Unfortunately, older case studies frequently mixed evidence and interpretation. This practice may still be excusable when doing a unique case study or a revelatory case study, because the insights may be more important than knowing the strength of the evidence for such insights. However, for most case studies, mixing evidence and interpretation may be taken as a sign that you do not understand the difference between the two or that you do not know how to handle data (and hence proceeded prematurely to interpretation).

D. CASE STUDY DATA ANALYSIS

Case study analysis takes many forms, but none yet follow the routine procedures that may exist with other research methods. The absence of any cookbook for analyzing case study evidence has been only partially offset by the development of prepackaged computer software programs. They can support the analysis of large amounts of narrative text by following your instructions in coding and categorizing your notes or your verbatim transcripts. However, unlike software for analyzing numeric data, whereby an analyst provides the input data and the computer uses an algorithm to estimate some model and proceeds to produce the output data, there is no automated algorithm when analyzing narrative data.

Whether using computer software to help you or not, you will be the one who must define the codes to be used and the procedures for logically piecing together the coded evidence into broader themes—in essence creating your own unique algorithm befitting your particular case study. The strength of the analytic course will depend on a marshaling of claims that use your data in a logical fashion.

Your analysis can begin by systematically organizing your data (narratives and words) into hierarchical relationships, matrices, or other arrays (e.g., Miles & Huberman, 1994). A simple array might be a *word table,* organized by some rows and columns of interest and presenting narrative data in the cells of the table. Given this or other arrays, several different analytic techniques can then be used (see Yin, 2009a, pp. 136–161, for a fuller discussion). Discussed next are four examples. The first three are *pattern matching, explanation building,* and *time-series analysis.* Multiple-case studies, in addition to using these several techniques within each single case, would then follow a *replication* logic, which is the fourth technique.

Techniques for Analyzing Case Study Data

If selecting your case(s) to be studied is the most critical step in doing case study research, analyzing your case study data is probably the most troublesome. Much of the problem relates to false expectations: that the data will somehow "speak for themselves," or that some counting or tallying procedure will be sufficient to produce the main findings for a case study. Wrong. Instead, consider the following alternatives.

You actually made some key assumptions for your analysis when you defined your research questions and your case. Was your motive in doing the case study mainly to address your research questions? If so, then the techniques for analyzing the data might be directed at those questions first. Was your motive to derive more general lessons for which your case(s) are but examples? If so, your analysis might be directed at these lessons. Finally, if your case study was driven by a discovery motive, you might start your analysis with what you think you have discovered.

Now comes a "reverse" lesson. Realizing that key underlying assumptions for later analysis may in fact have been implicit at the initial stages of your case study, you could have anticipated and planned the analytic strategies or implications when conducting those initial stages. Collecting the actual data may lead to changes in this plan, but having an initial plan that needs to be revised (even drastically) may be better than having no plan at all.

For instance, one possibility is to stipulate some pattern of expected findings at the outset of your case study. A *pattern-matching* logic would later enable you to compare your empirically based pattern (based on the data you had collected) with the predicted one. As later presented in Chapter 10, the prediction in a community study might have stipulated that the patterns of outcomes in many different economic and social sectors (e.g., retail sales, housing sales, unemployment, and population turnover) would be "catastrophically" affected by a key event—the closing of a military base in a small, single-employer town (Bradshaw, 1999). The analysis would then examine the data in each sector, comparing pre-post trends with those in other communities and statewide trends. The pattern-matching results should be accompanied by a detailed explanation of how and why the base closure had (or had not) affected these trends. By also collecting data on and then examining possible rival explanations (e.g., events co-occurring with the key event or other contextual conditions), support for the claimed results would be strengthened even further.

Second, a case study may not have started with any predicted patterns but in fact may have started with an open-ended research question that would lead to the use of an *explanation-building* technique. For instance, Chapter 10 includes a second case study that focused on the demise of a high-tech firm that, only a few years before its demise, had been a *Fortune 50* firm (Schein, 2003). The purpose of the case study was then to build an explanation for the demise, again deliberately entertaining rival explanations.

A third technique mimics the *time-series analyses* in quantitative research. In case study research, the simplest time series can consist of assembling key events into a *chronology*. The resulting array (e.g., a word table consisting of time and types of events as the rows and columns) may not only produce an insightful descriptive pattern but also may hint at possible causal relationships, because any presumed causal condition must precede any presumed outcome condition.

Assuming again the availability of data about rival hypotheses, such information would be used in examining the chronological pattern. When the rivals do not fit the pattern, their rejection considerably strengthens the basis for supporting your original claims.

If the case study included some major intervening event in the midst of the chronological sequence, the array could serve as a counterpart to an *interrupted time series* in experimental research. For instance, imagine a case study in which a new executive assumed leadership over an organization. The case study might have tracked the production, sales, and profit trends before and after the executive's ascendance. If all the trends were in the appropriate upward direction, the case study could begin to build a claim, crediting the new leader with these accomplishments. Again, attending to rival conditions (such as that earlier policies might have been put into place by the new executive's predecessor) and making them part of the analysis would further strengthen the claim.

When Sufficient Quantitative Data Are Relevant and Available

The preceding example was deliberately limited to a situation where a case study did not attempt any statistical analysis, mainly because of a lack of data points other than some simple pre-post comparison. However, case study analyses can assume a different posture when more time intervals are relevant and sufficient data are available. In education, a common single-case design might focus on a school or school district as a single organization of interest (e.g., Supovitz & Taylor, 2005; Yin & Davis, 2007). Within the single case, considerable attention might be devoted to the collection and analysis of highly quantitative student achievement data. For instance, a study of a single school district tracked student performance over a 22-year period (Teske, Schneider, Roch, & Marschall, 2000). The start of the period coincided with a time when the district was slowly implementing an educational reform that was the main subject of the study. The available data then permitted the case study to use statistical models (ordinary least squares) in reading and in mathematics to test the correlation between reform and student performance.

Cross-Case Synthesis for Multiple-Case Studies

Discussed earlier was the desire to apply a *replication logic* in interpreting the findings across the cases in a multiple-case study. The logic for such a cross-case synthesis emulates that used in addressing whether the findings from a set of multiple experiments—too small in number to be made part of any quantitative meta-analysis—support any broader pattern of conclusions.

The replication or corroboratory frameworks can vary. In a *direct replication,* the single cases would be predicted to arrive at similar results. In a *theoretical replication,* each single case's ultimate disposition also would have been predicted beforehand, but each case might have been predicted to produce a varying or even contrasting result, based on the preconceived propositions. Even more complex could be the stipulation and emergence of a typology of cases based on a multiple-case study.

E. GENERALIZING FROM CASE STUDIES

Apart from the techniques just described, a final analytic challenge is to determine whether you can make any *generalizations* from your case study. One available procedure applies well to all kinds of case studies, including the holistic, single-case study that has been commonly criticized for having little or no generalizability value. To understand the process requires distinguishing between two types of generalizing: *statistical generalizations* and *analytic generalizations* (Yin, 2009a, pp. 38–39). For case study research, the latter is the appropriate type.

Unfortunately, most scholars, including those who do case study research, are imbued with the former type. They think that each case represents a sampling point from some known and larger population and cannot understand how a small set of cases can generalize to any larger population. The simple answer is that a single or small set of cases cannot generalize in this manner, nor is it intended to. Furthermore, the incorrect assumption is that statistical generalizations, from samples to universes, are the only way of generalizing findings from social science research.

In contrast, analytic generalizations depend on using a study's theoretical framework to establish a logic that might be applicable to other situations. Again, an appealing parallel exists in experimental science, where generalizing about the findings from a single or small set of experiments does not usually follow any statistical path to a previously defined universe of experiments.[4] Rather, for both case studies and experiments, the objective for generalizing the findings is the same two-step process, as follows.

The first step involves a conceptual claim whereby investigators show how their study's findings have informed the relationships among a particular set of concepts, theoretical constructs, or sequence of events. The second step involves applying the same theoretical propositions to implicate other situations, outside the completed case study, where similar concepts, constructs, or sequences might be relevant. For example, political science's best-selling research work has been a single-case study about the Cuban missile crisis of 1962 (Allison, 1971; Allison & Zelikow, 1999). The authors do not generalize their findings and theoretical framework to U.S.-Cuban relations—or to the use of missiles. They use their theoretical propositions to generalize their findings to the likely responses of national governments when involved in superpower confrontation and international crises.

Making analytic generalizations requires carefully constructed claims (e.g., Kelly & Yin, 2007)—again, whether for a case study or for an experiment. The ultimate generalization is not likely to achieve the status of "proof" in geometry,[5] but the claims must be presented soundly and resist logical challenge. The relevant "theory" may be no more than a series of hypotheses or even a single hypothesis. Cronbach (1975) further clarifies that the sought-after generalization is not that of a conclusion but, rather, more like a "working hypothesis" (also see Lincoln & Guba, 1985, pp. 122–123). Confidence in such hypotheses can then build as new case studies—again, as with new experiments—continue to produce findings related to the same theoretical propositions.

In summary, to the extent that any study concerns itself with generalizing, case studies tend to generalize to other situations (on the basis of analytic claims), whereas surveys and other quantitative methods tend to generalize to populations (on the basis of statistical claims).

F. COMMENTS ABOUT THE POSITIONING OF THE CASE STUDY METHOD

The preceding refresher has pointed to the potential relevance of both qualitative *and* quantitative data in doing case study research. This duality reinforces the positioning of the case study method as a method not limited to either type of data. An important correlate is that case study investigators should be acquainted with collecting data from a variety of sources of evidence as well as using a variety of analytic techniques.

Such a realization also runs contrary to two common stereotypes of the case study method. The first is that the method is one of the strands of qualitative research—along with such other strands as narrative research, phenomenology, grounded theory, and ethnography.[6] The second and older stereotype is that the case study method is but one of the designs in quasi-experimental research.[7] Neither stereotype is acceptable today.

Rather, case study research appears to be based on its own separate method, related to but not wholly part of the qualitative or quasi-experimental domains. The case study method has its own design, data collection, and analytic procedures. As one indicator of the separateness of the method, contemporary students and scholars are now able to start and complete their own case studies by using qualitative or quantitative techniques as pointed out throughout this chapter. The existence of the separate craft is readily acknowledged every time someone says she or he would like to do a "case study" as the *main* method for a new study—not unlike the alternative choices of saying one wants to do an experiment, a survey, a history, or a quasi-experiment. Case studies also can and have been used as a companion to these other choices as part of *mixed methods studies*.

At the same time, the case study method is still evolving. New contributions are needed to improve the method's design, data collection, and analytic procedures. Such tasks pose the ongoing challenge of doing case study research.

NOTES

1. The latter also has been called an "extended case study" (Bromley, 1986, p. 8; Buraway, 1991).

2. Note that the embedded arrangement would pertain only as long as the entire study and its main research questions were about the organization in its entirety (e.g., the employee data are used in some way to corroborate the organization's overall condition). However, if the findings about the employees (but not the organization) become the main findings of the entire study, the original data about the organization as a whole likely will become merely a contextual condition for what in the end would be a study of employee characteristics, not a case study.

3. For a typology of truly substantive rivals, such as rival theories and rival explanations, see Yin (2000). For a parallel discussion in relation to quasi-experimental research, see Rosenbaum (2002).

4. Similarly, experimental psychology has had to address the fear that, from a sampling standpoint, the main generalization from any experiment using college sophomores as subjects can be only to the universe of college sophomores. Recent reviews have extended this concern into a cultural domain, suggesting the potential fallacy of automatically generalizing to universal populations when psychology studies mainly have used white, English-speaking, and middle-income people as subjects (e.g., Henrich, Heine, & Norenzayan, 2010).

5. Statistical generalizations also do not achieve the status of "proof" in geometry but by definition are probabilistic statements. In like manner, a "working hypothesis" as an analytic generalization is a probabilistic statement, too, just not expressed in numerical terms.

6. One popular textbook on qualitative research indeed treats case studies as a separate strand within qualitative research, along with the four other qualitative strands listed in the text (Creswell, 2007).

7. This stereotype was promoted by an early reference to the one-shot–post-test-only design in quasi-experimental research, made in a classic work coauthored by Donald Campbell (Campbell & Stanley, 1966). Though such a design does exist, Campbell later corrected the misperception with the statement, "Certainly the case study as normally practiced should not be demeaned by identification with the one-group post-test-only design," which then appeared in the textbook that was the successor to the classic work (Cook & Campbell, 1979, p. 96).

2

FIELD NOTES

Note taking of some sort will be common to virtually every case study. The notes may be based on different sources of evidence—whether open-ended interviews with participants, documents that have been reviewed, or, as with the present application in Chapter 2, observations that have been made in a field setting. In doing a case study, therefore, you need to know how to take good notes.

The initial notes may assume the form of "jottings." They may not involve complete sentences and may be written in a peculiar scrawl, legible only to you. The jottings also may include brief tallies or hand-drawn sketches that contain numbers and charts and not just narrative text. Regardless of the condition of the jottings, you should render them into more formal writing as soon as possible. In most case studies, such rendering occurs nightly during the fieldwork period. Adopting such a regimen can enhance your recollections from the day's work and also reduce the embarrassing occasions when you cannot decipher or interpret your own jottings.

The more formal writing may not become part of any published work. In this sense, the writing does not have to be polished or finely edited. The goal is to capture the interview, archival, or observational evidence in a methodic manner, later to be compiled and then used as part of the analysis of all your case study data.

The application in this chapter exemplifies a formal text (not a jotting). The text was written after a day spent accompanying a field participant in an urban neighborhood. (Similar texts were written following the other days in the same field setting.) The example tries to describe the field setting from a neutral perspective, not attempting to capture the view of the participant or of the author. In a few instances that appear in parentheses, the author expressed his own commentary as part of the original field note. The few portions of text appearing in brackets are side comments added expressly for this chapter; all names in the chapter are fictitious.

AUTHOR'S NOTE: The field notes in this chapter come with light editing from a set of notes written by Robert K. Yin and retrieved from his research files.

Introductory Note

Rather than giving a chronological account of the day's activities in the field, I have organized the text topically to make it appear more coherent (see **BOX 1**).

BOX 1

Direct Observations in Field Settings

The field notes in this chapter capture the observations made in a real-world field setting. Doing such fieldwork is one of the highly valued aspects of doing case studies.

In making these observations, the fieldworker is the primary research instrument. Although the observations are genuine, fieldworkers must work hard to avoid tainting them with the premature introduction of concepts and categories. Good fieldworkers nevertheless know that direct observations come with their own methodological challenges.

First, the fieldworker as an instrument will still have some unavoidable cultural and personal perspectives that affect how the field conditions are observed, interpreted, and reported. Second, the fieldworker's presence may inadvertently affect the participants being observed, so what appears as their routine behavior may contain a reflexive element. Third, the fieldworker cannot observe all locations at every point in time, and choosing where and when to make field observations represents another discretionary decision. For these and other reasons, most case studies do not rely on field observations as their sole source of evidence, as invaluable as they are.

(For more information, see Yin, 2009a, Chapter 4, sections on "Direct Observation" and "Participant-Observation.")

Lt. Harry Erroll

Harry Erroll has been with the city's fire department for about 25 years—the first 20 on fire duty (mostly in high-alarm neighborhoods) and the last four or five in community relations (limited-duty status due to injury). He is one of the more unusual persons one will meet in the department, having (a) grown long hair (which he readily admits he combs back any time he is to meet with his fellow firefighters), (b) accepted a Taoist-like philosophy of life (the only button he wears is one with the yin-yang symbol), and (c) otherwise accepted the ways of the people (he also writes poetry). A personal change seems to have occurred gradually over the past 10 years and is not based on any revelatory incident (as far as I can tell) but reflects the same interests in serving the community as those that led him to join the fire department in the first place.

In his role as community relations officer, Erroll serves one of the larger regions in the city, with three men [their names appear here] working with him. Together, they attend community meetings, give lectures to school children and adults, and otherwise keep in touch with neighborhood events. Apparently, the four determine their own schedules, filing activity reports before and after any given period of time. The three other men cover designated subregional areas; Lt. Erroll freelances.

Firehouse No. 10

Erroll has a desk here, which is also regional headquarters and hence has many men on limited duty on the top floor of the firehouse. I spent the first hour of my fieldwork here, with Erroll showing me samples of the routine reports, materials, and pictures that he uses.

Some of the topics we covered briefly included the following: harassment (the kids tell Harry that it's fun and when told that they endanger other people's lives at fires, say they now throw rocks at the firefighters only when they are clearly *returning* to the firehouse); the slight delay in response time caused by a new need to lock the firehouse because of the union requirement that all persons be on fire duty; and some paperwork in which Erroll has been trying to encourage more neighborhood kids to think about job opportunities with city agencies and to encourage the agencies to develop adequate training programs.

Neighborhood Streets

The main feature of the streets around the firehouse [specific cross-streets given here] and in the whole neighborhood is the garbage. I saw enough garbage to last for a long while. Most of it is not in garbage cans or jiffy bags and appears to come from a number of conditions. First, there are too many cars (including abandoned ones) blocking any garbage truck's routine access for collecting the garbage on the sidewalks. Second, the stores dump as much garbage as do the residents (evident from the number of crates and boxes among the garbage). Third, not being in garbage cans or bags, the garbage is even more difficult to pick up. Fourth, the neighborhood's empty lots attract dumpers.

The parking problem is a source of aggravation between the firefighters and the community because the firefighters drive to work and like to park close to the firehouse. According to Harry, they consider their own violations of the parking regulations as part of their work, and there has been at least one fight between a firefighter and a local resident over a parking space. One outcome of the parking problem around the firehouse is that the firehouse's street is one of the dirtiest in the area.

Three Community Organizations (a study in contrasts?)

We called on three different community organizations: the Youth and Community Center, the Gotham Boys Club, and the Urban Task Force [cross-streets and addresses of each organization given here]. The first is run by an active group of African-Americans, is well furnished in spite of having a "poor" storefront (carpet, desktop computers, modern furniture, sizeable office copy machine), and has a good deal of business, with a staff of about four or five persons [names and titles of each person listed here]. The office is about 20 months old, active in developing neighborhood programs, supported by some sort of private foundation fund, and seeking further support.

The second is run by an old man, Mr. Mantos, and has a gym and other recreational facilities within the same building. The club is sponsored mostly by people with Italian names and includes summer camp programs. It is about 11 years old, and Mr. Mantos said that the first few years were the hardest because the staff had to overcome the hostility of the local gangs. The club discontinued dances about five years ago, but except for this change, I got the impression that things have improved, especially in comparison to the first few years. The fire department has recently started a "class" in the club, conducted every two weeks, in which the kids are taught about fire hazards and fire prevention. Harry characterized the club's staff as relatively strict and old-fashioned, and he said that he and the other firefighters running the classes make sure that the staff is not part of the classes.

The third organization is run by Al Ball of the city's youth agency and a secretary. Ball is a very "bourgeois" (Harry's word) African-American, and the office is very poorly furnished. Ball had a great deal of difficulty trying to relate the fire problem to other community problems. The minutes of one of the task force meetings (I have the minutes from the past five meetings) give some idea of the routine work of the task force (it does not appear to work closely with the Youth and Community Center). Both the task force and Mr. Ball seem to be unsettled in their roles and not really involved in the community.

Around the Neighborhood

We drove and walked around many of the worst-appearing parts of the area [specific cross-streets given here]. Harry showed me a vacant lot that he had asked to be tarred over because it provides rocks that the kids throw at nearby buildings (and firefighters), but with no result. We ran into one of Harry's street friends [presumed name given here], about 17 years old, who was on his way to the court to bail someone out. He was not very talkative, but he was extremely friendly (he had once helped Harry in avoiding a confrontation between the firefighters and neighborhood residents). He thought things had gotten much worse in the seven years he had lived in the area [area boundaries given here] but could point only to garbage as a concrete example of the deterioration (our conversation took place next to a pile of burnt rubbish and beer cans about four feet high, which he said had been there for about a month).

We drove by one of the better parts of the area [specific streets given here], which has many frame houses and thus presumed homeowners. The street has a block association that is apparently highly active. In addition, we called on one of the schools where Harry had given a talk in the past week. During our visit, Harry gave pictures of the earlier occasion to a teacher and in return was given a copy of a news clipping from the past Sunday's *Dispatch* about one of the fire dogs.

Mama Almonte's [cross-streets given here] is an excellent place for lunch. The "sandwich Cubano" beats anything from downtown carry-outs. On the way there, we also saw a little of the [name] area, which also is in pretty bad shape.

Fire Hazards

Most people mentioned poor electrical wiring as the main cause of fires. The old apartment houses were not built to accommodate irons, toasters, air conditioners, or other common electrical appliances. Mr. Ball of the Urban Task Force, being more knowledgeable about the housing situation, also said that there was little that a land-lord stood to gain by improving his or her buildings, because the rent could be increased only by small amounts. However, no one on my visit (except for the fire-fighters) mentioned any other fire problems, such as the occurrence of false alarms.

On the prevention side, Harry mentioned that there had been a well-staffed fire department program that addressed individual classrooms at various schools. As a result of union pressures, this program had been reduced. Now, Harry and the other community relations officers are usually in a school's auditorium with a large audience, and Harry feels there is less communication with the kids than when he used to visit individual classes. He also tries to distinguish between the roles of the fire and police departments, and he finds the firefighter's uniform to be a hindrance, because it is much like that of the police. However, Harry admits that the other firefighters probably prefer not to be dissociated from the police; many of the firefighters simply do not understand the need for communicating with the people or the kids in the neighborhoods.

Concluding Remarks

There are several things left to be said about Harry Erroll. His views, as I have indicated, are much closer to those of the community than to those of the firefight-ers, and he has been trying to educate both.

Harry is not highly opinionated, complains little about the services provided by other city agencies in spite of several frustrating experiences, and though obser-vant, does not stereotype his observations. I felt that I was able to see things for myself, and Harry did not in any way offer any running commentary. At the same time, he does have a few ideas, which he did try to promote.

The first is that better community relations would have to depend on more staff and money (but he doesn't belabor the point). The second is that the city's employment must be opened much more to the city's residents, especially low-income residents, and that too many of the current employees do not live in the city or in the neighborhood they serve, and hence they are parasites of a sort. Third, he feels that landlords are obsolete and that perhaps the only way of getting people involved in their neighborhood is to have condominium or cooperative arrangements, without any kind of absentee ownership or management. This is probably not a new idea, but I found the thought intriguing in light of a recent, well-publicized report calling for greater financial returns for landlords.

Harry's involvement in his job is entirely on a personal basis. He can retire any time but enjoys his activities. His work can be understood only by observing his daily routine, as he is not prone to verbalizing it.

On the next fieldwork opportunity, I have asked him to show me around other neighborhoods that have not yet deteriorated as much as the ones we saw today. We also will try to visit some of the block association leaders (there is at least one highly active group, composed of tenants, which came up in our discussions with Ball).

INSIDE STORY FOR CHAPTER 2

Posing Initial Research Questions

The field notes in Chapter 2 came from the outset of a new study of street life in an urban neighborhood. The notes record the first of a series of introductory visits. After this introductory phase, the full study then involved extensive participant-observation in the neighborhood over a three-month period.

You may have observed that the notes do not contain any research questions. Nor do the notes appear to have much substantive direction, other than the visits to the community organizations. In fact, known at that early juncture was only that the study was to be about the relationships between firefighting officers and the communities they serve—because such relationships had declined to an unacceptably low point: Residents had been harassing the fire officers (e.g., throwing objects at the officers when they were fighting a fire), sending many false alarms that caused fire trucks to respond unnecessarily, and causing other forms of minor havoc. However, at the time of the first visit, as captured in the field notes, no specific research questions had been articulated. At that moment in time, no one knew how the study was to be designed or conducted or even what types of data would be collected.

For Class Discussion or Written Assignment

Develop a list of research questions that might have been addressed in the ensuing phases of this case study. The questions should illuminate the community relations between firefighting officers and the residents they serve, and the data should be assumed to come from fieldwork based on participant-observation. After compiling the list, prioritize the questions to see whether, in the aggregate, addressing them will produce a suitably strong case study.

3

THE ROLE OF THEORY
IN DOING CASE STUDIES

Reliance on theoretical concepts to guide design and data collection remains one of the most important strategies for doing successful case studies. Such theoretical concepts can be useful in conducting exploratory, descriptive, or explanatory case studies.

Your goal is to explore some preliminary concepts at the outset of your case study. One purpose served by such concepts, as with any other empirical study, is to consider how your case study might relate to an appropriate research literature so that the case study's findings may more readily advance knowledge about a given topic. Other purposes, possibly more important for case studies than for other types of research, are to assist in the following: defining the "case" to be studied; identifying the criteria for selecting and screening the potential candidates for the cases; and suggesting the relevant topics of interest and, therefore, possible data to be collected. Guidance from preliminary theoretical concepts can make all these choices easier, even if you later need to reposition your case study based on your early data collection.

How theory was used in five different case studies is the subject of the present chapter. The topics of the case studies cover the following topics: (1) organizing local services and routinizing innovations, (2) forming and maintaining interorganizational partnerships, (3) implementing initiatives in special education (the education of students with disabilities), (4) attracting high-tech firms to locate in research parks, and (5) explaining how and why findings from natural hazards research are eventually put into practice.

AUTHOR'S NOTE: This chapter is an expanded, adapted, and edited version of a paper written by Robert K. Yin that first appeared in Huey-tsyh Chen and Peter H. Rossi (Eds.), *Using Theory to Improve Program and Policy Evaluations* (1992, pp. 97–114), an imprint of Greenwood Publishing Group, Inc., Westport, Connecticut. Used with permission.

WHAT IS THE ROLE OF THEORY IN DOING CASE STUDIES?

Continued interest in the role of theory in doing evaluations (Chen, 1990; Chen & Rossi, 1989; Sutton & Staw, 1995) has had a counterpart in the role of theory in designing and doing case studies. Theory can be important to case studies in many ways, helping in the following areas:

- Specifying what is being explored when you are doing exploratory case studies
- Defining the nature of the "case(s)" to be part of your case study
- Defining a complete and appropriate description when you are doing descriptive case studies
- Stipulating rival theories when you are doing explanatory case studies

From this perspective, the term *theory* covers more than cause-effect relationships. Rather, *theory* means the design of research steps according to some relationship to the literature, policy issues, or other substantive source. Excluded would be considerations of access, convenience, logistics, or nonsubstantive issues. Good use of theory will help delimit a case study inquiry to its most effective design; theory also is essential for generalizing the subsequent results (see **BOX 2**).

BOX 2

Using Theory in Case Study Research

As pointed out and illustrated throughout the five applications in the present chapter, theoretical considerations can help at many stages in doing case study research. However, how you might develop such theory, especially prior to collecting any data, is sometimes an elusive matter. The desired theory should by no means be considered with the formality of "grand theory" in social science but should simply provide a blueprint for your study, such as developing "a [hypothetical] story about [*how* and] *why* acts, events, and structure occur" (Sutton & Staw, 1995, p. 378; italics added).

As one example, if you are at the stage of selecting the case(s) to be studied, the emerging theory might be about the (substantive, not logistical) quality of the case(s) that draws attention to itself. *How* and *why* the case seems to have special meaning would represent the start of an important theoretical statement. You could then link the statement, if desired, to related literature and thereby increase the potential contribution of even a single-case study.

As a second example, if you are at the stage of trying to generalize from the findings of your case study, having an emerging theory beforehand might point to *how* and *why* the eventual findings might be expected to be relevant to other similar situations or conditions. Focusing on the *how* and *why* of these and other questions can go a long way toward helping you increase the value of your case study.

(For more information, see Yin, 2009a, Chapter 2, section on "The Role of Theory in Design Work.")

The purpose of this chapter is to provide five specific illustrations of theory-based applications to case study research. Included are applications of theory to exploratory case studies, case selection, descriptive case studies, and two types of explanatory case studies.

EXPLORATORY CASE STUDIES

The exploratory case study has perhaps given all of case study research its most notorious reputation. In this type of case study, fieldwork and data collection are undertaken prior to the final definition of study questions or specific methodological procedures. Research may follow intuitive paths, often perceived by others as sloppy. However, the goal justifiably may be to discover theory by directly observing a social phenomenon in its natural form (Glaser & Strauss, 1967). Moreover, when the final study questions and methodological needs are settled, the final study may not necessarily be a case study but may assume some other form. Therefore, the exploratory case study (see **BOX 3**) has been considered a prelude to much social research, not just to new case studies.

BOX 3

Exploratory Case Studies

A major problem with exploratory case studies arises when investigators wrongly use the data collected during the exploratory phase as part of the ensuing case study. You could then be accused of having conducted a case study in which you found what you were looking for. Thus, you should not permit such slippage from the exploratory (pilot) phase into the actual case study to occur.

(Continued)

(Continued)

An exploratory study should be conducted as a separate task. You may have started your exploratory work because you were initially uncertain about some major aspect of your anticipated case study—the questions to be asked, the hypotheses of study, the data collection methods, the access to the data, or the data analytic methods—and, therefore, needed to investigate one or more of these issues. Once investigated, the pilot or exploratory phase should be considered as having been completed. Now, you are ready to start the real case study from scratch with a complete research design, a whole new set of sources of information, and a fresh set of data.

(For more information, see Yin, 2009a, Chapter 2, section on "Study Propositions.")

An illustrative application of the exploratory case study occurred as part of a final study on how innovations in urban services become routinized (Yin, 1981, 1982). (Contemporary interest in this topic falls under the related concept of "sustainability.") Service agencies were experiencing difficulties in making such innovations survive beyond the adoption phase. This meant that an innovation might be put into place for a two- or three-year period, show promising results, but then stop being used. The policy relevance of the study was to determine how to avoid such an outcome.

The exploratory cases were part of a pilot test for the final study, which ultimately involved 12 case studies and a telephone survey about innovations at 90 other sites. In the pilot study, the study team spent an extended time collecting substantial data from seven sites (none of which were used in the final study). Such a high proportion of pilot to final case study sites (seven to 12) is exceptional, but the study team had important questions in need of answers.

The Exploratory Issue: The Need to Create a Framework of Study

Only the broad features of the final study design had been determined ahead of time. First, the study team knew it was to select different types of innovations, but none of the innovations had been predetermined. Second, the team was to follow a retrospective design: The sites to be studied would be those in which the routinization of an innovation was known to have occurred so that the entire routinization life cycle could be studied, even though the data had to be collected retrospectively. Third, the study team would emphasize actual behavioral events in the routinization life cycle, in contrast to an alternative focus on people's perceptions of such processes. However, within these broader themes, the specific design and data collection methods were unspecified. Thus, a pilot test was designed to determine the innovations and services to be studied as well as the conceptual framework and operational measures to be used.

A key ingredient was the use of a special pilot protocol that elaborated alternative features about the life cycle of an innovation. The study team understood that adoption-implementation-routinization potentially constituted the entire life cycle but had not developed specific hypotheses or measures to facilitate empirical study. In this sense, the protocol fostered the development of operational concepts, not just methodological issues.

The study team modified this pilot protocol after every pilot site study was completed. The iterative process forced the team to address several questions repeatedly: Had sufficient information been learned that an existing exploratory question could now be dropped? Had new problems emerged, requiring the framing of a new question? Did an existing question need to be modified? The team also deliberately explored a variety of innovations, ultimately leading to the selection of the final six types. More important, the pilot study helped refine the conceptual framework for the final study. Ultimately, the research questions and instrumentation for studying an innovation's life cycle emerged.

Illustrative Results and Key Lessons

The pilot testing helped identify six innovations in three urban services (law enforcement, education, and fire protection) that were ultimately studied at more than 100 sites. However, the most important result of the pilot testing was the development of a conceptual framework and operational measures of a hypothesized routinization process. Measurable organizational events were identified as "cycles" or "passages," as illustrated in Exhibit 3.1. Furthermore, certain cycles and passages were predicted to occur earlier in the routinization process and others later. The framework pointed readily to the data to be collected and enabled the final study to proceed.

Another important result of the pilot testing was the finding that, whereas a single protocol could be used for the case studies, the study team had to design six separate questionnaires for the telephone survey, one for each type of innovation. For phone interviews, the terminology and events were sufficiently different that a generic set of questions could not be used. This discovery created much unanticipated work for the study team; in fact, the team resisted the finding throughout the pilot phase because of the known consequences in workload. However, no single questionnaire would work.

This experience with pilot testing shows how explicit explorations can elaborate key conceptual topics in some previously identified broad subject area. The use of a pilot protocol is strongly suggested as a tool for ensuring that the exploration is following some exploratory theory and that you are not merely wandering through the exploratory phase.

Exhibit 3.1   Organizational Passages and Cycles Related to Routinization

Type or Operation of Resource	Passages	Cycles
Budget	Innovation supports changes from soft to hard money	Survives annual budget cycles
Personnel: Jobs	Functions become part of job descriptions or prerequisites	—
Incumbent turnover	—	Survives introduction of new personnel; survives promotion of key personnel
Training: Prepractice	Skills become part of professional standards, professional school curriculum	—
In-service	—	Skills taught during many training cycles
Organizational governance	Innovative activity attains appropriate organizational status	Attains widespread use
Supply and maintenance	Supply and maintenance are provided by agency or on long-term (contract) basis	Survives equipment turnover

CASE SELECTION AND SCREENING:
CRITERIA AND PROCEDURES

The elaboration of theoretical issues related to the objectives of study also can provide useful guidance when you are selecting the case or cases to be studied (see **BOX 4**). The difficulties of this process and how they were overcome are shown in the second of the five illustrative applications, which was a study of local job training and economic development efforts.

BOX 4

Screening Candidate Cases

Selecting the cases for a case study should not simply be a matter of finding the most convenient or accessible case (or field setting) from which you can collect data. The case selection should be based on a clear, if not strong, substantive rationale. For instance, you may desire to have exemplary instances of the phenomenon being studied, or you may want multiple cases that include contrasting conditions.

Whatever the reasons, the candidate cases should be screened beforehand, and you need to anticipate this as a step in your work plan. The screening process will involve collecting sufficient data to decide whether a case meets your pre-established criteria. The most desirable screening process will identify an array of candidate cases but without actually collecting so much data that the screening begins to emulate the conduct of the actual case studies. In other words, you need to be careful to avoid allowing the screening procedure to become too extensive or too expensive.

(For more information, see Yin, 2009a, Chapter 3, section on "Screening the Candidate Cases for Your Case Study.")

The Research Issue: Linking Job Training and Economic Development at the Local Level

The study objective was to investigate how linkages between local job training (for the hard-to-employ) and local economic development efforts can produce distinctive outcomes (COSMOS, 1989). The potential advantage for the training participants is that placement is more likely to occur in jobs in growing industries and occupations, resulting in more enduring job placements. Conversely, for employers in growing lines of business, a larger pool of appropriately trained employees is created, thereby making recruitment easier. Without such linkages between job training and economic development, neither advantage is likely to be realized: Job training efforts alone can easily lead to placement in low-growth jobs for the hard-to-employ; economic development efforts alone can focus too heavily on employers' facilities and capital needs, overlooking their potential employment needs. A series of case studies was intended to examine these linkage situations and how these outcomes were produced. However, although linkage was simple in concept, it was difficult to define operationally. What kinds of cases would be relevant?

Unit of Analysis

An initial challenge was to define the "case." The study team readily understood that this unit would not necessarily be a single organization or initiative. To study linkage, a joint organizational effort (between two or more organizations) or joint initiatives (job training and economic development) would likely be the "case." The identification of such joint efforts, therefore, became the first task, before any case selection could be possible.

A troubling characteristic involved the context for such joint efforts. At the local level, such efforts can be represented by at least three different options: a joint project, a joint program, or an interorganizational arrangement. *Joint projects* included a community college offering a course focusing on the skills needed for the entry-level jobs of specific local firms in a high-growth industry, in collaboration with those firms. The study team found numerous examples of these joint projects in the published literature. *Joint programs* included statewide training programs for dislocated workers. In general, these programmatic efforts were more sustained than single projects. In the few years preceding the study, many states had taken such initiatives. In contrast, *interorganizational arrangements* did not necessarily focus on a single project or program. Rather, the qualifying criterion was that two or more organizations had joined in some arrangement—by forming a joint venture, initiating a consortium, or using interagency agreements among existing organizations—to coordinate training and economic development activities.

With regard to these three options, both theory and policy relevance played the critical role in the study team's final choice. First, the existing literature indicated that the three options were different—cases of one were not to be confused with cases of the others. For instance, programs call for more significant outlays than projects, and interorganizational arrangements may be the most troublesome but can then result in multiple programs and projects.

Second, the literature had given less attention to interorganizational arrangements, even though these had more promise of local capacity building in the long run. Thus, a local area with a workable interorganizational arrangement may sustain many efforts and may not be as vulnerable to the sporadic nature of single projects or programs.

Third, the study team was interested in advancing knowledge about interorganizational arrangements. Over the years, attention had been devoted to public-private partnerships, not just in employment and economic development but also in many services for specific population groups (e.g., in housing, education, social services, healthcare, mental healthcare, and community development). Yet, the available literature was shallow with regard to the workings of interorganizational arrangements—how they are formed, what makes them thrive, and how to sustain them.

Finally, a study of interorganizational arrangements also could cover component programs or projects—within the arrangements—as embedded units of analysis. In this way, the study could still touch on the other two options. For all these reasons, the study team selected the interorganizational arrangement as the type of case to be studied.

Criteria for Selecting Cases

The selection criteria started with the practical constraint that only a small number of cases could be the subject of study, because the study team wanted to collect data extensively from each interorganizational arrangement—collecting data directly from each of the participating organizations rather than covering just the lead organization. This constraint was based on the study team's desire to investigate the dynamics of each arrangement. The team suspected that no single organization would have accurate information on what might turn out to be a diversity of programs and projects within each arrangement.

A further constraint was the study's need to inform national policy. Although no representational sampling scheme could be used with such a small number of cases, some distributive factors still demanded attention. Overall, multiple cases were required, but only a small number could be studied, leading to the use of a replication logic to select the final cases.

In using the replication logic, the first selection criterion was that every case had to demonstrate—prior to final case selection—the occurrence of exemplary outcomes. This exemplary case design has been cited as an important use of case studies (Ginsburg, 1989). The basic replication question would then be whether similar events in each arrangement could account for these outcomes. A second criterion reflected the study's policy concern—some arrangements were to have a federally supported organization at their center, but other arrangements were to have such organizations in a more peripheral relationship. A third criterion was that the cases were to cover different regions of the country, emphasizing different economic conditions—reflected in the stereotypic notions of "sunbelt," "snowbelt," and "rustbelt."

As a result of these considerations, the study team sought six cases. All had to have documented and exemplary outcomes that could survive the study team's screening procedures. Three of the cases would have a key federally supported organization at their center; the other three would have such an organization in a more peripheral relationship. Together, the six cases would have to cover some distribution of different geographic and economic conditions.

Case Screening

The selection criteria led to a major effort for screening candidate cases. Such an effort is not an unusual adjunct of using the replication logic, and you must plan for sufficient time and resources to support the screening process. At the same time, if not properly controlled, the screening of any given candidate can become too extensive. The amount of screening data would begin to resemble the amount used in an actual case study—which would be far too much (you cannot do a case study of every candidate). Nevertheless, you must be prepared to collect and analyze actual empirical data at this stage.

The study team began its screening process by contacting numerous individuals in the field and consulting available reports and literature. These sources were used to suggest candidates that fit the selection criteria, resulting in a list of 62 nominees. The study team then attempted to contact these nominees both in writing and by phone. The team obtained information on 47 of them.

The information was based on responses to a structured interview of about 45 minutes, using a formal instrument. Each of the candidate arrangements also was encouraged to submit written materials and reports about its operations. The final analysis determined that 22 of the 47 candidates were eligible for further consideration. Exhibit 3.2 lists these 22 candidates (the exhibit also shows the 25 candidates that were considered outside the scope of further interest, and why). From these 22, the study team then selected the final 6 based on the thoroughness of the documentation and accessibility of the site.

Exhibit 3.2   Organizations Screened by the Project Team

Category	Name of Organization Contacted	Location/Belt	Type of Area
I. Within Scope of Further Interest			
Participation by local economic development agencies	Chester County Office of Employment and Training*	West Chester, PA/Rustbelt	Rural-Suburban
	City of Grand Rapids Development Office*	Grand Rapids, MI/Rustbelt	Urban-Suburban
	Columbus, Indiana Economic Development Board	Columbus, IN/Rustbelt	Rural
	Corpus Christi Area Economic Development Corporation	Corpus Christi, TX/Sunbelt	Urban
	Department of Community and Senior Citizens Services	Los Angeles, CA/Sunbelt	Suburban
	Department of Economic Development	Tacoma, WA/Mixed	Urban
	Office of Economic and Strategic Development	Merced, CA/Sunbelt	Rural
Participation by private industry councils or Job Training Partnership Act organizations	Northeast Florida Private Industry Council, Inc.*	Jacksonville, FL/Sunbelt	Rural-Mixed
	Pima County Community Services Department*	Tucson, AZ/Sunbelt	Urban-Rural-Suburban
	Portland Private Industry Council	Portland, OR/Mixed	Urban
	Private Industry Council of Snohomish County	Everett, WA/Mixed	Rural-Suburban

Category	Name of Organization Contacted	Location/Belt	Type of Area
	South Coast Private Industry Council	North Quincy, MA/Snowbelt	Suburban
	Susquehanna Region Private Industry Council, Inc.*	Havre de Grace, MD/Mixed	Rural-Suburban
	Western Missouri Private Industry Council	Sedalia, MO/Mixed	Rural
	Yuma Private Industry Council	Yuma, AZ/Sunbelt	Urban-Towns
Participation by other self-standing organizations	Cascade Business Center Corporation	Portland, OR/Mixed	Urban
	Daytona Beach Community College	Daytona Beach, FL/Sunbelt	Urban-Rural
	Greater Waterbury Chamber of Commerce	Waterbury, CT/Snowbelt	Towns
	Job Opportunities in Nevada	Reno, NV/Sunbelt	Urban-Rural
	Monadnock Training Council	Milford, NH/Snowbelt	Mixed
	Nevada Business Services	Las Vegas, NV/Sunbelt	Urban
	Seattle-King County Economic Development Council*	Seattle, WA/Mixed	Urban-Suburban

II. Outside Scope of Further Interest

Category	Name of Organization Contacted	Location/Belt	Type of Area
Sites with insufficient information about economic development activities	Cambridge Instruments, Inc.	Buffalo, NY/Snowbelt	Urban
	Community College of Rhode Island	Lincoln, RI/Snowbelt	Suburban
	Frost Incorporated	Grand Rapids, MI/Rustbelt	Urban
	Hawaii Entrepreneurship Training and Development Institute	Honolulu, HI/Sunbelt	Urban
	Indiana Vocational Technical College	Indianapolis, IN/Rustbelt	Mixed
	Metropolitan Re-Employment Project	St. Louis, MO/Rustbelt	Urban
	National Technological University	Ft. Collins, CO/Snowbelt	Mixed

(Continued)

Exhibit 3.2   (Continued)

Category	Name of Organization Contacted	Location/Belt	Type of Area
Single organizations operating both training and economic development activities	Coastal Enterprises, Inc.	Wiscasset, ME/Snowbelt	Rural
	Cooperative Home Care Associates	Bronx, NY/Snowbelt	Urban
	Esperanza Unida, Inc.	Milwaukee, WI/Snowbelt	Urban
	Focus Hope	Detroit, MI/Rustbelt	Urban
	Women's Economic Development Corporation	St. Paul, MN/Snowbelt	Urban-Suburban
Training institutions operating both training and economic development activities	The Business Development and Training Center at Great Valley	Malvern, PA/Rustbelt	Rural
	Catonsville Community College	Baltimore, MD/Rustbelt	Urban-Suburban
	Highlander Economic Development Center	New Market, TN/Mixed	Rural
	Job Services of Florida	Perry, FL/Sunbelt	Rural
	Luzerne County Community College	Nanticoke, PA/Rustbelt	Urban-Suburban
	Massachusetts Career Development Institute	Springfield, MA/Snowbelt	Suburban
	Niagara County Community College	Sanborn, NY/Snowbelt	Mostly Rural
	Pensacola Junior College	Pensacola, FL/Sunbelt	Metropolitan-Rural
State-level operations	Arizona Dept. of Economic Security	Phoenix, AZ/Sunbelt	Mostly rural
	Bluegrass State Skills Corporation	Frankfort, KY/Mixed	Mixed
	Delaware Development Office	Dover, DE/Rustbelt	Urban-Rural
	State of Iowa Dept. of Economic Development	Des Moines, IA/Snowbelt	Urban-Rural
	North Carolina Department of Community Colleges	Raleigh, NC/Sunbelt	Mixed

*One of six organizations selected for final study

Key Lessons

This stage of case study research can assume major proportions in a broader study. In the present illustration, the selection process consumed about 20% of the study's overall resources. Such major investments are not readily appreciated by funding sponsors. However, if the selection process is not properly conducted, even more trouble will result in the ensuing phases of the research.

One alternative not pursued in this case study but implemented in other studies can make the case selection step more formal but can produce even more useful information. This alternative is to define the screening process as a formal survey. Its design would depend on the ability to specify a universe and a sampling plan. However, the survey could cover the information for the selection criteria as well as additional descriptive features. Because of the representativeness of the sample, the descriptive features could be used as a backdrop for the final case study. In this manner, the survey would contribute to the entire study, not just to the narrower role of selecting the cases to be studied.

DESCRIPTIVE CASE STUDIES

Guidance about the development of descriptive theory has generally been overlooked in favor of guidance about explanatory theory. Yet, many case studies have description as their main objective. Such circumstances still can call for some theory to suggest the priorities for data collection. The typical atheoretic statement, "Let's collect information about everything," does not work, and without a descriptive theory, you may soon encounter enormous problems in keeping your case study within manageable proportions.

Multiple-Case Design

An illustrative use of descriptive theory was a study on special education (education for students with disabilities) in four states—Massachusetts, South Dakota, North Dakota, and New Jersey (Pyecha et al., 1988). The case study analysis followed a pattern-matching procedure: Data about each state's activities were compared with two rival, idealized, and theoretic patterns. The prediction was that two states (Massachusetts and South Dakota) would follow one pattern but not the other, whereas the other two states (North Dakota and New Jersey) would have the reverse result.

Thus, the case study design, even for a descriptive study, followed a replication logic. Without sufficiently strong theory, the differences or similarities between states would be difficult to interpret. In other words, the role of theory was to specify the descriptive differences between the two types of states that would be considered substantively critical. The key to the study design was the detailed and prior development of the rival theoretic patterns, portrayed as alternative *scenarios.* Experts helped develop and review these scenarios (or descriptive theories), against which the actual data were later compared.

The Research Issue: Categorical Versus Noncategorical Education

Elementary and secondary special education can commonly occur in *categorical,* self-contained classes. In this arrangement, students are first categorized according to disability; those with similar disabilities are then grouped and taught together for some if not all of their classes. This philosophy of education argues the following: (a) that different disabilities arise from different etiologies; (b) that students with different disabilities have different learning needs; and, therefore, (c) that different instructional methods must be developed and tailored to each type of disability. Furthermore, grouping the students according to their disabilities leads to more homogeneous classrooms, making instruction easier.

Logical as the argument appears, an alternative educational philosophy is that the educational needs and learning processes of students with disabilities are basically no different from those of other students with disabilities or from those of students without disabilities. Major differences may arise in the levels of achievement, but separate instructional methods are not relevant. Thus, except for limited supplemental situations, students with and without disabilities should share the same classrooms, curriculum, and instruction.

This alternative philosophy is known as *noncategorical* education, the implementation of which produces several benefits in comparison with categorical systems. First and foremost, a noncategorical system permits students with disabilities to remain in neighborhood schools, whereas categorical systems can lead to special classes (indeed, special schools) in remote locations, due to scalar requirements. Second, a noncategorical system is fully integrated with the regular education system, whereas a categorical system produces a dual system (one for regular education students and the other for students with disabilities). Third, a noncategorical system can avoid the potential negative consequences of labeling a student as having a disability.

Debate over these contrasting philosophies in education circles has been strong. During the 1970s and 1980s, two states chose to implement noncategorical systems—Massachusetts and South Dakota. A study of how such systems differ in practice from categorical systems had to be conceived as a multiple-case study.

The purpose of the study was not to determine which system was better. Instead, the purpose was descriptive—to define current practices in using noncategorical systems, determining whether such practices are indeed different from those in categorical systems.

Selection of Cases

Because state policy is a major organizing force for all local public education, the state department of education was the case in this third illustrative application. The study had to include Massachusetts and South Dakota automatically because they were the only states with noncategorical systems. For comparison purposes, the study team selected two geographically similar states to be paired with these first two states—New Jersey with Massachusetts and North Dakota with South Dakota.

In each state, educational services are delivered by local systems. Therefore, a sample of 28 such local systems also was selected for study in the four chosen states, representing an embedded unit of analysis. Data from the local systems were needed to ensure that differences in state policies actually resulted in different practices at the local level. For this reason, the selection of these 28 local systems was based on a state official's informed judgment that a district was implementing the state's policies with fidelity, so the selection of local systems again reflected a replication logic.

Development of Descriptive Scenarios

The design of the study required the careful development of idealized scenarios of the two types of systems. Draft scenarios initially were based on the research literature and consultation with experts. An expert advisory panel then reviewed the drafts, making important comments and modifications. The completed scenarios became the basis for developing data collection protocols.

The importance of these scenarios in the study design cannot be underestimated. Descriptive studies typically fail to specify a priori the critical ingredients of the phenomenon to be described. Data collection can then ramble as a result, and the ensuing case study may even contain undesirable, circular reasoning—the final description constituting a contaminated combination of what may have been expected and what was found. In contrast, the scenarios in the present application were intended to recapture the essence of what constituted categorical or noncategorical systems. The driving question underlying the development of the scenarios was, "What specific educational practices must a local school system have to be considered an example of categorical (or noncategorical) education?" The scenarios and their practices defined the relevant data collection: The presence or absence of a series of practices (10 for categorical and 17 for noncategorical education) was to be tracked in each of the 28 local school systems.

Note that under this scheme, unanticipated findings are not precluded. Revelatory or important information found outside the original scenarios can still be collected and analyzed later. However, the initial scenarios provide major support in structuring the data collection in the first place and avoiding an unending collection process.

Results

For most but not all of the proposed features, the 28 school systems in the four states followed the predicted pattern: Local systems in the two states with categorical policies were more like one another than like those in the two states with noncategorical policies. At the same time, a subset of features was not found, as postulated by the scenarios, to distinguish more sharply between the local systems in the categorical states and those in the noncategorical states. One example was a practice where special education was not found to be located in special facilities in the categorical states. Such a practice had been one of the 10 originally stipulated in the scenario for the categorical states. As another example, the cases revealed that principals in the noncategorical states did not control special education in their schools. Such a practice had been one of the 17 originally stipulated for the noncategorical states. Therefore, the overall findings were used to modify the original scenarios on the basis of the empirical findings.

Key Lessons

One lesson was that the scenarios could not have been developed had there not been an extensive literature and policy debate on categorical versus noncategorical systems. The literature and debate provided an array of practices, in highly operational terms, to be tested in the field. Many other topics for potential case studies may not have such rich sources, and a tentative descriptive theory may not be as easily developed. Under such circumstances, the actual case study may move toward being an exploratory rather than a descriptive case study.

A second lesson concerned the benefit of having rival theories. Without the categorical system as a contrast, any description of the noncategorical system could have become undisciplined and spilled over to other aspects of school system operations not critical to their noncategorical nature. The availability of a rival theory helped avoid such an expansive tendency, instead focusing data collection on the practices important to noncategorical systems.

EXPLANATORY CASE STUDIES I: FACTOR THEORIES

In quantitative analysis, one of the most common types of explanatory theories is a *factor* theory (Downs & Mohr, 1976; Mohr, 1978). Whether explaining some economic outcome (marketplace factors), individual behavior (psychological factors), or social phenomenon (social factors), this paradigm assembles a list of independent variables and determines those that are most highly correlated with the dependent variable. To the extent that the independent variables account for the variability in the dependent variable, the independent variables are said to "explain" the phenomenon of interest. To conduct the analysis and account for such complexities as the interactions among the independent variables, quantitative investigators may use factor analysis, regression analysis, and analysis of variance as illustrative statistical techniques.

The use of factor theories has its counterpart in case study research, although such an application is not preferred. However, if factor theories reflect the state of knowledge on a given case study topic, you may not be able to avoid this application. Many explanatory case studies have had to be done under these conditions. Therefore, this fourth illustrative application was included to show how a factor theory can be incorporated into a case study but also to suggest the limitations of this procedure.

The Research Issue: How to Attract High-Tech Firms to New Locations

Local economic development theory is a good example of a topic still dominated by factor theories. Firms are said to be influenceable in their decisions to locate or relocate due to the following illustrative factors:

- The availability of venture capital and other forms of start-up financing
- The local tax structure, including costs due to taxes and incentives due to tax breaks
- The physical characteristics of a place (physical capital)
- The labor force characteristics of a place (human capital)
- The governing laws and regulations covering wages, the formation of unions, depreciation, and numerous other items
- The preferences of key executives and their spouses

Within each general factor can be created long lists of specific factors, and local governments try to use these specific factors as policy tools in attracting firms. The most attractive locale is the one that can maximize as many factors as possible. However, rarely are these factors expressed in some coherent explanation of why firms relocate and how to get them to do so.

The illustrative application investigated a contemporary offshoot of this traditional situation by focusing on high-tech firms (COSMOS, 1985). The study asked whether high-tech firms respond to the same factors as any industrial firm or whether some other factors also are important. The study's goal was to identify such distinctive factors, if any, to provide advice to local governments desirous of attracting high-tech firms and not just industrial firms—a goal glorified by such classic high-tech successes as California's Silicon Valley, North Carolina's Research Triangle, and Boston's Route 128 corridor.

The study could have been designed as a survey or secondary analysis of economic data, both of which have been common ways of investigating this topic. However, such investigations do not permit in-depth examination of the factors themselves, focusing mainly on the outcome of whether a firm has decided to relocate. In contrast, the illustrative case study was intended to examine the factors more closely, thereby requiring data collection from a variety of sources and not just from the firm itself.

Data Collection and Findings From Firms in Nine High-Tech or Industrial Parks

To satisfy this objective, the study team conducted nine case studies. The cases were not firms. Rather, each case was either a high-tech park (mostly consisting of high-tech firms) or an industrial park (mostly consisting of industrial—e.g., manufacturing—firms). The team began with a long list of potential initiatives (or factors) used to attract firms. From this long list, the team determined the initiatives actually used by each park to attract firms, through interviews with the park's developers and local economic development officials as well as through an analysis of documentary evidence. The team then surveyed the firms in each park to ascertain the rationales for their locational choices and to confirm whether these mirrored the parks' initiatives. In all, the team conducted nine case studies and surveyed 232 firms, with responses from 200 of them (86%).[1]

The responses from the firms initially were used to confirm whether the parks were indeed dominated by either high-tech or industrial firms. Table 3.1 shows that Parks A, B, F, and I had more firms in research businesses than in manufacturing businesses and, therefore, were considered high-tech parks. Conversely, Parks C, D, E, G, and H had more firms in manufacturing than in research businesses and, therefore, were considered industrial parks.

The case studies were used to determine the initiatives (factors) undertaken by the developers of each of the nine parks to attract firms. Overall, certain basic factors (such as location near markets or transportation access) prevailed in all nine parks. However, in comparison to the five industrial parks, the four high-tech parks were found to have undertaken the following additional initiatives:

1. Exclusionary zoning or restrictive covenants, to produce a campus-like environment

2. University initiatives, to create collaborative efforts or personnel exchange between firms and local universities

3. Special utility capabilities, whether related to electrical power or telephone lines

Table 3.1 Number of Firms in Each Park, by Type of Business Conducted

Park	Research	Light Manufacturing	Heavy Manufacturing and Distribution	Other	Total
A	8	0	0	16	24
B	7	2	0	9	18
C	0	1	8	6	15
D	0	12	6	8	26
E	2	6	3	5	16
F	8	1	0	10	19
G	3	3	3	14	23
H	0	1	2	1	4
I	21	2	0	3	26
Totals	49	28	22	72	171

The identification of these additional initiatives permitted the study team to conclude that high-tech parks had pursued policies distinct from those of industrial parks.

The survey responses from the firms were analyzed to determine whether preference for these same initiatives distinguished high-tech from industrial firms. The results supported the importance of the university and utility initiatives to the acceptable degree of statistical significance, but they were neutral regarding the importance of a campus-like environment. Despite the lack of confirmation for this last initiative, the study team concluded that real-estate developers wanting to attract high-tech firms should focus on the three initiatives in addition to those used to attract industrial firms.

Key Lessons

This example demonstrates the use of a factor theory in an explanatory case study. The case study was able to identify individual initiatives to attract high-tech firms. Nevertheless, the limitations of this approach, with a factor theory available but to be tested using only nine cases, also should be evident:

- No deeper understanding could be developed regarding a firm's actual decision-making process in deciding to relocate.
- The initiatives (or factors) to be taken by the developers could not be ranked in any order of importance.
- The potential interactions among the factors—and whether these factors might have been part of the same, more general, factor—could not be determined.

Possibly, the latter two of these shortcomings can be overcome by using some method other than the case study. Factor theories generally thrive when there are a large number of data points to conduct extensive analysis among the factors, thereby favoring survey or secondary analysis rather than case study designs. The ensuing factor analysis or regression analysis can then be directed at determining the relative strength or importance of each factor as well as at the interactions between factors. However, the limited analytic possibilities when applying a factor theory to a case study create a less attractive situation.

EXPLANATORY CASE STUDIES II: "HOW" AND "WHY" THEORIES

In comparison to factor theories, explanatory theories—or what might be called "how" and "why" theories—are more suitable for designing and doing explanatory case studies. In fact, the more complex and multivariate the explanatory theory, the better. The case study analysis can then take advantage of pattern-matching techniques. Unfortunately, viable explanatory theories do not always exist for the topics covered by case studies, so you cannot always use this approach. However, a study conducted on the topic of research utilization benefited from the prior existence of several complex and rival theories—readily translatable into operational terms—and serves as this chapter's fifth illustrative application.

The Research Issue: How and Why Do Research Findings Get Into Practical Use?

The illustrative study focused on the key policy objective of making research more useful (Yin & Moore, 1988). Nine case studies were selected in which a funded research project was the main case. All projects were on a topic of natural hazards research and were known to have led to significant scientific publications, but the projects varied in their utilization outcomes. In the natural hazards field, such outcomes occur when engineers, planners, and government agencies use research findings to make actual changes in their practices or policies. The illustrative case study assessed and confirmed the occurrence and nature of any utilization outcomes, but it then went further to examine the explanations for these outcomes. Such explanations, in turn, were based on three major rival theories in the literature on research utilization: a knowledge-driven theory, a problem-solving theory, and a social-interaction theory.

The *knowledge-driven theory* stipulates that ideas and discoveries from basic research eventually result in inventions or advances in applied research, often leading to commercial products or services. Utilization is, therefore, the result of a linear sequence of activities following a "technology-push" process in which researchers continually produce the new ideas that get put into use.

The *problem-solving theory* also follows a linear sequence. However, the stipulated activities begin with the identification of a problem by some individual or organization in need of a solution, not by a research investigator. Even if the problem has been poorly or incorrectly articulated, it is communicated to a research investigator, whose task is to conduct the research needed to identify, test, and assess alternative solutions to the problem. The investigator also may redefine the problem. However, utilization is explained by a "demand-pull" process, reflecting the fact that the ultimate user of the research (a) helped define the initial problem and, therefore, (b) is waiting for and prepared to implement the solution (assuming a viable one emerges from the research).

The *social-interaction theory* does not stipulate a linear process. Rather, this theory claims that in high-utilization environments, research producers and users belong to overlapping professional networks with ongoing communications. The communications need not focus on any particular research endeavor. Instead, the communication exposes researchers and users to each other's worlds and needs, producing a rich "marketplace of ideas" (Yin & Gwaltney, 1981). Such communications can have serendipitous effects. For instance, research investigators may alter the focus of their studies or the early design of their research, based on dialogues with users. Or, as another example, users can project their future needs to reflect a sensitivity to ongoing research developments. In this milieu, utilization ultimately occurs because the continuous flow of communications increasingly leads to good matches between existing needs and emerging new research.

These three theories produced two critical conditions for the illustrative case study. First, they led to a predicted and complex course of events when utilization occurred as well as to the absence of those events when utilization did not occur. The existence of this course of events then could be traced in individual cases, with a pattern-matching analysis comparing the hypothesized with the actual course of events (Trochim, 1989; Yin, 2009a). The complex nature of the course of events made the relevant evidence more discernible. Second, the three theories led to rival courses that were nearly mutually exclusive. Therefore, empirical support for one theory could not be used to argue for support of another theory. In this sense, although the case studies were retrospectively conducted, the data actually permitted the testing of rival theories.

Results

The nine case studies followed a replication design—six cases having strong utilization outcomes, although the research covered different academic fields (e.g., engineering, mathematics, and urban planning), and three cases having negligible utilization outcomes. The main result was that those cases with the most extensive and diverse array of utilization outcomes all were found to have key ingredients of the social-interaction theory: Existing professional networks had created rich, ongoing producer-user dialogue. In some of the cases, professional associations had facilitated the exchange of ideas. In other cases, the exchange was simply the result of an active and communicative principal investigator who had either belonged to or even self-developed a broad network of scholars and practitioners. Overall, communications started earlier and continued far beyond the ending of a specific research project, in comparison to those projects with minimal utilization outcomes.

Key Lessons

The main lesson from this experience is that the presence of explanatory theories can facilitate theory testing with a rich and extensive data collection effort, including qualitative and quantitative evidence. Each of the nine cases was investigated by doing the following: reviewing pertinent documents; interviewing a wide array of individuals, including actual or potential users of the research; and observing the actual research processes or products. The case study protocol, tightly geared to testing the three theories, assured that the diverse data collection would involve converging lines of inquiry and triangulation of the evidence.

A key aspect of the theories was their complexity. This permitted the pattern matching of a series or sequence of events as the main analytic tactic in each of the cases. Without the theories or their complexity, data collection might have been undisciplined and pattern matching impossible. In this respect, the case study method may rely on "how" and "why" theories differently than do other methods. Whereas other methods may prefer single-variable theories and the incremental development of explanatory links over a series of studies, pattern matching in case study analysis permits case studies to test complex explanations in a single study.

CONCLUSIONS

These five illustrations show the multiple applications of theory to case study research. Critical to all illustrations was the development of such theory prior to the conduct of a case study. Furthermore, such development frequently required substantial time, resources, and expertise.

This approach to case studies mimics that used in most experimental science, where expert knowledge of prior research and careful hypothesis development precede actual experimentation. The approach, therefore, requires that you be well informed about the topics of inquiry and not simply dependent on a methodological tool kit. Moreover, the approach gives investigators an opportunity to reveal (and minimize) substantive biases that may affect the design and conduct of a case study. Finally, the approach produces case studies that can be part of a cumulative body of knowledge and not just isolated and short-lived empirical inquiries.

NOTE

1. The complete case study design, therefore, was a multiple-case study of nine parks, with a survey of a sample of the firms within each park being an embedded unit of analysis. The entire study design represents a strong example of combining the use of qualitative and quantitative methods in the same case study.

PART II

DESCRIPTIVE CASE STUDIES

Descriptive case studies have been among the most common case studies. They can offer rich and revealing insights into the social world of a particular case. These insights can then assume greater importance if the case being studied, as with many well-known case studies, covers the following: situations not normally accessible to social scientists (*revelatory* cases), instances of exceedingly successful ventures (*exemplary* cases), one-of-a-kind situations (*unique* cases), extreme conditions (*extreme* cases), or even ordinary conditions (*typical* cases).

Examples of these five kinds of situations are found throughout the case study literature. They also represent the criteria that can be used when choosing to do a descriptive case study in the first place. Of the three case studies presented in Part II, the one about an education leader (Chapter 4) might be considered an exemplary case, the one about citizens on patrol (Chapter 5) might be considered a revelatory case, and the one about a neighborhood organization (Chapter 6) might be considered a typical case.

As a research endeavor, doing descriptive work appears at first to demand only a low level of analytic activity. Everyone, even a nonspecialist, would seem able to produce a description of some sort, whereas other research endeavors such as statistical modeling would seem to call for more specialized and well-developed talents. As a result, in thinking about doing a descriptive case study, your first impression might be the ease of such a task. However, actually trying to describe a case—and covering its specific social scenes and interactions—likely will be more difficult than you initially might have thought.

The main difficulty comes from the need for you to establish the range of topics you will cover and the level of detail you will devote to the case study. Successful descriptions must mediate between trying to describe "everything" and being too sparse. Repeatedly referring back to your rationale for selecting the case being studied may provide some guidance for staying near a golden mean. The role of theory, previously discussed in Part I, now may seem to be more relevant and helpful. Even better results are likely to follow if you have had some experience in doing case studies.

The three applications in Part II present different degrees of detail and expanse. Befitting the purposes of the present book, the first two applications (Chapters 4 and 5) are deliberately short. Their goal is to give you a flavor of descriptive case studies in two different settings—education and residential crime prevention. Whereas the education case study was originally much longer and has been shortened for the present book, the crime prevention case study is presented in its original length. By comparison, the third application reflects a highly detailed and broad range of topics—possibly the most in this entire book. As a result, gaining an appropriate overview of the neighborhood organization requires you to "study" the case. Overall, the three case studies illustrate the variations in presenting descriptive case studies.

4

START-UP FOR A NEWLY APPOINTED EDUCATION LEADER

Many case studies can have an individual person as the subject or "case" being studied. Especially in psychology, such case studies have added invaluably to knowledge about human behavior. However, cases of individual persons also have been an integral part of other fields, such as education and management.

Leaders of organizations frequently serve as the subjects of case studies. The leaders are presumed to have followed some courses of action, made some decisions, or exerted some influence that offers important lessons to be learned. In education, the leader of interest may be a teacher (of a classroom), a principal (of a school), or even a superintendent (of a school system).

Chapter 4 presents a case study of a leader of a large, urban school system. The focus of the case study was on the leader's early tenure in this system. Because of the notoriously high turnover rate among urban school leaders and the pressure to show quick results in upgrading educational performance, many leaders are likely to experience this early phase. The experiences reflected in the current case study were intended to provide some lessons about the conditions other leaders who are new to their jobs are likely to confront.

AUTHOR'S NOTE: This application was written expressly for the present book and is based on a more extensive and earlier case study produced by Robert K. Yin.

INTRODUCTION: SCHOOL SYSTEMS IN THE UNITED STATES

The U.S. public school system consists of organizations known as "school districts." Nearly all districts are governed by a publicly elected school board. In this sense, districts are units of government, not just administrative units.

Schooling takes place in the individual schools that belong to each district. Some districts are extremely large, consisting of hundreds of schools. Other districts are tiny, having only a few schools. Districts also may be highly centralized, defining the curriculum, retaining the teachers, and providing all the support services for each school. Conversely, districts also may be highly decentralized, and the individual schools may define their own curricula, hire and retain teachers, and decide how district funds will be used to support other services.

Whereas the head of a school is a principal, the head of a district is a superintendent. A single district and its superintendent may, therefore, consist of many schools with many principals. All must work together to make the system work, as the normal progression of students means that they will move from elementary to middle to high schools in a feeder-like fashion. The major challenge for the public school systems across the country has been to deliver quality education to a large number of students who enter the system freely (only some schools have admissions requirements) and who receive a free education.

The following case study describes Alice Redding's early efforts in reforming the Steel City District, a large, urban, and underperforming district somewhere in Middle America. For the case study, a good deal of information was obtained in an extensive interview with Redding, a follow-up interview with her, and education articles appearing in Steel City's print media (see **BOX 5**).[1] (Pseudonyms are used for all names and places to preserve the anonymity of the superintendent and the district.)

BOX 5

Case Study Protocols: Aimed at the Investigator, Not Interviewees

A case study protocol serves as an essential tool for collecting case study data. The protocol contains questions that your case study will address.

Because most social science instruments contain questions for interviewees (or respondents), a frequent misconception is that a case study protocol has the same property. However, the case study protocol is, in fact, entirely different. It itemizes questions to be addressed by you as the case study investigator. The protocol also can describe the field procedures that you are to follow. In other words, a case study protocol serves as your own field agenda.

The data collection in the present case study followed just such a protocol. The protocol was developed prior to the fieldwork, and its questions were addressed by obtaining data from multiple sources—that is, by reviewing documents, making direct observations, and conducting interviews. A well-designed protocol will cover the questions of a case study in a systematic manner. As a result, a good protocol also can lead directly to the outline for the case study report.

(For more information, see Yin, 2009a, Chapter 3, section on "The Case Study Protocol.")

A MAJOR REFORM GOAL: DATA-DRIVEN SCHOOL SYSTEMS

The superintendent's main strategic goal was to revamp the district so that all its schools and school staffs would be able to make instructional decisions based on feedback about students' performance. In the school reform literature, this goal has been recognized as striving to create a "data-driven school system."

CONDITIONS CONFRONTED BY THE NEW SUPERINTENDENT

When Superintendent Redding started her tenure at the Steel City District, she brought with her a team of four other senior officials. They all had worked together when Redding was in her previous position as the superintendent of a smaller urban district. Redding easily likened her strategy to being "called into an emergency room" and "needing to have a support team," rather than believing one can "act like Dr. Kildare and try to succeed alone."

Upon their arrival, the team was surprised to find an extremely weak infrastructure at Steel City. Few of the district's key positions were filled—especially the research and assessment function that would be most critical in creating a data-driven system. The district had a chronic shortage of about 400 teachers. Some of the schools were not entirely safe, causing Redding to place armed resource officers in them, although she had opposed such an action earlier in her career.

Even more alarming, for a district that had a budget of about one billion dollars and nearly 11,000 employees, virtually every administrative system still relied on manual operations. (In retrospect, Redding recalled that, just before assuming her superintendency, she had been a paid consultant with the district and had wondered why her consulting checks were handwritten.) From Redding's point of view, everything needed to be fixed, but the world would not stop to allow time for the needed remedies to be put into place. In her words, "I knew how to knit, but I didn't know how to knit a sweater while wearing it."

An early initiative had to be devoted to teacher recruitment. To reduce the flow of teachers from Steel City into more lucrative jobs in the surrounding suburbs, district salaries finally had moved into line with those of the surrounding districts. Redding then spearheaded a recruitment drive that even reached to countries outside the United States. Although there were originally 466 vacancies, one year later, the district had only about 40 unfilled positions. As an important accomplishment, every science and mathematics classroom now had a certified teacher "for the first time in recent memory."

In the classroom, Redding's ideal was for teachers to have ready access to students' test scores, not only on different subjects but on different education strands within each subject. The scores would be used diagnostically, identifying the strands that a teacher might have to reteach to help students reach the next plateau. At the school and district level, the ideal was for principals and the superintendent to have ready access to a wide variety of data—including test scores but also covering enrollment, attendance, transfers, teacher turnover, and many other items—to boost individual schools and the system as a whole.

TRYING TO CREATE EARLY SUCCESSES AND SUPPORT

At the same time, Redding and her team knew that they had to gain broad community support for their administration. To do this, they started two high-profile educational initiatives. Both reflected Redding's deep conviction regarding the importance of literacy, which she viewed as the crux of teaching and learning and where she has kept a "laser focus."

Two Literacy Initiatives

The first was a summer literacy program that took place during the first summer of the new team's tenure. Whereas only 1,500 to 2,000 students had enrolled in such a program the previous year, students for the first time were not charged tuition to attend the program and also were offered transportation services. An oversupply of teachers also had been recruited because the teachers were able to earn extra pay, in part to offset the fact that they had not received raises for a couple of years.

The new summer institute ended up enrolling 12,000 students. It had adopted a rigorous, top-down, goal-oriented, and highly scripted literacy program. Even though the new data system was not in place to trace the effects of the program on students' reading performance, the summer program was nonetheless "a raging success." Even the unions "had got onboard" with the academic agenda.

The second educational initiative also was related to literacy. The district assigned a literacy instructional specialist (as well as a mathematics specialist) to every school. The district had provided training to both the specialists and the schools' principals so that they, in turn, could provide professional development and support the classroom teachers. Newly issued English Language Arts standards for every grade, along with a new district K–12 curriculum, were aligned with the state's proficiency tests. The curriculum emphasized a phonetic approach in the early grades, a spiraling curriculum, students' writing, and reduced dependence on textbook use.

Data-Driven Results

Meanwhile, the team had not ignored its initial strategic goal. Eventually, the efforts began to bear fruit. Newly installed data systems finally could define the number of students enrolled in the district and track student performance down to the classroom level.

In relation to the literacy initiative, the system provided test results with an item analysis to teachers, cross-walking the items with the new standards and enabling teachers to customize their subsequent instruction to prepare for the state's proficiency tests. The data began to show promising results in literacy performance, as Steel City's students improved three times as much as those in the state's seven other large urban districts—and two times the statewide average.

Community and Union Reactions

Redding received widespread public approval for her initiatives. Help for gaining such approval possibly came from her earlier experiences. She learned to maintain a constant posture of "public disclosure," keeping people fully informed about her actions. As she notes, "it is what it is, and when we make a mistake, we say 'oops' and move on."

At the same time, the union initially questioned the use of the literacy and mathematics specialists. Over a period of about two years, the union finally took ownership of the idea of placing such specialists in the most troubled schools, but also put the issue to a vote. The membership defeated the idea but did not try to prevent the district from instituting the policy on a district-wide basis.

REORGANIZING FOR REFORM

Reorganizing the District's Schools

During these early years, Redding also started other important initiatives. One included the placing of the district's 16 struggling schools into a special region, headed by its own regional superintendent. These schools receive extra resources but also must set high performance standards and pursue meaningful changes. The schools also receive especially close scrutiny and oversight. One of the schools later became sufficiently successful that it was able to leave its special status and return to its regular regional organization. The experience was a positive one, but the special status had become so meaningful that the school "was only reluctantly accepting its reassigned status."

Another effort involved reorganizing schools into a grades K–8 and then 9–12 system (the existing system had included a combination of grades K–5, 6–8, 6–12, and 9–12 schools). The goal was to improve student performance at all grade levels, but especially in the middle grades. Two schools were converted in the superintendent's second year, 14 more in the following year, and 21 more in the year after that. Early results suggested that test scores were starting to improve.

Reorganizing the District

After nearly four years in the school district and after having started the important initiatives just described, Alice Redding and her team were ready to reorganize the entire district in a data-driven direction. During this time, she already had appointed new principals in 75 of the district's 122 schools. A new reorganization plan, introduced after these appointments, pairs mentoring principals with those who are still striving to become instructional leaders. The pairs have been working together, and their success will be judged by classroom accountability. As a brief characterization of the desired relationship, the principals are to ask of one another, "Is X being done" and "How do you know?"

The aftereffects of the announced district reorganization took place after the completion of the case study.

NOTE

1. The present case study was part of a broader study that involved additional data not reported in this chapter. The broader study involved fieldwork that directly examined the literacy initiatives started in Steel City during Alice Redding's initial tenure. The fieldwork involved site visits to several schools, interviews of school staff, and reviews of school records. The results of this fieldwork provided a deeper understanding of the initiatives, also corroborating their depiction as reported by Redding herself in the current case study.

INSIDE STORY FOR CHAPTER 4

Elite Interviews

The term *elite interview* refers to those occasions when you are interviewing a person of high stature, such as an elected official, business executive, or other public figure. The person usually fills some unique role and can provide distinctive insights or information covering a whole set of issues and not likely to be obtained from other sources. A clear example of such a person is the school superintendent who was central to the application in the present chapter.

Doing elite interviews can be a challenging task. The elite person is likely to be an experienced interviewee, having been interviewed by media representatives or other researchers like you. As with other interviewees, you may have to penetrate a façade before feeling comfortable about the candor of the interview.

However, possibly different from other interviewees, the experienced interviewee also knows how to manage the interview process and especially the time made available for your open-ended interview. During the interview, you may be startled to find that the interviewee is graciously thanking you and exiting the interview before you have had a chance to cover all your planned topics (however, this did not happen in the present case study). Given the interviewee's elite status, you may then find the person inaccessible for any follow-up conversations. A word of caution, therefore, is to be ready to cover your important topics early in elite interviews, rather than "working up" to the topics as you might do in other interviews—although you may not have had the needed warm-up time.

For Class Discussion or Written Assignment

Discuss the tension, in open-ended interviewing, between the need to spend time on some preliminary "warm-up" topics and the need to cover the most important substantive topics, when the time for an interview is likely to be short. What are the best ways of settling or at least minimizing this tension?

5

CITIZENS ON PATROL

Many residential neighborhoods are known to have "eyes on the street," meaning that neighbors are maintaining casual vigilance over the neighborhood's public areas. The neighbors are watching for any untoward behavior whenever they look out the windows of their homes, sit on their porches, or take walks in the neighborhood. From the standpoint of public safety, such vigilance usually is considered to be a positive sign, also reflecting a degree of solidarity on the part of the residents.

Taking this volunteer activity one step further, the residents in many neighborhoods have organized themselves to operate formal patrols. The patrol members usually do not carry any weapons. The patrol routine involves systematically covering the neighborhood's streets and other public places, and the patrol members are ready to call the local police should they see or suspect any untoward behavior. Understanding how such patrols work and whether they might create their own problems, such as becoming "vigilante" groups, was the topic of a study covering many such patrols under a variety of neighborhood settings. The following chapter contains a description of but one of the patrols that were the subjects of separate case studies. As part of the same overall study, other patrols were the subject of a survey (see **BOX 6**).

AUTHOR'S NOTE: This application was written expressly for the present book. The application is based on an earlier case study that appeared, along with many other case studies, in *Patrolling the Neighborhood Beat: Residents and Residential Security*, Rand Corporation, Washington, D.C., March 1976, as part of a project designed and directed by Robert K. Yin and supported by the U.S. Department of Justice.

BOX 6

Case Studies as Part of a Mixed Methods Study

Mixed methods research consists of single studies that employ two or more different methods (e.g., a survey and a case study as part of the same overall study). The single-case study presented in this chapter was part of a fuller, multiple-case study that was a mixed methods study.

First, it involved 32 case studies, such as the one in the present chapter, and covered patrols across the country. Second, the research team conducted phone interviews with the patrol leaders of 100 other patrols. All this information became part of a cross-case synthesis and then the basis for drawing conclusions about the workings of citizen patrols.

Among other contributions, the findings included a newly articulated typology of patrols: patrols limited to buildings or residential compounds (*building patrols*); patrols of neighborhood streets more generally (*neighborhood patrols*); and patrols offering escort, delivery, and other community services (*service patrols*). Of the three, the neighborhood patrols are most prone to accusations of vigilanteism because the patrol members cannot readily distinguish the residents who live in the neighborhood from those who do not. The patrol in this chapter was one of the neighborhood patrols.

(For more information, see Yin, 2009a, Chapter 2, section on "Mixed Methods Designs.")

STUDYING CITIZEN PATROLS

Residential Crime Prevention

In the face of rising crime rates and a declining sense of security, residents may undertake their own crime prevention activities. Participation is entirely voluntary. Although some actions—such as adding locks and alarm systems—take place in private dwellings, other actions—such as organizing a surveillance routine around the neighborhood—take place in public settings. Both kinds of activities represent excellent opportunities for doing descriptive case studies.

With regard to crime prevention in public places, although residents demand greater protection from the local police, they also feel that their own preventive efforts can be important. For instance, you may have encountered *Neighborhood*

Watch signs when driving through some of the neighborhoods in your area. The signs alert passersby to the presence of a higher degree of residential vigilance, especially aimed at preventing burglaries, car thefts, and even robberies. The vigilance means that the residents maintain a more watchful orientation, paying attention to any irregular behavior that may signal a crime underway or suggest the prelude to a crime.

One of the more proactive activities arises when residents organize some type of patrol, either by foot or in cars. These *citizen patrols* raise new issues worthy of field-based research. Questions include, "How does a patrol operate?" "What connection does it have with the local police?" "Under what circumstances might a patrol slide from acceptable *vigilant* behavior to less acceptable *vigilante* behavior?" These and other related questions were examined through the following descriptive case study.

Defining Citizen Patrols

Unlike a school or a classroom, a citizen patrol is not a readily defined entity. Starting a study of a citizen patrol, therefore, illustrates well the problems of defining the "case" in a case study. Without careful definition, many other similar activities might be incorrectly labeled as citizen patrols, creating misleading findings and conclusions. Three criteria helped exclude those activities that were not considered as representing citizen patrols.

First, the activity of interest had to be aimed at preventing *criminal* acts. Not of interest were citizen groups organized to pursue personal or political interests, such as harassing particular social groups of people (e.g., Ku Klux Klan or neo-Nazi groups). Similarly, outside the realm of interest were groups that themselves engaged in nuisance if not illegal behavior, such as gangs that put graffiti markings on private and public property.

Second, the activity of interest had to be organized and implemented by a residents' group or organization—often a homeowners', tenants', or neighborhood association. If the residents or property owners merely hired an outside private security agency to do the patrolling, this situation did not qualify as a citizen patrol. That kind of case study would then have been about private security guards, who have different training and may establish different relationships with residents and the local police than might a citizen patrol.

Third, the prevention activity had to be primarily directed at residential, not commercial areas. Thus, crime prevention organized by a group of storeowners or business firms to protect the premises where people work rather than reside also fell outside the realm of interest.

After applying the preceding exclusion criteria, many types of activities still remain (see Exhibit 5.1). All these activities were deemed acceptable as the subject of case studies of citizen patrols. The following case study describes the workings of one such patrol (all names are fictitious).

Exhibit 5.1   Illustrative Activities Qualifying as Citizen Patrols

- A volunteer group patrolling neighborhood streets in cars
- A volunteer group patrolling neighborhood streets on foot
- A service for escorting pedestrians, staffed by residents
- Residents patrolling a housing compound or housing project
- Residents serving as watchmen or gatekeepers for a residential compound

THE RANGEFIELD URBAN CITIZENS PATROL

Origins

The Rangefield Patrol operates in a four-block area in the middle of a multiethnic community. The four blocks are dominated by renovated townhouses and their resident owners. The surrounding area, including adjacent neighborhoods, has faced constant threats from drug dealing, muggings, burglaries, and car thefts.

J. B. Compton, an artist and graphic designer, has lived in the neighborhood for nine years and is a patrol member. He has had several personal experiences with crime since moving to the Rangefield area. First, he was a victim of what he described as "a spectacular burglary" in which his house was "virtually cleaned out." Second, his car was vandalized several times, and third, tools were stolen from his backyard on three separate occasions.

Compton's experiences are not unique. Two years earlier, there was a rash of housebreaks and muggings, and the residents in the four-block section met to discuss ways of stemming the crime wave. The area already was highly organized by neighbors who had banded together around environmental and political issues affecting them, and people already had experience working together. David High, a recognized community leader who later initiated the Rangefield Patrol, noted that "it's a neighborhood where everyone knows each other and a spirit of unity exists" (see **BOX 7**).

BOX 7

Open-Ended Interviews

The numerous quotations of the words spoken by the participants in this case study represent one way of presenting the data from open-ended interviews. The quoted phrases and sentences help present the participants' perspectives and thinking. In other case studies, you may want to explore these insights more deeply. You can present lengthier renditions of quoted materials, representing whole paragraphs or even large portions of a chapter.

Of course, taking quoted words while actively participating in a field setting is a challenge. Without some kind of recording device, the quoted material is likely to be short, as in the present chapter. To use longer passages will either require you to use such recording devices or to develop a facile note-taking procedure. An alternative option, also found in many case studies, is to use longer passages but to paraphrase rather than directly quote the participants. Now, however, some of the value of having directly quoted materials is lost because the paraphrasing does not assure that a participant's exact mood, tempo, attitude, or content have been captured properly.

(For more information, see Yin, 2009a, Chapter 4, section on "Interviews.")

As an initial response to the crime wave, High said, the community at first requested additional surveillance by the local police. The community also discussed ways of increasing the residents' "security consciousness," resulting in many homeowners purchasing lights for the front and rear of their houses and installing burglar alarms. Although the local police promised increased protection, the residents felt no such increase, with several of them watching the streets and counting the presence of patrol officers and patrol cars.

"When we saw that we were getting no response from the police, we decided to see if we could stop crime in the streets ourselves," High recalled. Four residents volunteered to plan a citizen patrol. When they presented the plan at a neighborhood meeting, 15 to 20 persons immediately volunteered to participate. Soon, the volunteers numbered around 60. "It was not without some difficulty that we ultimately gained support from the broader community," High also noted. "Initially, we were charged with being vigilantes and as people with guns trying to preserve our homes."

The original and continuing goal of the Rangefield Patrol has been to make the four-block area safer. An independent organization, the patrol performs only crime prevention activities, although many of the members also belong to the larger Rangefield Neighborhood Association that sponsors many social, political, and service-oriented activities. All members of the patrol are adult males.

Patrol Operations

At the time of the case study fieldwork, the Rangefield Patrol worked from 9 p.m. to 1 a.m. every night but Friday (the local police have an augmented patrol on Friday nights). The four-hour shift is manned by two volunteers on a rotating basis.

The most important instruction to all patrol members is to remain visible. "Visibility," explained High, "makes residents feel secure and also deters potential criminals." The main activities of the patrol include these: walking and standing around the four-block area, talking to and greeting residents as they approach their homes, escorting people into their homes or around the block if requested, and periodically checking the back alleys of the blocks. Compton said he did not feel that his patrol activities were dangerous. "You have to be careful because you don't know if a passerby is armed or not," he said, "but a little common sense eliminates most of the danger in this work."

If a patrol member witnesses a crime, his instructions are to call the police, blow his whistle, but if at all possible, not to become involved in any confrontation. "We will confront a criminal if we have to," High said, "but so far, we haven't had to do that because our whistle campaign has been so successful. Our neighborhood's show of force has successfully intervened in several incidents." All residents, whether on patrol or not, carry tin whistles, and upon hearing the sound of a whistle, all neighbors are instructed to call the police immediately and then to go outside and lend assistance to the patrol and any victims. According to High, at least five or six muggings and several auto thefts have been broken up by residents responding to the call of a whistle. "Response to whistle calls has been fantastic, even late at night," High said.

The inexpensive whistles are essentially the only equipment used by patrol members. They wear no special uniforms or badges and do not carry weapons. High remarked, however, that he would like to see the patrol acquire claxon horns, which are easier to use than whistles and which emit louder sounds.

Patrol Organization

The patrol's current membership hovers around 60 adult males. A woman, however, serves as a patrol coordinator, and several other female residents assist in distributing flyers or doing other chores. The coordinator is responsible for shift scheduling, finding substitutes for absentees, keeping written records of patrol-related incidents, and convening the occasional meetings of the patrol members. In addition, she maintains close communication with the police and, as a representative of the neighborhood, frequently presents the local police with security-related requests and demands.

According to High, the patrol has no specific leadership positions or administrative infrastructure except for the coordinator's position. "Several of the more active volunteers have emerged, through their involvement, as patrol spokesmen," High explained, "but none have titles of any sort." Decisions, he added, usually are made by the coordinator or at meetings of the entire patrol. Likewise, Compton emphatically asserted that all patrol volunteers can have a voice in running the operation. "There are no real patrol leaders," he said, "and we usually have group meetings where people can criticize, make suggestions, or just talk out their problems."

During the past two years, the need for patrol recruitment has been minimal. The 60-person membership has remained constant. According to Compton, in order to join the patrol, all one must do is express an interest in getting involved. He himself joined the patrol a little over a year ago, hearing about it through the neighborhood grapevine. Most patrol members have joined because they are committed to making the area a safe, enjoyable place to live, he said, although some residents have not participated because they feel that the job is dangerous or because they are in poor health. "Others, especially renters, just aren't interested." When asked what members gain from being part of the patrol, Compton replied that more acquaintances are made with neighbors, fostering a heightened sense of community spirit. The greatest rewards, however, are passive ones, he noted, "such as everyone in my family simply being safe. When things are quiet, when nothing is happening, that's our best reward."

The only "dues" for patrol members are the hours pledged to patrol. High estimated that he spends about 12 hours per month on patrol efforts. Compton said that he usually patrols twice each month for a total of about eight hours. "The patrol certainly can be a burden," he remarked, "but I try to work out my schedule accordingly."

Each patrol member is expected to be level-headed and willing to participate. Each novice is trained by a veteran volunteer who accompanies the novice on his first few patrol shifts. No written rules or behavioral guidelines exist. "The general tone for our patrol activities was set in our planning discussions," said High, "and we all have a sense of what we should or should not do. Foremost is an understanding of being careful for our personal self and of only getting involved in absolute emergencies." Since the patrol has been in existence, no members have been disciplined or discharged for acting with poor judgment.

Incipient attendance problems may be starting to arise, however. High said that "people are getting bored because things are so quiet." When the patrol first began, patrol members intervened in several muggings and attempted auto burglaries and turned away countless suspicious-looking loiterers. Now, people are beginning to lose interest because there is very little activity on the streets.

In general, the patrol seems to be widely supported by residents. "We get tons of feedback from neighbors who personally thank us for making the area safer," High said. Compton said he also feels that most residents have a positive opinion of the patrol, but he added, "I have no idea" what the local police think about the group. "Because our direct contact is so minimal, I sometimes get the feeling that they don't care that we exist."

Relationships With the Local Police

The Rangefield Patrol sees itself as an organization that supplements the local police and that affords its neighborhood extra protection. Although there is no routine contact with the police, the coordinator keeps the police informed of all patrol activities. The police, in turn, try to provide the area with additional patrols on Friday nights. High rated the police as "fairly good" in responding to patrol calls and said that the quality of police protection probably has improved since the Rangefield Patrol began. "That may be, though, because our neighborhood has proven to be particularly vocal," High speculated. He added that overall police protection still is not adequate, "or we wouldn't be out there."

Officer Jon Lindh, the director of community relations at the local police station, said that the Rangefield Patrol has had no effect on the deployment of the local police in the area. Police officers are allocated according to crime levels in a neighborhood or in relation to police workload, he explained.

Officer Lindh said he has been in contact several times with members of the Rangefield Patrol. "As far as citizen patrols go, they behave themselves pretty well," he said, adding that he is unaware of any police complaints regarding the patrol's behavior or activities. However, contact between the local police and the patrol members is minimal. Officer Lindh said that the beat patrolmen stop occasionally to chat briefly with a patrol member, but that is the exception rather than the rule. He did mention, however, that patrol members have come to the station several times to talk with the captain or "to present a list of grievances about things happening in their neighborhood."

In discussing the patrol's accomplishments, Officer Lindh said that they primarily have been twofold: The patrol has fostered a sense of community awareness and concern and also has kept the police informed of neighborhood happenings. In general, however, he does not think the concept of citizen patrols should be supported because "these people can't take the place of the police. They usually don't know what to look for or how to handle a serious problem." Basic crime reporting, he added, is a good thing. "We encourage people to do that." He said the police also have praised other citizen patrols' efforts at various crime prevention seminars throughout the city.

Compton said that the success of the patrol has far exceeded his original expectations. There has been a visible reduction in the neighborhood's crime rate, and increased community cohesion has accompanied the concern about security. In discerning the effect that the patrol has had on crime in the neighborhood, High asserted that "boredom is success." "There have been no housebreaks, muggings, or other criminal activity in the last eight or nine months," he said, "and there is no telling how many potential criminals we have deterred." Regarding crime displacement, Officer Lindh said that, although no figures exist to verify his statement, he feels that because of the Rangefield Patrol's activities, some criminals might have avoided the Rangefield neighborhood and victimized other neighborhoods instead.

Personal Security When Doing Fieldwork

Studying citizen patrols, much less accompanying residents while on patrol, poses a potential threat to your own security. Although you will not be able to avoid unexpected events and will have to exert extreme caution and care if such events occur, some preparatory steps still can be helpful.

Two steps can be extremely important. First, you should have received appropriate clearance to do the study and to carry out your specific field routines. For citizen patrols, the providers of such clearance will be persons of authority, such as the main persons responsible for organizing the citizen patrol and also local police officials. The least desired situation would be if you had obtained clearance only from the member of the patrol whom you were accompanying. (Such need for the higher clearance has counterparts in doing other kinds of fieldwork; for instance, you would want to obtain clearance from the principal of a school even if you were going to study only a single classroom and that classroom's teacher already had agreed to your presence in it.)

Second, you would want to let a trusted colleague (or two) know about the exact time of your planned fieldwork but request that they not call you during that period of time. As part of this procedure, you also would want your patrol companion to know that you had alerted your colleague(s), to deal with any unanticipated communication need.

For Class Discussion or Written Assignment

Discuss other precautionary steps that might be taken when doing fieldwork in different settings. Speculate how fieldworkers should respond when an untoward event occurs (e.g., when a patrol member encounters a problem and confronts someone in some threatening manner). Should the fieldworker assist? Observe? Depart?

————————————◆————————————

6

A CASE STUDY OF A NEIGHBORHOOD ORGANIZATION

Neighborhood organizations exist throughout the country and have been important partners in neighborhood revitalization and development efforts. The organizations, usually drawing heavily on residents' voluntarism, may be found in all kinds of neighborhoods and can improve both the physical and social aspects of neighborhood life. As one result, case studies of such organizations—whether they are tenant, faith-based, education-oriented, or service organizations—frequently appear in the literature.

This chapter presents one such case study. Although the case is from an earlier era that might now be considered ancient by younger scholars, the case study demonstrates the continuing relevance of neighborhood organizations: Their work from the earlier era, in this case dealing with housing, still bears a strong resemblance to the work of counterpart organizations today.

Methodologically, the structure of the case study's text was deliberately designed to present narrative answers to a series of questions. The questions reflected the interest of the original sponsor of the case study. More important, the same questions—and their answers—were used to structure the case studies of more than

AUTHOR'S NOTE: This chapter is a highly condensed version of a case study that is one of more than 40 such case studies, all following the same research design and procedures, as part of a project developed and overseen by Robert K. Yin. All the case studies appeared in *People, Building Neighborhoods,* National Commission on Neighborhoods, U.S. Government Printing Office, Washington, D.C., March 1979. To keep the chapter to a manageable length, substantial portions of the original case study have been omitted, mainly shown by those instances where the response to a posed textual question has been omitted. Despite these omissions, all the questions have been included here to help readers understand the full flow of the original case study's line of inquiry. The original and complete case study was written by Kenneth Snipes. The portion presented in this chapter has been lightly edited for readability.

40 such neighborhood organizations. Although the resulting case studies may appear to have been rather mechanically composed, the format made it easier for the sponsor (as well as other readers) to find the answers to the questions of concern across all the case studies. In other words, a reader could examine the response to, say, Question 10 in each case study (because it was the same question) and effectively conduct a customized and targeted "cross-case" synthesis, without having to rely on an external analyst.

Furthermore, as the present chapter shows, the mechanical organization of the case study did not preclude a rich and in-depth description of each organization (see **BOX 8**). An added benefit is that the format facilitated the writing of the case studies. Fieldworkers could assemble their field notes and other data according to each question, rather than struggling with a more fluid, though potentially more creative, reporting structure. Last, this question-and-answer approach accommodated the fact that conducting more than 40 case studies within a reasonable time period required a group of fieldworkers—not just a one- or two-person team. The consistent structure of the case studies, therefore, made these fieldworkers' work less idiosyncratic. Overall, the question-and-answer format especially seems to help both the reading and writing of the case studies in a multiple-case study (see **BOX 9**).

BOX 8

Theories for Descriptive Case Studies

References to the use of theory usually involve the formation of hypotheses about cause-effect relationships. These theories would, therefore, be considered relevant to explanatory case studies. However, theories also can be important for descriptive case studies. In the present chapter, the section headings represent the "theory" of the important aspects of neighborhood organizations that needed to be described. The headings reflected topics of interest to the originators of the study as well as the need to gain an understanding of how the neighborhood organization worked.

The desired descriptive theory should cover the scope and depth of the case being described. If you were to describe an individual, an organization, or some other possible subject of a case study, where should your description start and where should it end? What should your description include, and what might it exclude? The criteria used to answer these questions would represent your "theory" of what needs to be described. This theory should be openly stated ahead of time, should be subject to review and debate, and even may later serve as the design for a descriptive case study.

(For more information, see Yin, 2009a, Chapter 2, section on "The Role of Theory in Design Work.")

> ## BOX 9
>
> ### Case Study Databases
>
> The question-and-answer format in this case study about a neighborhood organization is not just a way of presenting a case study report. The format also may be used to organize a database from which a more interesting and compelling case study can be composed. Thus, the current case study of a neighborhood organization could have been used as either the final case study (as presented in Chapter 6) or as the database for a separate case study to be composed afterward.
>
> Preserving the database in a question-and-answer form that reflects the questions from the case study protocol is analogous to the assembling of a survey database and strengthens any subsequent case study. The most formal version of a case study database would contain numerous citations, indicating the specific source of the data, such as a particular document, interview, archive, or date and place of a field observation. (Such citations were present in the original version of the current case study.)
>
> (For more information, see Yin, 2009a, Chapter 4, section on
> "Create a Case Study Database.")

INITIATION AND STRUCTURE OF THE ORGANIZATION

Organizational Origins

1. In what year did the organization come into being? Jeff-Vander-Lou, Inc. (JVL), formally came into being on October 24, 1966. On March 29, 1967, its articles of incorporation were officially amended, granting JVL broader legal capacity to engage in building, rebuilding, purchasing, selling, leasing, investing of funds, and other such activities geared to more specific undertakings in terms of its goal of community renewal.

JVL evolved out of the 19th Ward Beautification Committee created in mid-1964 in response to Lady Bird Johnson's efforts to encourage the beautification of America. The group initially was headed by local officials (19th Ward alderman and committeeman). However, later in 1964, three community activists were elected as its first major officers. The name *Jeff-Vander-Lou* is derived from three principal streets that bound the area—*Jeff* from Jefferson Avenue, *Vander* from Vandeventer Avenue, and *Lou* from St. Louis Avenue.

2. What caused its creation, and who or what was the main source of support in the creation? JVL was created as a result of a series of issues and events, and the union of the three principal individuals who emerged from community meetings, marches, and other such neighborhood activities. These three leaders were Macler C. Shepard, Reverend Hubert Schwartzentruber, and Florence Aritha Spotts.

Macler ("Mac") Shepard, owner of an upholstery shop, had been twice displaced by urban renewal projects. He decided to move no more. He ran unsuccessfully for 19th Ward committeeman. A committeeman is a nonpaid party functionary who is responsible for getting the vote out. In the spring of 1964, following the shooting of a youth by a police officer in a neighborhood schoolyard, Shepard mobilized a citizens' protest. It grew into a march of 5,000 to 8,000 people, which started from the JVL area and went through the Pruitt-Igoe housing project (since demolished) to police headquarters. Subsequently, Shepard served as spokesman in joint meetings with officials.

Hubert Schwartzentruber, a young Mennonite minister from a small rural section of Canada, was sent by his church to the near North Side black community of St. Louis. Until that time, he never had been in a large city nor had any personal contact with black people. He succeeded the pastor of a black Mennonite Church located near Shepard's upholstery shop. Schwartzentruber set up a coffeehouse called The Handle, where people from the neighborhood could discuss problems and concerns. It became a meeting place for residents and others interested in issues affecting poor and black people.

Florence Aritha Spotts, a retired schoolteacher, was among those who frequented The Handle. She had a reputation as an organizer and critic of politicians and the political process. She said she would fight anything she thought was wrong.

These three people joined forces in 1964 and were elected to major offices of the 19th Ward Beautification Committee. They attempted to use that committee to develop community improvement projects and, in particular, a housing rehabilitation program.

In an attempt by Mayor Cervantes's administration to befriend the 19th Ward neighborhood, paint was delivered to it. However, the 19th Ward Beautification Committee sent back the paint (along with a strongly worded message to the mayor), because it could be used only for the exteriors of buildings. The large number of deteriorating houses indicated that more serious help was necessary. Another promise of assistance for the neighborhood came from the Cervantes administration in the form of Operation Big Sweep, a cleanup campaign scheduled to begin in the 19th Ward in late 1965. When the mayor pushed an oversized symbolic broom, the handle broke. The JVL neighborhood still ranks cleanup, street paving, and sidewalk repair (along with other city services) among its top priorities in support of its housing development efforts.

During this same period (1964–1966), another government program designed to rescue poor people and neighborhoods was being implemented. The U.S. Office of Economic Opportunity (OEO) was preparing for antipoverty programs in the Yeatman District. The geographic boundaries of this area were much the same as the area identified with the 19th Ward Beautification Committee. The OEO program was established through its local agency, the Human Development Corporation, which in turn delegated implementation responsibilities to the Urban League of Greater St. Louis. The Urban League's first task was to organize a neighborhood advisory council to direct the efforts and resources available through OEO. During the process of organizing, conflicts surfaced between the existing, more traditional Urban League Federation of Block Units (block clubs) and the leadership of the 19th Ward Beautification Committee.

Against this backdrop of confrontation with the administration of Mayor Cervantes and the local entanglements of the antipoverty and soon-to-come federal Model Cities programs, two specific issues contributed most to the creation of JVL. Both issues surfaced in 1966.

The first issue started with the city's request for citywide support for a major $79.3 million bond issue. The bond issue was to provide improvements in most areas of the city *except* the JVL neighborhood, according to JVL respondents and writings. These facts became apparent after investigation by the Urban League organizers who were working closely with the beautification committee. Protests were made to the city, but the officials would not alter or commit the bond issue to specifically include the 19th Ward Beautification Committee/Yeatman area. JVL respondents who were active at that time indicated that the city's refusal strengthened the belief that the neighborhood actually was scheduled for complete demolition and redevelopment. At the base of this fear was that the area would become the site of new industrial development and permit the construction of a north-south distributor highway.

The determined efforts of Shepard and the JVL community, together with a group from the predominantly white South Side, forced the defeat of the bond issue in November 1966. For example, the city promoted the passage with a booklet titled "Let's Do It." The JVL community countered with a mimeographed booklet called "Let's Don't," which pointed out that some proposals provided for and passed in a 1955 bond issue were duplicated in the 1966 bond proposal. Also, the JVL community strongly opposed the north-south highway that could be constructed with passage of the bond issue. According to Shepard, the highway would further divide the black community, displace many people relocated two or three times before because of urban renewal, and be of primary benefit to county residents rather than those who lived in the city.

The second issue arose after the bond issue failed. In late 1966, JVL, together with the Urban League outreach staff, met with the St. Louis Building Commissioner to protest the lack of housing code enforcement in the JVL area. Again, there was refusal by the city to apply its resources to problems and concerns identified by those in the community. The city officials stated that buildings in the "slum areas" were inspected only on a specific complaint rather than a community-wide basis.

Homeowners in the JVL area began to submit complaints against violators, but the complainants then found that their own homes were being inspected. Respondents indicated that absentee owners were receiving minor fines, but owner-occupants were ordered to make extensive repairs. The legal and economic pressures on the residents threatened to discontinue the demand for community-wide code enforcement.

Workers in the JVL community spent the next three weeks collecting about 1,200 complaints against 13 real-estate dealers who owned or managed 85% of the property in the neighborhood. In this instance, all the complaints were filed by persons who lived outside the area. Later, the building commissioner announced that 75% of the area was "unfit for human habitation." Families were evicted. As the city evicted families, JVL moved them back in and, in addition, announced that it was setting up "refugee camps" in churches, community centers, and other such places.

Meanwhile, riots began in other major cities. The building commissioner stopped the evictions, public officials sought to negotiate a settlement, and JVL exacted a promise of no further urban renewal. This action provided JVL with the opportunity to purchase the structurally sound abandoned houses and to rehabilitate and sell them to the residents.

Simultaneously (in late 1966), Shepard, Schwartzentruber, and Spotts—along with the Reverend Donald Register of the United Presbyterian Church, the Urban League staff organizers, and other neighborhood people—planned for the creation of Jeff-Vander-Lou, Inc. (incorporation of JVL), designed to be an independent citizen-controlled organization. It was incorporated on October 24, 1966. Macler Shepard was elected president of its board of directors.

Despite the creation of JVL as a separate organization, its supporters and directors continued their attempts at influencing the use of OEO resources through the Yeatman Advisory Council.

The struggle for control of the advisory council resulted in the disqualification of the election results on three different occasions by the Human Development Corporation. During this period, JVL gained neighborhood support to act as the OEO Yeatman District Advisory Council. According to a JVL administrative assistant, the Human Development Corporation was against JVL controlling the Yeatman Council, and elections were held until the JVL influence was diluted. The executive director of the Yeatman Corporation recalled that the disqualifications resulted from JVL protests and their resistance to open elections with a broad-based council, as required by OEO. In the spring of 1967, prior to the formation of the Yeatman Corporation but following the incorporation of JVL, the Urban League terminated its staff organizers. Several of those individuals continue to play key roles in JVL today.

Finally, in the fall of 1967, election results were certified. The JVL constituency obtained 13 seats, and the remaining 47 were won by others with no prior experience in neighborhood organizations, according to the Yeatman Corporation's executive director. During 1967, the JVL constituency on the Yeatman Council discovered that it could not adequately influence the council's decisions and actions.

3. What was the original source of funding? JVL had no formal funding sources at its creation. According to Macler Shepard and other respondents, personal funds from the leadership itself were used to cover various operational expenses. Some printing and other such costs were paid for by neighborhood groups, including the Franklin Avenue Businessmen's Association. The Urban League staff organizers provided primary technical assistance from 1965 to 1967.

Because funding had been from private (not public) sources during its initial period, JVL was able to engage in politically active matters that it considered vital to the survival of the neighborhood.

According to a JVL staff member, the first house renovation was undertaken in 1967 at a cost of about $18,000. The financing of the two-family dwelling was provided through funds loaned by the Lindell Trust Company, which has offices in the area. Additional financial assistance came from local businessmen (the Franklin Avenue Businessmen's Association, now called the Martin Luther King Redevelopment Association, after the street name was changed) and other neighborhood people.

Once underway in 1967, JVL, Inc., received a $30,000 interest-free loan for housing rehabilitation from the Mennonite Church (the Mennonite Mutual Aid Fund). Also, the Mennonites' Minority Ministries Council made a grant of $30,000 to hire a construction supervisor for a three-year period. The Mennonite Disaster Services sent skilled craftsmen into the JVL neighborhood to rehabilitate houses, and the Illinois Mennonite Youth Fellowship raised funds to help purchase and rehabilitate a house.

According to one respondent, a professor at Washington University, students from that college, and others have worked in the JVL area since 1967. The type of technical assistance provided by students and faculty alike included grant development, research, and analysis. For instance, individuals from the university researched state requirements for day-care programs (e.g., the needed ratio of space to the number of students, nutrition, the criteria for selecting youngsters, and the financing of day-care services).

Another example of outside resources was the funding of a trip to Washington, D.C., by the Franklin Avenue Businessmen's Association, for JVL representatives to present their proposals to officials of the U.S. Departments of Housing and Urban Development (HUD); Health, Education, and Welfare (HEW) [now Health and Human Services]; and Labor. All early proposals were rejected. HUD, in particular, made it clear that JVL needed to acquire experience in handling funds and to demonstrate the capacity to undertake housing rehabilitation projects before it would seriously consider JVL's proposals.

Among outside technical resources available to JVL in 1968 and 1969 was a Mennonite farmer from Washington State who had special expertise in large-scale projects and the ability to figure out government regulations. While working in St. Louis, he supplemented his income by teaching. According to the pastor of the Mennonite Church, the clergy also has been important to JVL in getting ideas into workable form.

In 1967, a successful St. Louis businessman took a special interest in JVL. According to a later article in the *Globe Democrat* (December 5, 1977), "The founder and president of the Tier-Rack Corporation and Arrowhead Products Company set up a tax-deductible corporation, called the Arrowhead Foundation, to provide Jeff-Vander-Lou with seed money for constructing a staff office, warehouse space, and a site for tenant relocation and homeowner training." A similar later report in the *St. Louis Post-Dispatch* (November 15, 1976) indicated that the Arrowhead Foundation's founder called the private sector "tools" and the community residents "crafts people." The article stated that in the preceding six years, Arrowhead had given JVL about one million dollars in grants and interest-free loans.

4. Was either mandated citizen participation or formal, legal grants of authority involved in initiating the target organization? [The responses to this and other questions posed throughout the remaining text have been omitted to reduce the length of the present chapter. However, the original questions still have been presented to enable the reader to get a sense of the entire set of questions addressed by the original case study.]

5. What was the early orientation of the organization?

6. What was the organization's main leadership structure?

7. What was the organization's membership and structure?

Organizational Evolution

8. How has the organization changed since the early days? The changes in JVL have been in terms of size of staff, intensity, and greater organizational structure stemming from the general increase in the number of activities, programs, and projects. The intensity of JVL's housing development activities led to the creation of a separately incorporated entity in 1970 called JVL Housing Corporation. JVL Housing is exempted under IRS Section 501(c)(3), so the organization has received tax-deductible contributions that have boosted its housing development efforts. JVL Housing evolved from negotiations with HUD, which (during 1967–1970) insisted on a co-sponsor for a particular housing development of 74 new units under HUD's 236 rental housing program. Businesses and foundations gave extensive support following the establishment of JVL Housing.

Structural change came with the staffing and funding requirements of each JVL, Inc., program component, also resulting in the functional spread of JVL. Because JVL from its founding had set its mission along comprehensive activity lines, these developments are seen as fulfilling the neighborhood plan rather than as changes. The evolutionary direction, therefore, has been one of overcoming setbacks as JVL has attempted to carry out its reinvestment and survival plans for its neighborhood.

Outside the housing field, important transitions by JVL have been as follows:

- In 1969, JVL set up an employment screening and referral office for the Brown Shoe Company, which had built a new factory in the JVL area.
- Early in the 1970s, JVL made public improvements through the Model Cities program, working with the Franklin Avenue Businessmen's Association.
- Also in 1970, JVL established a housing management program.
- In 1973, day-care activities were formalized.
- Later in 1973, the JVL Senior Citizens' Center was started.

- In the spring of 1974, JVL published its first paper, called the *Jeff-Vander-Look* [*Look* magazine was a prominent national magazine in the United States at that time]. In November 1975, the paper was reorganized with *Proud* magazine's assistance and renamed *JVL News*.
- In 1976, JVL began its Summer Youth Program, funded by the U.S. Department of Labor. An economic development staff was added that same year.
- In 1977, the JVL Communications Center, an outgrowth of the summer program, received funding.

Each of these activities, along with many issue-oriented tasks, caused changes in the organization, in turn helping assure both supervision and continuity by providing for professional staffing and appropriate facilities. Throughout, JVL's geographic boundaries have remained the same, and housing development continues to be a high priority.

9.   *What were the events that led to these changes?*

10.   *Overall, has the organization become more independent or dependent?*

REVITALIZATION ACTIVITIES AND THEIR SUPPORT

11.   What activities have been completed or are currently underway? JVL has had many accomplishments, especially in housing development:

- *1968:* Renovated first building, a 12-room house; completed five housing units repaid through a HUD mortgage insurance program; brought 10 private insurance companies together, agreeing to spread the risk of loss among themselves through a rotation process, to meet JVL's insurance needs to cover 88 units until the Missouri Fair Plan was created in 1969–1970
- *1969:* Rehabilitated "Opportunity House," a complex consisting of six apartments completed at a cost of $85,000; renovated the Sheridan Medical Building, which was then operated by doctors for the benefit of the JVL area; convinced the Brown Group, Inc., to build a shoe factory in the JVL neighborhood and began handling employment screening and referral for a peak employment level of 450 workers
- *1967–1970:* Completed a total of 81 units under a HUD program; units were sold to families in the community with interest subsidy ranging from 1% to 3%
- *1970:* Set up housing management component with a grant from the national Self-Development of People Committee of the Presbyterian Church, allowing for the payment of salaries for the manager of the Spotts Apartments, a chief executive, and an administrative assistant
- *1971:* Completed construction of the Aritha Spotts Apartments, a 74-unit new construction project costing $1.5 million, including a two-story office and community building (the project was JVL's first development using a HUD

rental housing program); also completed seven units of homebuyers' housing under a related HUD program

- *Early 1970s:* Persuaded the Model Cities program to invest funds in public improvements in the Martin Luther King shopping district, resulting in improved streets, sidewalks, bus stops, parking, and other public areas
- *1973:* Opened the Aritha Spotts Child Care Center in the Spotts apartment complex, serving 32 children and initially operated with a HEW grant in conjunction with the Early Child Care Development Corporation
- *1974:* Opened the JVL Senior Citizens' Center to house existing programs for the elderly, such as home-delivered meals, with funds from Model Cities, the city of St. Louis (after direct confrontation with the St. Louis commissioner on aging and a hearing by the governor), and some HEW funds; also began publication of the neighborhood newspaper *Jeff-Vander-Look,* with the assistance of four students from Washington University
- *1975:* Opened a second day-care center at the Bethesda Mennonite Church and in the process effected changes in the state licensing law (a regulation requiring windows in a day-care facility was finally waived, allowing for the establishment of the center in the church basement); reorganized the JVL publication into a 12-page monthly newsletter (renamed *JVL News*) published in cooperation with *Proud* magazine; completed two more HUD 236 rental housing projects, totaling 123 additional units of scattered-site rehab housing (according to a JVL report, every housing package proposed through this period initially was rejected by city officials and local and regional HUD staff, with approval coming only after interminable haggling, recalcitrance, and a general attitude of "it will never work"; the report further states that JVL's successes were seldom recognized and then only as exceptions or miracles that could never happen twice)
- *1976:* Began rehabilitation of 98 units (completed in mid-1978) of scattered-site housing under a HUD program in conjunction with the National Housing Partnership
- *1977:* Received initial funding for the JVL Communications Center—a $148,000 grant award from the Mott Foundation for renovation, equipment, and program start-up costs—to provide curricula in television, radio, photography, and motion pictures in cooperation with the St. Louis public school system
- *1978:* Currently, JVL is exploring tax-sheltered syndications for further developments in the community, and three more housing packages are in various stages of processing: package #16, 88 units of scattered-site infill new construction, already underway; package #17, a 100-unit HUD-supported elderly and handicapped project; and packages #18 and #19, 114 units of rehabilitated and newly constructed units

12. How did the organization become involved in these activities?

13. How were these activities planned?

14. How were these activities implemented?

15. Have there been difficulties with continued or new funding for these activities?

16. Were different leaders/staff involved in the process of program planning and implementation as contrasted with the founding of the organization?

17. *What choices were required, if any, among the various activities?*

18. *What problems has the organization chosen not to confront?*

19. *What has been the effect of activities on the organization's basic character over time?*

RELATIONSHIP TO VOLUNTARY ASSOCIATIONS AND NETWORKS

20. *Make a list of other organizations or individuals who have voluntarily assisted the organization in a major way.*

21. *Name three major occasions on which the target organization has voluntarily assisted other groups.*

22. *Has the organization ever worked in collaboration with other organizations in the same neighborhood?* JVL is especially neighborhood-bound. Housing rehabilitation, child care, and programs for the elderly all have involved joint planning and implementation with the Bethesda Mennonite Church. Mennonite labor and funds went into the earliest housing projects, and one of the JVL child-care centers is located in the church.

JVL's "meals on wheels" program for the elderly was created through the joint efforts of JVL and the Yeatman Corporation. This project was first conducted with resources from the Model Cities program and later received St. Louis Area Agency on Aging funding. The JVL Communications Center, funded in part by the U.S. Department of Labor and the Mott Foundation, is being developed as a neighborhood resource and learning center in collaboration with the St. Louis public school system. Students in the program will spend part of their regular school day at the JVL Communications Center, with 64 youngsters studying such curriculum areas as television, radio, photography, and motion pictures. Their work will include material for the public schools' FM radio station, production of instructional films, creation of a tape library of neighborhood cultural history (stories by elders), and the recording of neighborhood landmarks. For instance, while researching an old school building, several structures (houses) were found to appear on maps indicating that they had been built prior to 1870.

23. *Is the organization part of a large umbrella organization?* None of the respondents or any of the written material indicated that JVL is formally associated with a large umbrella organization. Through its principal leader, Macler Shepard, JVL is, however, included on many boards and councils. For instance, Shepard is a commissioner on the Bi-State Development Agency and a board member of the Mennonite Mutual Aid, the North Side Team Ministry, and the United Way, to mention a few such appointments.

24. *Is the organization part of a larger citywide, regional, or national network?* JVL entered into a joint venture with the National Housing Partnership in 1976, which provided for the financial guarantees required to undertake 98 units of housing. There were no indications that JVL has been a formal member of a network, but through its staff and volunteers, it maintains functional contacts

with other development corporations and neighborhood organizations in St. Louis. JVL has worked on specific issues with neighboring communities and tenant organizations in Carr Central, Vaughn, Murphy-Blair, Pruitt-Igoe, and Montgomery-Hyde Park.

25. Describe the relationship between the target organization and other local organizations. JVL has the respect and admiration of other local organizations in terms of its accomplishments in housing development and other positive projects for the betterment of the JVL area. However, a leader of the Lucas Heights Village housing development summarized the sentiments expressed by other respondents who are associated with the Yeatman Corporation and the Ward 19 alderman. Basically, areas of conflict and competition seemed to surface when discussing what can be accomplished as compared with what can be only dreamed about. Specifically, JVL is thought to be creating an island without adequate ties to other projects such as Lucas Heights, located within JVL's boundaries. Also, JVL depends heavily on HUD funds. These community leaders stated that JVL is very "turf" oriented and is unwilling to change the direction of its development plans to tie into the Lucas Heights project. A political leader expressed what might be considered jealousy among several strong-minded groups. Most respondents thought that the city should assume the role of developing cooperative planning among the several groups.

There were no signs of conflict between JVL and resident groups or the Martin Luther King Business District Association. They have worked together on the market study and several early housing rehabilitation projects.

26. Overall, have outside organizations played an important role in the target organization's life history?

RELATIONSHIP TO CITY GOVERNMENT

27. Does the target organization have any relationship with specific officials or offices in city government? JVL experienced severe negative relationships with city government in its inception period. Confrontations with city government on bond issues, highway development, industrial park land, code enforcement, Community Development Block Grant uses, and junkyard permits left a trail of hard feelings and uneasiness between JVL members and city officials.

Relationships with city government, however, persisted and appear to be improving. Macler Shepard maintains a relationship with Mayor Conway and his top aides. Other JVL staff members work with the St. Louis Community Development Agency (CDA) and its executive director, assistant deputy director, and neighborhood planner. Another JVL staff person oversees ties with the St. Louis Agency on Training and Employment, which coordinates U.S. Department of Labor funds. Ninth District police officers have been featured in *JVL News* and given special commendation for their efforts to provide better services. There is also a link between JVL and the mayor's office for senior citizens.

In spite of these and other ties to city government, JVL does not hesitate to oppose any action by city government deemed harmful to the JVL area. For example, JVL opposed a bill in early 1977 that would have allowed for certain tax relief for developers, stating that it would bring about neighborhood blight. Further, in 1978, JVL sought action against the St. Louis Board of Adjustment because it supported a junkyard permit, another example of blight according to JVL. JVL often will use the public media and its own *JVL News* to state its case against a government official or agency. Much communication between JVL and city government is formal, due to the existence of pressure and confrontation.

The mayor appointed a CDA Citizens' Advisory Committee to receive citizen proposals and municipal agency proposals that are reviewed and rated. The committee's recommendations are given to the city's Neighborhood Betterment Committee and other city departments for review and recommendations. Final approval of proposals is made by the Board of Estimate and Apportionment, the Board of Aldermen, and the mayor. The city's neighborhood planner recommends the selection of the JVL area representative for the advisory committee. The planner makes an independent recommendation and does not seek advice from JVL, Inc.

28. Is the relationship formal or informal?

29. Has this relationship been productive? Mayor Conway indicated that JVL has been able to persuade both federal and private sources to be supportive. He said that the city recognizes JVL's positive contribution and that the city has no quarrels with JVL, generally. However, actions by JVL that have generated conflict were its opposition to both the north-south distributor highway and the rehabilitation of the Cochran Gardens public housing project. With the latter, JVL questioned the St. Louis Housing Authority's plans to rehabilitate one Cochran building at a cost of three million dollars, after the authority had opposed a JVL plan to use similar financing mechanisms for four buildings in Pruitt-Igoe at a cost of $5.5 million. The mayor suggested that JVL's actions may have been to gain leverage. However, the mayor noted that the problem has been resolved to some extent, and JVL presently has a cooperative relationship with the Housing Authority.

An assistant to Mayor Conway said that the city's relationship with JVL has declined because JVL goes to the media in the middle of negotiations or discussions. He said he thinks that JVL becomes antagonistic rather than seeking advantages. Further, he went on to describe political alliances that have been in opposition to the 19th Ward alderman, creating other sources of conflicts.

Despite the tensions and pressures that characterize the relationship between the city and JVL, the respondent said that JVL housing packages #16 and #18 had recently been placed at the top of the review list, indicating the city's desire to work with JVL. In spite of such tensions, there are signs of a functional and productive relationship. A reporter for the *Globe Democrat* said that Macler Shepard has the respect of city officials.

30. Are there any examples of city government having thwarted the emergence of community organizations? St. Louis currently has many community organizations. The city has established a process of actively assisting such groups. Two requests for proposals have been developed by the CDA—one to develop organizational capacity and the other to fund housing development projects. Also, in early 1977, the CDA formed the St. Louis Local Development Company with a $100,000-community development block grant to assist small businesses in obtaining incentive financing.

The city of St. Louis has a neighborhood improvement program funded by a federal $10.1 million public works grant. The grant is administered by the CDA. The primary emphasis is on street and parks improvements. JVL is included in this program, as it is focusing on those areas with extensive private housing rehabilitation.

31. Has the city made any structural changes in its own organization to be more supportive and competent with respect to neighborhood preservation and revitalization goals generally? CDA was reorganized two years ago. The reorganization resulted in the establishment of 18 planning districts as a citywide basis for neighborhood planning. Seven neighborhood planners are assigned to the 18 districts. Their role is to assess the districts' priority needs. The planners dialogue with neighborhood representatives and conduct field inspections. The planners are expected to consult with neighborhood leaders, and the plans emanating from this process guide block grant improvements in the neighborhoods.

The neighborhood planner who works with JVL indicated that the city did not provide site improvement funds to assist neighborhood improvement projects until 1977. The planner noted that it happened as a result of public demand.

32. What are the target organization's main relationships outside the city?

33. Overall, has the city government played an important role in the target organization's life history?

OUTCOMES

Condition of the Neighborhood

34. During the lifetime of the organization, has there been any tangible evidence of neighborhood improvement? Neighborhood improvement in the JVL area surveyed over its lifetime is significant, visible, and dramatic. Even those respondents whose views were critical of JVL's methods and plans clearly acknowledged its accomplishments. Housing development, both new and rehabilitated, is the foremost achievement of JVL. Housing units are developed in what is referred to as a "package" assembled by technical experts, including architects, general contractors, lending institution executives, insurance agents, and others, under the guidance of the JVL staff and board of directors. To date, 18 packages have been developed, containing a total of 623 units of new or rehabilitated housing. The packages have ranged in size from four to 100 units. Months of detailed work and negotiations are devoted to the creation and development of these packages.

The writer observed many of the housing improvements during several tours of the JVL neighborhood. Capital improvement, with the exception of dwelling units, was not as evident. In the early 1970s, JVL advocated the use of Model Cities funds to improve the Martin Luther King shopping district. Improvements such as street paving, new sidewalks, tree planting, bus stops, and off-street parking were undertaken at a cost of several hundred thousand dollars, according to a JVL report. In 1976, the *JVL News* reported that the area suffered from neglect and poor maintenance. The plaza still lacks proper upkeep. JVL has included further developments in the area as part of its economic reinvestment plan. According to the *JVL News,* the target organization has been responsible for getting the Metropolitan Sewer District to provide more and better service to the area.

This writer observed that sidewalks and curbs are greatly deteriorated throughout the area. Vacant lots are trash-ridden and overgrown with high weeds. JVL puts continuous pressure on city departments to combat such problems. The *JVL News* is used effectively to criticize when nothing is done and to announce results as they occur. Currently, much of JVL's effort is focused on sidewalk improvements and construction of infill housing—new housing units on vacant lots.

In 1968, JVL influenced the Brown Shoe Company to build a shoe factory in the neighborhood. The factory provides 300 to 450 jobs. In the November 1976 edition of *JVL News,* the plant supervisor reported a 97% attendance record. Brown Shoe also has a training program for both foremen and supervisors. JVL maintains a personnel office to screen and test applicants for jobs. In terms of law enforcement, JVL summarizes resident complaints and periodically has identified the current "hot spot"—a corner or street that is then highlighted in the *JVL News* and reported to the police. Any subsequent improvements also are reported.

35. Has there been any evidence of the organization having blocked or prevented some change in the physical condition of the neighborhood?

Residents' Perceptions

36. What do residents feel about the target organization? Many respondents noted that the activities and accomplishments of JVL have contributed to the significant decrease in every category of crime between 1970 and 1976. The decrease is evidenced by police statistics contained in the 1977 market study.

According to a reporter from the *Globe Democrat,* the JVL neighborhood lacks stores, shops, and cultural events and institutions of the type that would attract young, middle-income persons into the neighborhood, with the exception of those committed to repopulating the North Side and those believing in self-help in the black community. He said that such persons also would be willing to take more risks—referring to a widespread belief that the JVL area is unsafe, despite the reported decrease in crime. The reporter does not live in the JVL area, but his reporting assignments include JVL.

A resident whose comments summarized the sentiments of a number of persons living in the JVL neighborhood said that, to him, the neighborhood is like a frontier. He noted that the people who own their homes take better care of them. He indicated that the basics for power (unity of the people in an organized effort) are in the JVL neighborhood. Residents said they felt positive about JVL, most often citing the physical improvements in housing and the continuous advocacy role played by JVL on behalf of the area. Several respondents described easy access to participation and involvement. For example, one resident went to a monthly meeting to hear about plans to improve vacant lots. He presented an idea, and city bulldozers arrived within 10 days. The resident now keeps the lot clean.

37. Do residents feel that the target organization has addressed the neighborhood's problems? All the residents interviewed said they felt that JVL has addressed the most significant area problems. Commercial development as well as general maintenance and cleanup are problems that were most often mentioned. Commercial reinvestment is anticipated based on the completion of the Martin Luther King Business District market study. Most respondents said they believe that JVL is presently working near its capacity, so commercial ventures must be delayed until new funding sources and other resources are obtained. Problems of inadequate city services have been attributed to the belief that the city has attempted to eliminate sections of the North Side community to allow for the development of an industrial park and a new highway.

38. Have the activities of the target organization resulted in increased residential activity? JVL activities for older adults have generated new and varied services for many elderly. Films, speakers, transportation and escort services, shopping assistance, and welfare problem assistance bring together hundreds of elderly persons weekly. Teens and young adults have greater access to both recreational and educational activities as a result of the Summer Youth Program. The summer activities of the young people focused on the neighborhood. For instance, a visual arts project on display showed their own concepts for a new recreational facility. Also, a film produced by the youth featured familiar locations in the area. The awards ceremony was filled to capacity with persons of all ages from the JVL neighborhood.

JVL holds monthly community meetings at the Mennonite Church. Respondents stated that the attendance fluctuates, based on the interest in the topics being discussed. The topics have included tax increases (with top city officials present), vacant lot programs, health issues such as alcoholism and sales tax on medicines, the election of JVL's board of trustees, as well as JVL's program plans. JVL residents contact city officials through formal meetings, telephone, and other direct interaction in part because JVL discloses the identities of the city officials directly responsible for various services. JVL publishes a telephone guide in the *JVL News* that gets heavy use, according to respondents. The guide includes many city hall telephone numbers.

According to JVL's leaders, JVL works with many block clubs and their parent organization, the Federation of Block Units. However, there has been no indication of JVL having created additional clubs. Several organizations such as the Congress of Neighborhood Organizations in North St. Louis and the North Side Team Ministry include some JVL leadership. The congress has helped air issues through press conferences and information gathering. It has dealt with issues such as social services, housing, neighborhood betterment, citizen participation, programs for low- and moderate-income families, and the distribution of government funds. The ministry serves as a weekly outreach and community feedback channel for JVL, as well as for the clergy.

39. Are there any specific instances of a resident having become more influential outside the neighborhood because of the target organization?

40. Is there increased unity or fragmentation in the neighborhood since the founding of the organization? JVL's contribution to neighborhood unity seems to border on the spiritual. Macler Shepard at times appears to be a preacher and the neighborhood his congregation. The respect that he appears to enjoy is reinforced by a warm admiration felt for him by persons throughout the neighborhood. Shepard himself is certainly among the unifying factors in the JVL neighborhood. JVL has a reputation for being, in one word, "tenacious," according to respondents (including Mayor Conway and other city officials).

Race and Social Justice

41. How has the organization dealt with neighborhood problems of race and poverty? JVL's entire roster of activities has related to the plight of poor and black people. Its record of accomplishments deals with the problems of being poor and black in a large and older American city. This whole case study is a response to the issues of race and poverty.

42. How has the target organization responded to patterns of neighborhood transition—that is, displacement, integration, and resegregation? JVL has attempted to retain older residents through the development of newly subsidized housing for the elderly. In other cases, JVL has sold property back to renters under highly favorable terms, after renovation. JVL has sought to rehabilitate older, but sound, structures for habitation by persons in the middle- and upper-income levels. There is a clear pattern of economic integration underway in the JVL housing development program.

According to respondents who are white, there is no racial integration occurring in the JVL neighborhood. Although they live and work at a church in the area, they have broad contacts through the neighborhood. Prospects of racial integration may be related only to a school desegregation case that has been in the courts for several years. No other prospects seem imminent. The business community in the JVL area is integrated and works cooperatively with the organization. The JVL workforce also is integrated.

43. Have problems of race or ethnic division arisen in the target organization? Leaders and other respondents indicated that such divisions have not arisen. The unique team that provided the initial leadership for JVL was composed of black and white as well as female and male persons. Leadership and support workforce members share similar diversity today. Problems that were mentioned related to personality differences.

44. Over time, have there been any changes in the organization's policies or activities with regard to any of the issues in the preceding four questions?

45. How do the organization's leaders or members describe the accomplishments and disappointments from JVL's activities? [A list of 22 principal accomplishments appeared in the original case study, most of them already covered in earlier responses.]

The following are the principal disappointments:

- Demolition of the Pruitt-Igoe public housing complex and, in particular, the four buildings in the complex that JVL proposed to rehabilitate and manage
- Demolition of other landmarks, such as the Divoll School, built in 1872
- Rejection of the Opportunity House funding request by the United Way of Greater St. Louis
- Failure to cause the city to take action against illegal junkyards and other blight scattered throughout the JVL area
- Failure to win local government support for large-scale funding of public improvements to enhance housing developments

46. How has the organization enhanced community leadership or increased the involvement of residents?

47. Does the organization have a capability of dealing with multiple issues simultaneously?

48. During the lifetime of the organization, what situations, if any, threatened the survival of the organization? The principal threat to JVL's survival over its lifetime has been the need to raise money to survive, according to its leaders. JVL has dealt with that threat by continuously developing new funding sources and structuring the organization's fiscal practices along the lines of business and industry, striving for increased levels of self-generated or self-controlled revenues for a $200,000 core budget.

Other threats have come from the constant battle with local government. JVL has a history of confronting local political issues directly and mobilizing its base of support and respect in the JVL neighborhood, according to both JVL writings and respondents.

49. Are there any specific incidents that best characterize the work of the organization? Macler Shepard claims that "we dedicated ourselves to the community," and words such as "inspiration" and "dedication" characterize much of the JVL spirit. One young adult respondent who plans to reside in the JVL area said that she wants "to build equity in the neighborhood and realize a return from it—not money, but the sense of satisfaction that comes when you go home in the evening and say, 'I've accomplished something'—whether it's picking up trash or responding to the questions of young people who involve themselves at the [Communications Resources] Center."

LIST OF RESPONDENTS AND ANNOTATED BIBLIOGRAPHY

[The original case study listed 25 persons, with detailed titles, addresses, and telephone numbers, as well as complete references to 34 documents, reports, and printed materials.]

INSIDE STORY FOR CHAPTER 6

Being the Subject of Questions, Not the Questioner

Although neighborhood organizations tend to be accessible to outsiders, studying these organizations is not always easy. You need to develop a degree of trust among the organizers, and they may want to test you as part of the process.

One surprise can occur when you have arranged to interview one of the organizers but, upon arriving at a planned meeting location, find that a bunch of the organizers are present, ask you to sit, and proceed to interview you. They may want direct answers to such questions as the motives and sponsor (if any) of your study; your own personal views toward neighborhood organizing, or even their particular organization; and your own background and qualifications for doing the study. (Similar questions also can arise when you are with a single interviewee, either obtaining the person's agreement to participate in your study as part of your human subjects procedure or conversing with the person as part of the interview.)

The general caution is that, when doing fieldwork, you are working in a real-world setting where other people have their own routines and can reach out to you. Doing fieldwork is not like working in a laboratory or even administering a structured questionnaire.

For Class Discussion or Written Assignment

For a research study (not necessarily a case study) that you either have done or are thinking about doing, discuss how you would respond to the following questions that might arise, either when obtaining *informed consent* from a participant or as spontaneous queries by a participant during your fieldwork: Why are you doing this study? What are your qualifications for doing it? How will the results of your study be used? How will the participant (who is posing these questions) be affected (or not) by the results?

◆

PART III

EXPLANATORY CASE STUDIES

Explanatory case studies are the most difficult and may be the most frequently challenged. Each case study seeks to explain *how* and *why* a series of events occurred. In real-world settings, the explanations can be quite complex and can cover an extended period of time. Such conditions create the need for using the case study method rather than conducting, say, an experiment or a survey—even though those methods can help answer other important questions (e.g., Shavelson & Towne, 2002, pp. 99–106).

Part III (Chapter 7) begins by modeling an explanatory pattern by presenting a "nutshell" example. The example should illustrate the difference between descriptive and explanatory case studies by showing how the latter attempts to engage in causal reasoning. In the case of the "nutshell" example, the causal path suggests that the availability of external funds shifted the focus in the computer science research being done by different faculty—followed by a broader department-wide transition from "a theoretical, pencil-and-paper research operation to one with a high degree of experimental computing." In a parallel manner, the applications in Chapters 8 and 9 follow the same kind of explanatory reasoning: In Chapter 8, three brief case studies all attempt to define the conditions that led to certain drug prevention outcomes; in Chapter 9, a complete case study attempts to explain how a manufacturing firm improved its business outcomes.

Challenges to explanatory case studies arise when the case studies appear to cover the same cause-and-effect relationships that might have been covered by using the experimental method. Can case studies, especially single-case studies, prove anything? The answer is, "Not with the certainty of true experiments." However, the explanations contained in a case study usually can enrich the understanding of a cause-and-effect relationship beyond what can be discerned by using experiments or quasi-experiments alone. Whereas these other methods may be able to formally test a cause-and-effect relationship and establish whether there appears to be one, a case study can explain the relationship as well as its absence. Therefore, experiments and case studies—as with other distinctive research methods—may be considered complementary methods. You might use them within the same (mixed methods) study, to take advantage of their complementary roles.

You can strengthen the credibility of an explanatory case study enormously by practicing one other essential technique: searching for and testing *rival explanations*. When case studies include the investigation of such rivals, and if the prevailing evidence can support their rejection, you can place greater confidence in your case study's original explanation and conclusions. Chapter 10 recognizes the importance of engaging in rival explanations by presenting two applications that explicitly attended to such rivals.

7

A NUTSHELL EXAMPLE

The Effect of a Federal Award on a University Computer Science Department

This illustrative application was not originally a case study. Rather, the application comes from an abstract to the final report of a research grant, written by its principal investigator. The writer attempts to attribute significant organizational changes in a university computer science department to the use of funds from a federal grant. Serendipitously, the abstract's logic contains the essential ingredients of an explanatory case study. Because of its original one-page length, the abstract does not contain sufficient data or evidence to support its logic. However, the essence of the logic serves as an excellent point of departure for understanding how to develop an explanatory case study.

To demonstrate the usefulness of the logic, the present author has added methodological commentary (see the bracketed items) to the original text written by the principal investigator.

From 1980 to 1986, the Computer Science Department at Cornell was radically transformed from a theoretical, pencil-and-paper research operation

AUTHOR'S NOTE: This chapter is based on a one-page abstract from a final grant report for Award No. DCR81-05763 from the National Science Foundation to Cornell University, covering the period from June 1, 1981, to November 30, 1986. The abstract was written by the principal investigator of the grant, David Gries, and is dated February 27, 1987. The abstract is presented in its original form, with methodological comments added by Robert K. Yin to one with a high degree of experimental computing. The departmental computing facility grew from a VAX/780 and a PDP11/60 to an integrated complex of almost 100 workstations and UNIX mainframes. All faculty and graduate students now use computing daily **[a sequentially earlier outcome, further itemized below]**, and much research that was hitherto impossible for us is now being performed **[a sequentially later outcome, operationalized further below]**.

The change in emphasis was due to the maturing of computer science **[a concurrent condition that also can be a rival explanation]**, to commensurate changes in the interests of the faculty **[another concurrent condition]**, and to hardware and software advances that made flexible computing available at an affordable price **[a third concurrent condition]**. However, without the National Science Foundation's five-year CER (Coordinated Experimental Research) grant DCR81-05763, it would not have been possible **[main hypothesized intervention]**. The CER grant provided the wherewithal that allowed the department to change with the times; it provided equipment and maintenance, gave us leverage with vendors for acquiring other equipment, and funded staffing of the faculty **[critical how-and-why explanation for how the grant worked to produce the outcomes observed next]**.

The influence of the grant can be seen by mentioning just a few of the more important projects that it has stimulated. Turing Award winner John Hopcroft changed his interests from the theory of algorithms and computational complexity to robotics and now heads a growing and forceful group that is experimenting with robotics and solid modeling **[operationalized outcome]**. Theoretician Robert Constable and his group have been developing a system for "mechanizing" mathematics. This system, which has inspired many theoretical as well as experimental advances, has as one of its goals the extraction of a program from a mathematical proof; it gives a glimpse into how professional programming might be done 20 years from now **[a second operationalized outcome]**. Tim Teitelbaum and his group generalized his work on the well-known Program Synthesizer into a system that is able to generate such a programming environment from a formal description of a language; the resulting Synthesizer Generator has been released to more than 120 sites worldwide **[a third]**. Ken Birman's group is developing an experimental distributed operating system for dealing with fault tolerance **[a fourth]**. And visitor Paul Pritchard used the facility for his work on prime numbers, resulting in the first known arithmetic progression of 19 primes **[a fifth]**.

The CER grant enabled the department to attract bright young faculty who would not have joined a department with inadequate facilities **[yet another outcome]**. As a result, the department has been able to branch out into new areas, such as VLSI, parallel architectures and code optimization, functional programming, and artificial intelligence **[a second]**. The CER program did what it set out to do: It made it possible for the department to expand its research activity, making it far more experimental and computing intensive while still maintaining strong theoretical foundations **[general outcome]**.

Self-Reported Data

The material in the present chapter was retrieved from the official files of a government agency. The agency had provided grant funds to support a computer science department. The abstract was part of a longer report in which the department presented much more detail about the changes that took place as a result of receiving the grant funds. Although such reports still represent "self-reported" data, the contents may be slightly more credible because of the report's official nature and a grantee's obligation to account accurately for the funds that have been received. Reviewing these reports when they are available, therefore, can be an excellent way of preparing for working in the field (and corroborating the critical events in the report).

For Class Discussion or Written Assignment

Discuss the pros and cons of relying on self-reported information, such as the document in this chapter. Identify whether there are some circumstances when such information can be accepted as being more trustworthy and other circumstances when the information should be considered less trustworthy.

8

ESSENTIAL INGREDIENTS OF EXPLANATORY CASE STUDIES

Three Drug Prevention Examples

These three illustrative applications were developed specifically for case study train-ing purposes. To this end, the text contains special markings. First, key evidence in the text has been italicized. Second, the topics listed in the margins represent a running commentary that tracks the presumed line of an explanatory argument being made by the case study.

The applications were written in a deliberately abbreviated manner and with the running commentary, to show the essential logic underlying explanatory case studies. The basic claim underlying each case is that (1) a community formed (2) a partner-ship that in turn supported (3) activities leading to (4) reductions in substance abuse (see **BOX 10**). Arraying data to present these presumed "how" and "why" links is the main challenge of each abbreviated case study. (See Chapter 13 for a case study evaluation on a similar topic.)

The abbreviated versions are based on an original set of case studies that were much more extensive and contained greater detail and additional evidence, based on extensive fieldwork (all names in the abbreviated versions are anonymous).

AUTHOR'S NOTE: This chapter contains highly condensed versions of case studies produced by staff members of COSMOS Corporation under the direction of Robert K. Yin, as part of a project for the U.S. Department of Health and Human Services. Later, the team also produced the condensed versions specifically for the purpose of illustrating explanatory case studies. The condensed versions have been used successfully in numerous case study training sessions and were edited for inclusion in this chapter.

BOX 10

Logic Models

The hypothesized sequence of the four activities and outcomes for the case studies in the present chapter comprise a conceptual array known as a *logic model.* Case study data then can be collected and analyzed to examine the plausibility of the hypothesized sequence, to determine whether the actual sequence of events emulates the hypothesized one.

Articulating the logic model even can be considered an end in itself. For instance, in studying public programs or organizational changes such as those in Chapter 8, sometimes the articulation of a logic model may reveal that a planned change is illogically related to its desired outcomes on intuitive grounds alone, prior to collecting any empirical evidence (Wholey, 1979). The establishment of a compelling logic model, therefore, is helpful in two ways. First, it can guide the implementation of any planned change. Second, case study teams can establish that a hypothetical logical model makes common sense before committing to data collection and the remainder of a case study.

(For more information, see Yin, 2009a, Chapter 5, section on "Logic Models.")

The lengthier case studies clearly are stronger, providing more evidence, but the purpose of the abbreviated versions is to illustrate the essential explanatory logic, not to provide detailed evidence.

Despite their brevity, the illustrative applications also illustrate the use of rival explanations. Some rivals deal with the newness and distinctiveness of the partnership; others with whether the partnership in fact was the main instigator of the critical activities; and, finally, yet others with the link between the activities and drug prevention outcomes. The more such rival explanations are identified and rejected, the stronger the resulting explanation—again highlighting the ability of case studies to explain the possible relationships between how-and-why causes and their presumed effects.

The three applications are not intended to be part of any cross-case logic. However, you may view them as attempted replications of the same theory—the importance and role of community partnerships. From such a standpoint, the more cases that can be arrayed in similar replicative fashion, the stronger the aggregate evidence in support of this broader theory.

SIMPLIFIED CASE EXAMPLE NO. 1:
TOWN MEETINGS GALVANIZE ACTION AGAINST DRUG DEALING

In 1992, Bordertown, USA, recorded its highest homicide rate in history. Similarly, drug arrests and drug-related crimes were at high levels and had been steadily increasing. A new partnership—the Community Partnership Coalition (CPC)—charged its Anti-Drug Task Force to work with the community to identify the causes of crime and identify solutions. The CPC, located in the Mayor's Office, organized a town meeting to hear citizens' opinions on crime. *This was the first attempt to bring together city residents to address these issues.*

The meeting, which attracted more than 1,000 participants in November 1992, focused on several problems in the city, including drug dealing, abandoned houses, lack of community involvement, and various quality-of-life issues. *The CPC sponsored 15 follow-up neighborhood meetings among residents, police, public works officials, and others, to identify specific problems and prioritize plans to address these problems.* In all but one neighborhood, residents cited drugs and drug dealing as the highest concern. These residents were asked to identify specific examples, such as the addresses of the abandoned houses and the exact street corners on which drug dealers were loitering.

With the information provided by community residents, the CPC brought together town officials, the Bordertown Police Department, and the Department of Public Works. *This was the first time these parties had collaborated.* The result was the design of Operation Eliminate in May 1993, a two-pronged strategy that combined (1) specialized drug operations targeting both drug dealers and users and that involved drug sweeps, sting operations, and buy-busts and (2) a streamlined process for demolishing abandoned buildings. The enforcement component was built on existing narcotics enforcement practices; however, *the unique aspect of this new strategy was the involvement of the CPC, residents, and public works to identify targets.*

Operation Eliminate is funded in part by the town. The CPC also was able to secure corporate contributions to support the effort. The success of this effort has been contingent on the active involvement of community members, starting with the CPC-sponsored neighborhood meetings, which have continued.

A possible rival notion that Operation Eliminate resulted from a preexisting community policing initiative is not supported because the initial police division involved with Operation Eliminate was the narcotics division (which made drug arrests and seized drugs), not the community policing division.

Preexisting substance abuse problem

Partnership-initiated collaborative intervention

Partnership planning

Distinctiveness of the collaboration

Collaborative activities

Rejection of rival sources of support for intervention

Quantifiable outcomes and
impacts

Outcome

Outcome

Rejection of major rival explanation
for outcomes and impacts

Additional outcomes and impacts

Rejection of additional rival
explanation

As of April 1994, Operation Eliminate had resulted in *1,278 drug arrests and confiscations of 311 weapons. Overall, drug arrests in the city increased by 150% between 1992 and 1993, 43% of which are directly attributable to Operation Eliminate* (see Table 8.1). Statistics from the drug court, which is responsible for processing all drug offenders, indicate that *the quality of arrests also has improved, with guilty pleas for felony offenses increasing 41% after June 1993.* As a result of these arrests, *the police department has seized $678,962 in illegal narcotics. Also, since June 1993, when Operation Eliminate was implemented, the number of drug-related homicides has dropped by one-third citywide.* In contrast to these trends, *other crime rates have remained the same or increased, providing no support for yet another rival explanation.*

The second prong of Operation Eliminate resulted in a reduction in the backlog of abandoned houses scheduled to be demolished, from 336 in 1993 to none in 1994. The time required to process building demolitions also decreased from eight to six months, and the costs per building dropped from an average of $2,000 in 1992 to $1,155 in 1993. Another positive indication of community involvement is the increase in the number of offenses reported to the police and to public works. Reported drug offenses increased 36%, and calls for service increased an average of 6% in high-crime areas in the six months immediately following the implementation of Operation Eliminate. *The case study team explored but found little support for rival explanations, including changes in the amount of drugs entering the city and the ongoing implementation of other police enforcement programs.*

Table 8.1   Town Meetings Galvanize Action Against Drug Dealing

		Pre-1992	Post-1993	% Increase From 1992 to 1993
Law enforcement	Drug arrests	1,020	2,547[a]	149.7
	Marijuana seized	482 lb	2,452 lb[b]	408.6
	Cocaine seized	16 lb	349 lb[c]	2,029.8
Drug court	Jury trials	17	74	355.5
	Judge trials	2	0	0.0
	Guilty pleas	574	808	40.7

a. 42.5% of drug arrests were logged by the Operation Eliminate unit.
b. 11.0% of marijuana seizures were recorded by the Operation Eliminate unit.
c. 4.0 % of the cocaine seizures were recorded by the Operation Eliminate unit.

SIMPLIFIED CASE EXAMPLE NO. 2:
INTERAGENCY COLLABORATION TO REDUCE BWI INCIDENTS

Until 1990, boating-while-intoxicated (BWI) incidents in the waters surrounding Seaside, USA, had been rising steadily. No apparent actions had been taken to address the problem. For instance, the U.S. Coast Guard, by mandate, focuses on water safety—not enforcement. The waterway enforcement agencies (Coast Guard, Harbor Patrol, and State Environmental Police) had been following an "enforcement by demand" policy, with little attention to BWI incidents and hardly any arrests. There were no BWI-specific patrols, blockades, or checkpoints by any of the three waterway enforcement agencies, nor were there any other related prevention actions.

Preexisting substance abuse problem

A new partnership, the Seaside Prevention Network (SPN), was formed in January 1991. In initiating action, the SPN project director contacted the Coast Guard to identify ways of collaborating. Water safety (including substance-abuse–related issues) was viewed as a point of common interest. Soon after, the SPN formed the Water Safety Coalition in February 1991. The Coalition chose to focus its efforts on collaboration, community awareness, and training for boaters. These activities began almost immediately, with the SPN supporting community awareness campaigns and staff support for the Water Safety Coalition.

Partnership-initiated collaborative intervention

Earlier, *in 1988, the first federal regulation prohibiting the operation of a vessel while intoxicated went into effect. In 1992, an amendment established behavioral standards for determining intoxication.* The Water Safety Coalition's goal was to use this law to raise awareness and carry out preventive activities; no changes ever were attempted in enforcement practices.

Supportive contextual events

The Water Safety Coalition brought the three participating agencies together for the first time in their histories. When large recreational events were planned, the agencies would now coordinate their patrol efforts. *As another example, in 1993, the State Environmental Police and the Coast Guard developed an interagency agreement describing the role of each in concurrent jurisdictions.*

Absence of prior collaborative history

Distinctiveness of the collaboration

The *community awareness activities* led to the placing of 300 BWI posters on marine gas pumps throughout the Seaside waters. The Coalition also mailed BWI information and safety tips to all mooring permit holders in Seaside and continues to do so on an annual basis. Related activities included bumper stickers, public service announcements, newspaper articles, and education films for cable television.

Partnership activities

The Coast Guard Auxiliary, also a member of the Coalition, taught boating skills to junior operators by *coordinating junior*

Additional partnership activities

Rejection of rival sources of support for intervention

Quantifiable outcomes

operators' classes for state certification. Thus far, 62 youths have received training to qualify for junior operator's licenses from the state. Throughout these activities, the SPN continued to provide funding, leadership, and staff support, which continues to this day. *The individual agencies also provided support, and no other sponsors were involved.*

By 1993, a total of 14 BWI incidents (boardings resulting in arrests, accidents, or deaths) were reported by the Coast Guard, the Harbor Patrol, and the State Environmental Police, compared with a total of 35 reported incidents in 1990 (see Table 8.2). Normalizing these incidents by the total boat traffic (monitored by a local bridge authority) also shows this downward trend, from 0.16% in 1990 to 0.05% in 1993.

Table 8.2   Changes in Number of BWI Incidents

Law Enforcement Agency	1990	1991	1992	1993
U.S. Coast Guard	30	19	10	8
Local	3	5	1	5
State	2	0	0	1
Total BWI incidents	35	24	11	14
BWI incidents as percentage of total boat traffic	0.16%	0.10%	0.06%	0.05%

SIMPLIFIED CASE EXAMPLE NO. 3: DESIGNATED DRIVER PROGRAM, DELIVERED THROUGH VENDORS

Preexisting substance abuse problem

Summertown, along with surrounding vacation communities, has experienced sharp seasonal increases in alcohol-related automobile injuries and deaths. Arrests for operating under the influence (OUI) have exceeded the state average and have caused concern among residents who want to maintain the tourist industry but also maximize the safety of local citizens and visitors.

Partnership formation

The Summertown Partnership to Reduce Substance Abuse was formed in 1991. The issue of alcohol abuse was a primary concern, and efforts began immediately to find an effective remedy that would not undermine the tourist industry. A designated driver campaign had been planned and was in the early stages of implementation in surrounding communities. *The partnership adopted and expanded the campaign, developing the Safe Driver Program.*

Partnership-initiated collaborative intervention

The partnership drafted *two drinking/driving policy initiatives* that were adopted—after testimony before local lawmakers and provision of safe-driver training and literature for the alcohol vendors and servers—by the town and the sheriff's department. The first policy was embodied in a local ordinance requiring applicants for one-day alcohol sales to include a plan to prevent drinking and driving away from the event. The second policy strongly endorsed participation in the partnership's Safe Driver Program, and the sheriff's department implemented the policies by informing all alcoholic beverage vendors and serving establishments.

Partnership activities

From the outset, change in OUI arrests was considered the criterion outcome measure. Furthermore, although effective initiatives might have been expected to lead to an initial rise in such arrests, eventually they must decline in order for an initiative to be deemed successful. Thus, data have to be available over an extended period of time.

In Summertown, multiyear baseline data for the period prior to introduction of the program were compared with multiyear data for the period following implementation. The data showed that, *compared with a rapid rise during the baseline period, OUI arrests began to decline slightly between 1990 and 1994* (see Table 8.3).

Quantifiable outcome

Implementation of the Safe Driver Program was widespread, primarily because the partnership enjoys active support from the local law enforcement office and also from businesses that serve alcoholic beverages. *Because of the collaborative effort, an intervention was designed that enhanced the law enforcement effort to reduce drunk driving without damaging business interests.* Moreover, the OUI data—necessary for verifying the program's impact—were accessible to the partnership because of the collaboration of the local law enforcement department, which is a partnership member. *This collaborative relationship did not exist prior to the formation of the partnership.*

Attribution to collaboration

Absence of rival collaborative history

The state launched a campaign against drunk driving during the period that the Safe Driver Program was being implemented. *However, other vacation communities reported an increase, rather than a decrease, in the number of arrests during the same period.*

Discussion of major rival explanation for outcome

Table 8.3   Outcomes From Designated Driver Program

	OUI Arrests, June–August (1988–1994)	
	Year	**Number of Arrests**
Prior to program	1988	52
	1989	69
	1990	88
After program inception	1991	72
	1992	76
	1993	65
	1994	62

Shortened Case Studies

The length and density of most case studies can test most readers' patience in following a text and absorbing information. As a result, the three short case studies in the present chapter were created in an attempt to provide an abbreviated format for presenting case study material. However, their brevity also produced an undesirable effect—skepticism on the part of readers regarding the credibility of the case studies—because the presentations were so short and the material was insufficiently detailed.

To overcome these challenges, a generally accepted procedure is for you to develop both a short and a long version of your case study. Note that the short version still would differ from the more conventional *abstract* or *executive summary,* because the short version would present only the actual case study. In other words, the short version—as with the three applications in the present chapter—would not discuss other matters such as the research methods or other background information normally found in abstracts and executive summaries. In this sense, your complete long version could still contain its own abstract or executive summary, in addition to having a short version of your case study.

For Class Discussion or Written Assignment

Discuss the minimal topics in a shortened case study that would still retain readers' confidence in a case study's findings. Consider whether graphics or tables of any sort might be a helpful part of the shortened case study. Suggest topics that might have been added to the three applications in the present chapter, still keeping the versions short but enhancing the credibility and trustworthiness of the findings.

———————◆———————

9

TRANSFORMING A BUSINESS FIRM THROUGH STRATEGIC PLANNING

Research on business firms frequently has assumed the form of case studies. This chapter's application demonstrates how explanatory case studies about such firms may be designed and conducted. The firm was one of many that were chosen for study[1] because it had successfully transformed itself, as follows.

The firm was a family-owned machine shop and components manufacturer. It had been pressured by its major customer to improve its production system or risk losing business. Implementation of cellular manufacturing solved the firm's initial production problems and resulted in a 300% capacity increase and a rise in employee skill levels and problem-solving capabilities. In addition to the improved manufacturing processes, the firm's management team developed a shared, common direction about what to do with the company's extra capacity. The team undertook a strategic planning process that set the course for achieving important long-range company goals and objectives in marketing, information systems, manufacturing, and human resources.

The case study documents the changes undertaken by the firm, showing how the combined effect of the changes went far beyond mere manufacturing improvement—effectively transforming the whole firm and its original organizational culture. Besides describing these processes, the case study explains how they led to the firm's successful growth in sales and profits.

AUTHOR'S NOTE: This chapter is based on a case study that appeared in *Transformed Firms Case Studies,* issued by the National Institute of Standards and Technology, U.S. Department of Commerce, Gaithersburg, Maryland, April 1999. Robert K. Yin designed and directed the entire case study project, although each individual case study was conducted by a different person. The original Rheaco case study was conducted by Jan Youtie. Robert K. Yin condensed and edited the version in this chapter.

Methodologically, the case study presents evidence from multiple sources. In many instances, the reported course of events represents a triangulation of the data from these multiple sources (see **BOX 11**).

BOX 11

Triangulation

Most research investigators know the original derivation of the concept of *triangulation:* A point in three-dimensional space may be established by specifying the intersection of three vectors (not two or one, and four would be redundant). This concept has been borrowed for dealing with social science evidence: The most robust evidence may be considered to have been established if the data from three independent sources all coincide.

Consider the difficulty of establishing the occurrence of an event if you were unable to observe it directly yourself. You would be more confident in saying that the event had occurred if your study showed that information from interviews, documents, and archival records all pointed in the same direction. Most of the events reported in the present case reflect such a condition. This type of triangulation is the most desired pattern for dealing with case study data, and you should always seek to attain it. An important clue when doing fieldwork is to ask the same question of different sources of evidence, as well as asking the same questions of different interviewees. If all sources point to the same answer, you will have successfully triangulated your data.

(For more information, see Yin, 2009a, Chapter 4, section on "Triangulation: Rationale for Using Multiple Sources of Evidence.")

COMPANY PROFILE AND CONDITIONS LEADING TO CHANGE

Rheaco, Inc., is a family-owned, privately held machine shop and components manufacturer. Located in the heart of the Dallas-Fort Worth Metroplex in Grand Prairie, Texas, Rheaco provides full-service machining and metal fabricating, primarily for defense customers. About 90% of its business is in the defense industry.

Defense Industry Consolidation, Leadership Change, and Rising Production Volumes Spur Changes

Rheaco's internal and external business environment experienced major changes in the early 1990s. Rheaco's founder and president turned the company over to his son, Rhea E. Wallace, Jr., in 1992. The same year and following the Gulf War, Rheaco's major customer, Lockheed Martin, began aggressively consolidating its supply chain, reducing the number of its vendors from roughly 1,600 to 400 over a two-year period.

Having survived this round of cuts, Rheaco had new opportunities to supply parts to Lockheed Martin. Rheaco received orders for several thousand additional parts, but the new orders choked Rheaco's production system, which emphasized long production runs, long setup times, manufacturing to inventory, and the shipping of parts regardless of their quality. In an earlier interview, Wallace had stated, "The company worked seven days a week for a year, with no letup."[2] Wallace had trouble locating orders and did not have enough file cabinets for all the paperwork. Work in process was so extensive that walking through the facility was difficult. Occasionally, Rheaco's quality rating dipped below Lockheed Martin's supplier specifications. Wallace's initial solution (to buy shelves and file cabinets) added to the clutter. He even formed a team of 25 expeditors to meet each morning, to determine the jobs needed to be completed by the end of the day.

Change Process Begins With Solving Production System Problems

Wallace said, "It wasn't fun to come to work." He recognized the need for change but did not have a specific plan. Instead, he took steps to solve his immediate problem, which ultimately led to broad-based changes. Wallace turned to third-party resources for problem-solving assistance and for validating the ideas he had read about. Lockheed Martin provided some help—seminars and hotlines—but it did not have an assistance program in the manufacturing process area.

At about that time, Wallace and his management team attended a breakfast workshop series cosponsored by the Automation and Robotics Research Institute and the Texas Manufacturing Assistance Center (TMAC). The workshop series stressed creating a vision, changing company culture and dealing with human resource issues, and then adopting process and technology improvements. The series ended with a call for volunteers for in-company assessments, to be conducted by TMAC or its affiliates.

Wallace volunteered his company for such an assessment. A specialist from one of TMAC's affiliates later conducted the assessment. As part of the assessment, the specialist helped Wallace set up a process improvement team. The team first decided to work on paperwork issues and the ability to locate order information. The team, however, found that the paperwork problems were symptomatic of deeper production-floor problems.

In mid-1993, Wallace toured another small manufacturer, InterTurbine, which had experienced similar problems. InterTurbine had solved its production problems with cellular manufacturing, so Wallace concluded that cellular manufacturing was what his operation needed. Cellular manufacturing emphasizes small production runs, groupings of diverse equipment and machines, and manufacturing functions performed in close proximity to workers. These attributes represented a significant change from Rheaco's production system. Wallace decided to begin by implementing a three-person prototype cell in the metal extrusions area. That cell was successful, achieving a 200% improvement in throughput by its second week of operation.[3]

Because of this success and spurred by requests from other Rheaco workers to become involved in cells, Wallace implemented cellular manufacturing throughout the facility during the following year. Rheaco's workers took two months to design the new facility layout. The two months of preparation allowed Rheaco employees to implement the new cells speedily, with minimal financial losses and downtime. Employees tore down the old workplaces overnight and implemented the new cells within a week. They created five manufacturing cells, one assembly team, and two plating teams, supported by five functional teams responsible for scheduling, quality, human resources, maintenance, and supplies.[4]

The rollout also involved training managers and production-level workers in team processes and problem solving so that the cells could assume responsibility for each part. This level of responsibility required further training to enable team members to operate several types of machines and to manage different processes. Wallace set a goal of two qualified operators for each piece of equipment in each cell and promoted on-the-job cross-training to meet this "two-deep" goal. Designed to be self-directed, the teams eliminated the need for a foreman and moved the company toward a flat organizational structure.

Within the first year after converting to cellular manufacturing, Rheaco saw significant process improvements. Cellular manufacturing reduced work in process by 65%, material transport by 35%, and lead time by 87%. First-run yields improved by 77%. Cycle times for videoconferencing card products declined from 120 days to three days, and production capacity increased by 300% without additional equipment or personnel. These improvements also led to a reduced need for inventory, freeing 5,000 square feet of additional space.

Productivity improvements also reduced the need for workers, so 36 workers were terminated. Other employees, unable to handle the changes, decided to leave on their own. Shop-floor workers themselves made the remaining staffing decisions, based on factors such as performance, skills, and ability to be a team player.

STRATEGIC PLAN TRANSFORMS THE BUSINESS

Manufacturing processes had improved, but Rheaco's management team had no shared vision of what to do with the company's extra capacity. In the past, the company's founder had made all decisions about where to allocate company resources. However, Wallace's management style, as evidenced by the manufacturing cells and self-directed work teams, was more participatory. Among the management team, members held diverse ideas about where to take the company and where its resources should be invested. The sales manager suggested that investments be made in new equipment, based on his discussions with customers about upcoming opportunities. Wallace's experience with cellular manufacturing identified the need for major expenditures on workforce training and quality certification. He said, "Management was going in many different directions because we disagreed and lacked focus."[5]

Once Wallace was able to spend less time solving daily production problems, he turned his attention to the development of a strategic plan. In the spring of 1996, he asked a TMAC manufacturing specialist to facilitate the strategic planning process for the company. The planning process involved developing a statement of purpose, assessing external strengths and weaknesses (including a customer profile), assessing internal strengths and weaknesses, establishing strategic goals, identifying obstacles to realizing the goals, and developing actions for overcoming the obstacles. Members of the management team—representing human resources, finance, operations, customer service, and quality control—met weekly to produce the document.

The primary benefit of the strategic planning process was not just the planning document. Management team members reported that communications had improved. Team members achieved consensus on issues of company direction and allocation of company resources. "We were all on the same page," Wallace said. The customer service manager said that the planning process "brought everything to light."

The team decided to move from the company's traditional production-driven strategy to one oriented to customer needs. An analysis of costs and revenues by customer and by product identified those customer needs that resulted in the most profitable business for Rheaco. To obtain this business, the planning team identified desirable strategic attributes: performing quick turnaround; developing advanced capabilities, such as five-axis machine technology for complicated surface parts; providing whole subassemblies; and offering full-service in-house capabilities in areas such as machine shop, painting, and plating. These attributes distinguished Rheaco from other machine shops. The impact of the strategic plan on other aspects of Rheaco's business is described below and summarized in Exhibit 9.1.

Marketing: Targeting Valued Customers

In the marketing area, defense industry cutbacks and lack of long-term relationships with key customers made the company believe it had to "respond rapidly to the constant, unanticipated changing needs" of its customers.[6] Rheaco's move to cellular manufacturing made it more agile so that the account managers could "quote anything if the quantity was large enough." This approach produced large numbers of buyers to deal with and quotes to develop. Managing these multiple diverse relationships was difficult and time-consuming. Account managers had less time to prepare quotes and understand customer needs. Wallace, who served as account manager for most smaller accounts, endeavored to treat these 60 to 70 customers equally in terms of account management and delivery dates promised. This effort diverted his time from broader leadership efforts and impeded service to larger accounts.

Exhibit 9.1   Rheaco's Systems Before and After Improved Strategic Alignment

Area	Before Strategic Planning	After Strategic Planning	Results
Management	• Lack of consensus about allocating company resources	• Single direction toward customer-oriented manufacturing	• President focuses on longer-range issues • Improved communication among management team • Involvement in community activities, such as apprenticeship program sponsorship
Marketing	• Difficulty prioritizing 54–70 customer jobs • Quoting inaccuracies	• Focus on a few key customers to become preferred supplier • Customer diversification initiatives	• Improved quotes • Sole-source provider for a number of parts • More sales at higher margins
Manufacturing	• Cellular manufacturing improved efficiency and capacity, and freed up space	• New business opportunities guided plant layout and investment decisions—for example, investment in new penetrant inspection room • Pursuit of D1-9000 certification • Purified plating discharge • Achieved OSHA exemption	• Manufacturing capabilities match company strategy and market demand • Environmental, health, and safety measures support community commitment value in strategic plan
Information Systems	• MRP system did not integrate with accounting system • Weekly cash flow status not available • Materials were purchased late • Sometimes already stocked items were purchased	• New MRP system integrated manufacturing and accounting systems	• Material orders on time or ahead of schedule • On-time delivery of parts and components to customers improves, consistent with quick-turnaround customer satisfaction goal in strategic plan • Ordering material already in stock eliminated • Weekly assessment of financial status available

Area	Before Strategic Planning	After Strategic Planning	Results
Human Resources	• Investment in machinery and equipment favored over employee training • Cellular manufacturing emphasized flat organization, self-directed teams	• Invested in people—for example, hired penetrant specialist and retrained welders in penetrant inspection—as well as equipment to implement its new penetrant cell • Departed from flat cellular organizational structure by hiring general manager • Participated in developing community-wide apprenticeship program	• Human resources supports manufacturing, market demand, and company strategy • New general manager relieves president of ongoing shop-floor management • President focuses on strategic issues • Apprenticeship program supports community commitment value in strategic plan

The strategic plan showed that Rheaco had a small number of key profitable customers. Rheaco's customer services unit changed its practices to focus on these customers. The customer services manager now had time to produce more accurate quotes and could obtain in-depth understanding of the customers' current and future needs. For example, Lockheed Martin had shared information with its Rheaco account manager about the amount of business it expected to subcontract in certain product areas. Rheaco became a sole-source provider to Lockheed Martin for a number of parts and has been selling a larger number of products at higher margins. Monthly revenues from major customers tripled in late 1998, from $20,000 to $60,000. Becoming a preferred provider effectively reduced the uncertainty in Rheaco's sales revenues. Focusing on major customers also enabled Wallace to devote less time to minor customer account management and more time to broader strategic issues.

Rheaco's strategic plan also called for diversifying into commercial aerospace markets. Rheaco's planning team determined that the commercial aerospace industry was a good fit with its existing defense business. The plan called for understanding the needed qualifications for doing business with aerospace firms. Rheaco then targeted its marketing and quality efforts at this new customer segment.

Manufacturing: Supporting Customers' Needs

Rheaco's traditional approach to manufacturing systems was to invest in machines that could run large volumes of parts. With the introduction of cellular manufacturing, the company arranged equipment and workers to improve efficiency and free up space, but what the company was to do with its additional capacity and space was not clear.

The strategic plan played an important role in guiding the company to use this newly found capacity. A significant number of new business opportunities now guide plant layout and investment decisions. For example, the improved understanding of a major customer's plating needs led Wallace to purchase new plating equipment. Another example involves Rheaco's new "penetrant inspection" cell, built in 1998 to conduct nondestructive testing for cracks, leak paths, and other structural defects. An account manager had learned that Lockheed Martin needed quick turnaround service in this area. Wallace decided to use the excess space from the cellular manufacturing implementation to build a penetrant inspection room. These two examples illustrated Rheaco's ability to rearrange manufacturing cells based on the likely sources of new sales and revenue.

To meet the other goal of the strategic plan—diversifying into commercial aerospace markets—Rheaco's quality manager pursued Boeing D1-9000 certification. Wallace said that, before the process changes and strategic plan, "I didn't even have enough confidence to get certified." Rheaco met Lockheed Martin's quality requirements and those of other major defense customers. Earlier, Rheaco had won various quality awards, such as the 1993 Loral Vought Systems Subcontractor of the Year Award (even as the company was converting to cellular manufacturing) and the 1994 Small Business Administration's Administrator's Award for Excellence. However, the company never had undergone standards certification. The plan identified quality certification as a major goal and the lack of Boeing D1-9000 certification as an obstacle to customer diversification. Rheaco's quality manager led the quality team in assessing manuals, training, and conducting audits and worked with TMAC quality specialists to achieve Boeing D1-9000 certification.

Pursuing Boeing D1-9000 certification and making facilities investment decisions based on customer needs demonstrate the alignment between the production system and Rheaco's strategic plan. Although the cellular manufacturing implementation had solved Rheaco's production capacity concerns, manufacturing capabilities matched company strategy and market demands only after Rheaco completed its certification.

Investing in Human Resources

In the human resources area, the strategic plan addressed hiring options. Despite the human resource changes associated with Rheaco's cellular manufacturing initiative, the planning process revealed that the company's investment emphasis on machinery and equipment over human resources hindered the accomplishment of the strategic goals. Rheaco's managers decided to allocate resources based on skills needed to bring in specific business. For example, Rheaco wanted to deliver penetrant inspection services, but it lacked in-house expertise. Therefore, Rheaco hired a specialist to help design a penetrant inspection cell for the shop floor and provide training. To implement its new penetrant cell, Rheaco invested in people as well as equipment.

In addition, Rheaco hired a general manager in 1998 to deal with the day-to-day responsibilities of the manufacturing operation. Although this addition conflicted with Wallace's desire for a flat organization, the management team reached consensus in the planning process that the shop floor needed a general manager. The new general manager quickly relieved Wallace of ongoing shop-floor management responsibilities.[7]

Information Systems: Improving Customer Service

In the information systems area, the strategic planning process revealed problems with Rheaco's old manufacturing resource planning (MRP) system. This system was not integrated with other systems and was not regularly used. Consequently, the purchasing department made errors in ordering materials. For example, sometimes orders were not placed until after the final delivery date, and at other times the purchasing department ordered materials already in stock. The strategic plan called for an integrated information system.[8]

In 1998, Wallace purchased a new MRP system that combined manufacturing and accounting systems. The new system significantly improved the purchasing function. The purchasing manager now orders and receives materials on time or ahead of schedule, which has improved the on-time delivery of parts and components to customers. These improvements have enhanced Rheaco's ability to be a quick turnaround shop and to meet its customer satisfaction goal of 100% on-time delivery. Wallace also uses the system to assess the company's financial situation weekly, rather than waiting until the end of the month.

Enhancing Community Involvement

One of the strategic plan's major goals was to "be actively involved in our community."[9] Community involvement, according to the management team, included environmental, health, and safety compliance, as well as participation in community programs. In 1998, Rheaco participated in the Safety and Health Achievement Recognition Program and received a Certificate of Recognition award from the U.S. Department of Labor's Occupational Safety and Health Administration (OSHA), exempting the company from programmed OSHA inspections—a first for Rheaco. Wallace joined with 15 other small manufacturers and Bell Helicopter in sponsoring an apprenticeship program in the Fort Worth Independent School District. Rheaco hired three graduates from the first two graduating classes.[10]

Results: Sales and Wages Increase, Along With Supplier Consolidation in Tight Labor Market

Total sales increased 56%, from $3.5 million in 1992 to $5.4 million in 1997. Sales per employee improved by 90% over the same period (see Figure 9.1).

Figure 9.1   Rheaco's Sales and Wages per Employee

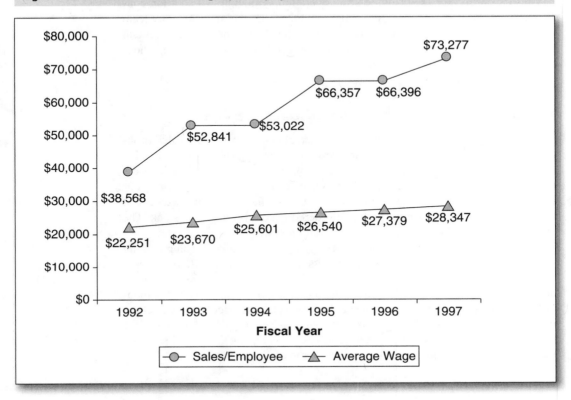

Value added per employee (revenue minus wages, per employee) increased 175%, from $16,317 in 1992 to $44,930 in 1997.

Rheaco's sales increase arguably may have resulted from changes made by Lockheed Martin, whose supply chain consolidation provided opportunities to Rheaco and other preferred suppliers, including higher value-added components and subassemblies business. Nevertheless, Lockheed Martin's supplier management practices cannot fully explain Rheaco's sales increases. Without its extensive changes, Rheaco could have been eliminated as a supplier in later rounds of consolidation. Lockheed Martin's additional specialized needs might have been missed without Rheaco's strategic goals in the account management area. Clearly, Rheaco's new customer orientation in marketing and other areas resulted in substantial sales increases.

Rheaco's consistent sales increases have allowed it to recruit additional employees. The number of employees has risen from a low of 67 to 85—starting to approach pre-layoff levels. Nevertheless, payroll expenses as a share of sales revenue dropped from 58% to less than 40% from 1992 to 1997, reflecting Rheaco's increased productivity (see Figure 9.2). Wage increases also occurred,

Figure 9.2 Rheaco's Business Performance

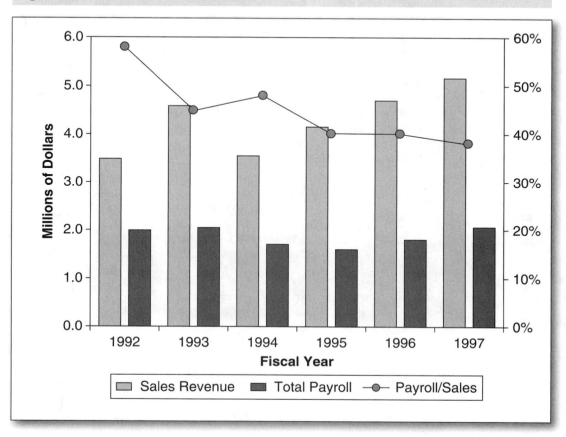

in part, because of a tight labor market: The unemployment rate in the Fort Worth-Arlington area dropped to 3.1% in October 1998 (compared with 4.4% nationwide).[11]

Conclusion: Strategic Planning Leads to Multiple Changes, Making Rheaco a Transformed Firm

Rheaco transformed itself because it made multiple changes throughout all major company systems. The firm had been operating soundly prior to these changes and had survived Lockheed Martin's massive supplier consolidation. Rheaco also had won quality awards prior to or simultaneously with converting to cellular manufacturing—and well before it initiated strategic planning.

Nevertheless, even recognizing these accomplishments, Rheaco had been experiencing fundamental production problems that threatened its customer relationships. Cellular manufacturing initially addressed these problems. Ultimately, however, it was the strategic planning process that led to multiple and interrelated changes—for example, improving the alignment in the company's systems in support of market needs and business strategies.

The totality of the transformation produced Rheaco's significant gains in financial performance. Lockheed Martin's supplier consolidation gave Rheaco opportunities, but Rheaco could not have exploited these opportunities, much less profitably expanded them, without its broad-based and interrelated changes. By aligning the company's systems, Rheaco moved from a capacity-driven job shop to a customer-driven, high-precision supplier. Consequently, the total effect of the changes on firm performance became greater than the sum of the effects of individual changes (see **BOX 12**).

BOX 12

Exemplary Case Designs

The Rheaco case was chosen to be the subject of a case study because the firm was believed, ahead of time, to have transformed itself successfully. The case selection criterion represents an example of an *exemplary case* design.

This design can be used in doing a single-case or multiple-case study. In the multiple-case situation, the use of the exemplary case design means that all the cases in the case study will reflect strong, positive examples of the phenomenon of interest. The rationale suits a replication logic well because the overall investigation then may try to determine whether similar explanatory events within each case produced these positive outcomes.

The use of the exemplary case design, however, also requires you to determine beforehand whether the specific cases indeed have produced exemplary outcomes. Extensive case screening may be needed, and you must resist permitting the case screening process to become a study in itself.

(For more information, see Yin, 2009a, Chapter 2, section on "What Are the Potential Multiple-Case Designs?")

CHRONOLOGY

1991–1992: Felt pressures of defense downsizing, which threatened business with largest customers

Early 1992: Rhea E. Wallace, Jr., took over as company president; company had 94 workers; Wallace and other Rheaco managers attended Breakfast Workshop Series co-sponsored by TMAC

Late 1992: Small Business Development Center for Enterprise Excellence (SBDC) representative conducted an in-company assessment

February–March 1993: SBDC representative helped Rheaco set up process improvement team; team decided to focus on paperwork processing problem

June–July 1993: Managers visited InterTurbine

August–September 1993: Implemented prototype manufacturing cell in metal extrusions area; SBDC representative provided training for 25 managers and shop-floor workers; won Loral Vought Systems Subcontractor of the Year Award

November 1993–February 1994: Implemented cells throughout production floor and set up team structure

May 1994: Won U.S. Small Business Administration's Administrator's Award for Excellence

End of 1994: Workforce dropped to 67 workers

1995: Work in process declined by 65%, material transport reduced by 35%, lead time dropped by 87%, first-run yields improved by 77%, cycle times for videoconferencing cards reduced from 120 days to three days, and production capacity increased by 300%

November 1995: Won Blue Chip Enterprise Initiative Award

Spring 1996–1997: Management engaged in strategic planning process, facilitated by TMAC representative; established "two-deep program"; developed plan for effective quoting system; partnered with Bell Helicopter and 15 other companies to offer machinist apprenticeship program and hired three program graduates

First quarter of 1998: Participated in the Safety and Health Achievement Recognition Program

April 1998: Qualified for exemption from programmed OSHA inspections

Second half of 1998: Hired penetrant inspection specialist and built penetrant inspection cell; began pursuit of D1-9000 certification; hired new general manager; bought new MRP system; had 85 workers

December 1998: Welders received penetrant inspection training

 INSIDE STORY FOR CHAPTER 9

Chronologies

Chronologies of the sort found at the end of this chapter can play a helpful role in orienting readers. The presentation of key events in such a summary form makes it easy to peruse their sequence, compared with having to extract similar information from the text of a case study. However, creating a chronology is not a straightforward task.

In an earlier version of the case study in the present chapter, the initial chronology was too detailed. The lengthy list of events paradoxically made it difficult to derive coherent meaning from the flow of events, as key events were interspersed with unimportant ones. Conversely, an initial chronology can be too sparse, providing insufficient information on which to build any understanding of a case. There are few if any guidelines on the amount of detail that needs to be presented in a chronology, and you must be prepared to struggle to complete what at first might have appeared to be a rather simple task.

For Class Discussion or Written Assignment

Locate two (or more) existing chronologies that might have appeared at the end of two (or more) published case studies. Peruse the case studies to get an idea of their coverage and theme(s). Discuss whether the existing chronologies are helpful for creating a mental sketch of the events in the case study, especially raising the issue of whether the chronologies were too detailed or insufficiently detailed. Also discuss how to minimize any unwanted selectivity in deciding what to include or exclude from a chronology.

NOTES

1. This case study also is part of the cross-case analysis in Chapter 14.

2. *Transformed Firms Case Studies.* (1999). Rheaco, Inc. (p. 63). Gaithersburg, MD: National Institute of Standards and Technology.

3. Underdown, Ryan, & Mills, John. (1995, June 15). Agility: A Small Defense Manufacturer Can Do It Too! *Manufacturing News,* p. 9.

4. Company documents: "Old Rheaco Floor Plan" and "World Class Rheaco."

5. Rheaco Strategic Plan, "Internal Weaknesses," 1996.

6. *Transformed Firms Case Studies,* op. cit., p. 72.

7. Organization Chart, Rheaco, Inc.

8. Rheaco Strategic Plan, "Strategic Goals," 1996.

9. Rheaco Strategic Plan, "Values," 1996.

10. *Transformed Firms Case Studies*, op. cit., p. 71.

11. U.S. Bureau of Labor Statistics, December 1998.

10

RIVAL EXPLANATIONS

An invaluable function of case studies is their ability to examine alternative or rival explanations directly. To do this, case studies must collect evidence supporting an explanation of what occurred in a case as well as other evidence explaining what might have occurred instead. Comparing the strength of the two sets of evidence would lead to a stronger conclusion than if only one set had been considered.

This chapter presents two separate applications of the use of rival explanations. The first, covering the economic impact of the closure of a military base, examines two directly competing rivals: that the closure produced a "catastrophic" impact—or that it did not. The second covers the reasons why a well-known *Fortune 50* firm went out of business. However, the two rival explanations in this second application are overlapping—that is, both may be part of a broader and more comprehensive explanation. Such overlapping rivals are commonly found in the literature.

The chapter differs from the preceding ones by starting with a preliminary discussion, prior to introducing the two separate applications. The preliminary discussion distinguishes between two kinds of rivals, *craft* rivals and *substantive* rivals. The discussion should be especially helpful because the prevailing methodological texts rarely address substantive rivals. Yet, good case studies need to cover both craft and substantive rivals. You probably already know how to deal with craft rivals. However, regarding substantive rivals, how to frame those that are *plausible*—not just any old alternative explanation—remains the challenge of creating a compelling explanatory case study.

AUTHOR'S NOTE: This chapter draws on a previously published article, "Rival Explanations as an Alternative to 'Reforms as Experiments'" (Yin, 2000), whose original text has been adapted and abbreviated. However, readers still may want to refer to the original article for additional background information on the use of rival explanations, especially when doing case study evaluations. The summaries of the two illustrative applications then were written expressly for this chapter by Robert K. Yin, based on the original works (Bradshaw, 1999; Schein, 2003).

In a key sentence to the foreword of my book on *Case Study Research: Design and Methods* (Yin, 2009a), the noted methodologist Donald Campbell asserted the following:

> *More and more I have come to the conclusion that the core of the scientific method is not experimentation per se, but rather the strategy connoted by the phrase, "plausible rival hypotheses."*

Campbell's reference to the scientific method referred to applications in physics, chemistry, and the other natural sciences. However, his real focus was on the importance and usefulness of engaging in rival thinking—in posing and investigating *plausible* rival hypotheses—as an essential function in social science analysis, whether such analyses are quantitative or qualitative.

Campbell noted that, in quantitative research, perfectly executed experiments can rule out virtually all rival hypotheses. They are "controlled" out even though they are not identified. By ruling them out, experimental designs can provide a high degree of certainty about a study's main conclusions.

Case study research cannot employ such designs or rule out all rivals. Nonetheless, Campbell's remarks highlighted the notion of *plausible* rivals. He made the point that, in any given case, the number of plausible rivals in fact may be small. Thus, investigating them directly still can fall within a manageable case study. By doing so—that is, by identifying the most plausible rivals and collecting data to determine whether the rivals can be rejected—a case study can reach an acceptable degree of certainty about its conclusions, though not as airtight as in an experiment. Therefore, entertaining and directly examining individual rival hypotheses can markedly strengthen a case study's analysis and deserves serious consideration (see **BOX 13**).

BOX 13

Rival Explanations

No concept is more helpful in conducting research than the concept of *rival explanations.* Yet, existing texts rarely point to the importance of this concept, much less give guidance on how to articulate or investigate such rivals.

The most common rival explanation has been the null hypothesis. A null hypothesis is simply that the observed effect or outcome occurred by chance alone and not because of any hypothesized intervention. However, in doing case studies, the more important rivals are those that point substantively to other *plausible* conditions or forces that might explain what really happened in a case. When you have identified rival explanations in this sense, you can collect data to examine the competing explanations and compare the results through a pattern-matching process. The better and more numerous the rivals that can be investigated in this manner, the stronger your case study will be—whether the bulk of the evidence supports your original explanation or not.

(For more information, see Yin, 2009a, Chapter 5, section on "Examining Rival Explanations.")

Unfortunately, few existing works provide any guidance on how you might start to think about the plausible rivals in your own case study research. Much of the research literature does address methodological or *craft* rivals. These largely stem from the undesired artifacts of research design and procedure. However, little has been written to help you with the *substantive* rivals that pose serious threats to the conclusions from your research and that are the plausible rivals requiring attention. In fact, craft and substantive rivals differ in their source and in the amount of attention that they have received.

Investigating rival hypotheses or explanations should become a routine part of your own analyses, especially when you are dealing with case studies. The ideal case study will confront both *craft* and *substantive* rivals. Therefore, they are reviewed next—but with greater attention given to the substantive rivals.

CRAFT RIVALS

Craft rivals might be considered the more basic of the two because studies with flawed designs or procedures are unacceptable. Therefore, scholars have documented craft rivals with some frequency, and most of you are aware of them and can be sensitive to them in your own research.

The classic craft rival in all of social science is the null hypothesis, with statistical "chance" being the rival explanation for a presumed "effect." Understanding and using the null hypothesis has been a basic tenet of statistical work and has been discussed in every methods text.

A second commonly understood craft rival is actually a group of rivals—those enumerated when experimental or quasi-experimental designs are used (e.g., Campbell & Stanley, 1966; Cook & Campbell, 1979). For instance, the conventional threats to validity relate to concerns over the *internal validity* of a research design, but such threats also have been called rivals or alternative explanations (e.g., Reichardt & Mark, 1998). Among the threats, the potential artifacts due to "history," "maturation," "testing," "instrumentation," "selection," and so on have been discussed in nearly every methods text and should be well known to all of you.

A third type of craft rival occasionally, but not always, appears on a list of threats to internal validity. The rival covers the situation in which an investigator's theories, values, or preconceptions—in some unknowing and unacceptable way—produce in laboratory studies an "experimenter effect" (Rosenthal, 1966). In case studies, as with other field-based research, such potential bias has its own counterpart: the effect of the research on the setting or participants being studied, generally known as "reflexivity" or "reactivity" (Maxwell, 1996, pp. 90–91). Again, most investigators are highly familiar with this third type of craft rival.

SUBSTANTIVE RIVALS

Less well understood has been the range of substantive rivals. For guidance on these kinds of rivals, the existing methodological literature has bordered on nonexistent. Pick up any social science textbook and you will find virtually no discussion of substantive rivals or whether useful types of substantive rivals deserve to be recognized. Yet, substantive rivals—though not producing flawed designs or procedures—will compete with the main interpretation of your study's findings and, therefore, can dramatically affect your study's conclusions. The substantive rivals represent alternative explanations for the observed phenomenon or results of your study. For instance, in case study evaluations, the critical rivals will deal with claims that, although the measured outcomes may have been well documented, the targeted intervention did not produce them. Rather, other conditions (i.e., rivals) could have led to the observed outcomes.

Although a hard and fast typology of substantive rivals has yet to emerge, and although six types of rivals can be identified when doing case study evaluations (e.g., Yin, 2000), most of the logically possible rivals seem to fall into two groups:

1. When the rivals compete directly with each other

2. When the rivals differ but may overlap

Directly Competing Rivals

When rivals directly compete, if one rival is accepted the other(s) must be rejected. For instance, Hooks's (1990) case study examined whether the U.S. government had helped subsidize the early development of the computer industry—or not. The prevailing wisdom had been that Japanese industries had successfully competed internationally—and had an unfair advantage—because they had been subsidized by the Japanese government. In contrast, U.S. industries had to make themselves competitive through their own private means, unassisted by government support.

Using the computer industry as a "case," Hooks's (1990) study found that U.S. private industry had been responsible for a major breakthrough—the invention of the integrated circuit in 1959. However, although the U.S. government had not directly financed this invention or its development, once these prospects had emerged, the U.S. Department of Defense "energetically financed production refinements . . . and not only did this guarantee a market for costly integrated circuits, but it proved their utility" (p. 358). Hooks's main conclusion, therefore, supported a rival explanation—that the U.S. government indeed had supported industrial development in a manner parallel to that of the Japanese government.

When properly stated, directly competing hypotheses epitomize the ideal rival explanations: They need to be mutually exclusive. Such an ideal helps increase the certainty of a case study's findings, and if the study can address (and reject) several plausible competing hypotheses, the certainty in the case study's findings can be high even in the absence of an experimental design.

Unfortunately, most case studies are not able to identify rival explanations that follow such direct confrontations. Rather, the stated rivals may coexist or overlap.

Overlapping Rivals

For instance, education studies have found that adults in rural areas may only passively support their children's homework needs. One explanation is that the adults are preoccupied with their own household and occupational work and do not have the time to cajole, coach, or comfort their children who are doing homework. A rival explanation is that the adults have an underlying fear that, with successful education, their children eventually will leave the rural community, to lead productive lives elsewhere. In the long run, such outmigration would threaten the longevity or at least quality of life in the rural community.

Although these two explanations may in some ways represent rival explanations, the ultimately satisfying explanation may involve some of both. To this extent, the explanations are not really mutually exclusive. The tendency toward overlapping rather than strictly rival explanations is commonly found in research, whether using case study or other methods.

To show how the two types of rivals can work, the following two applications illustrate two different conditions—when rivals are mutually exclusive and when they differ but are not mutually exclusive.

AN EXAMPLE OF DIRECTLY COMPETING EXPLANATIONS IN A CASE STUDY

Whether Military Base Closures Produce Catastrophic Impacts or Not

Military bases throughout this country not only fulfill important military functions but also can make valuable contributions to local economies. By employing portions of the local civilian population and consuming local resources, and especially by being located in small jurisdictions, a military base can play a substantial economic role in these jurisdictions.

When such bases are then closed, usually in relation to the reorganization and consolidation of the country's bases, the closures pose a dire threat to the local economy. Such was the case with an Air Force base in a rural county in California, and the base's closure was the subject of a case study by Ted K. Bradshaw (1999).[1]

Hypothesis 1. The initial hypothesis was that the base closure would have a "catastrophic" impact on the county, for the following reasons.

The base was a well-established Strategic Air Command facility for B-52 bomber and K-135 tanker crews. It employed more than 6,000 persons (5,000 military and 1,000 civilian), making it the county's largest employer, representing 10% of the county's employees. Similarly, 11,000 military personnel, spouses, and dependents were associated with the base, representing 6% of the county's population. Moreover, the county's broader economy was dominated by agriculture and related industries and did not have other large employers or other federal government facilities to which the base's 1,000 civilian employees could transfer.

The base closure, following the typical congressional and public objections over such closures, had been one of those recommended by the Base Realignment and Adjustment Commission. As a result, the base's operations and most of its personnel were transferred to other military installations located in Oklahoma and Louisiana, during the year prior to the formal closing of the base.

At that time, a formal task force report predicted the dire economic consequences that soon would occur. The report said that the county would suffer a loss of 3,700 civilian jobs, a population loss of 18,000 persons, and a loss of $105 million in retail sales. The county's unemployment rate, already chronically high at 14.4%, was predicted to rise to 21.7%. All these potential job, population, sales, and unemployment levels were considered to represent a *catastrophic outcome* for the county's economy.

Hypothesis 2. In support of a contrary hypothesis, Bradshaw's article started by pointing to the findings from studies of other base closures that had taken place several years earlier.

One of the studies examined the impacts of closures of three bases in the same state as the Strategic Air Command facility. This study as well as the others all suggested that these base closures had not been accompanied by catastrophic effects, even in the short run. Although some economic decline did occur, the impact was not as severe as had been predicted. Furthermore, in the long run, the abandoned base facilities also provided the opportunity for renewed economic development.

Bradshaw's case study then examined the two competing or rival hypotheses. He collected and presented a variety of economic data before, during, and after the year of the base closure, in a number of important economic sectors: retail sales, local equipment suppliers, hospital and healthcare services, employment and unemployment, housing, and population change (see **BOX 14**). In each

> ## BOX 14
>
> ### Archival Sources of Data
>
> The case study of a military base closure shows the invaluable nature of archival sources of data, depending on the topic being studied. Although the case study included evidence from the author's own fieldwork and interviews with people at and around the military base, the bulk of his data came from economic records maintained by a variety of sources, including the local chamber of commerce (these sources are detailed and fully cited in the case study as it was originally published but have not been included in the briefer rendition in the present chapter).
>
> One clear benefit of using these archival data is to permit a case study to extend its reach over a longer period of time. With the military base closure, relevant annual trends were presented over a five-year period. Such a period may go well beyond the reasonable commitment of time for doing the fieldwork for a case study, and in this sense archival data can help elongate the time perspective and provide a firmer basis for drawing the conclusions from a case study.
>
> (For more information, see Yin, 2009a,
> Chapter 4, section on "Archival Records.")

sector, the case study found that strong negative effects had been avoided, and the main conclusion was that the closure had not produced a catastrophic impact.

From the standpoint of the present chapter, and as an illustration of an explanatory case study, more important were the author's explanations of why the catastrophic impact had not occurred. These explanations were based not only on the economic data but also on Bradshaw's interviews with key local officials, community and business representatives, and military staff. Illustratively, for the purposes of the present chapter, the experiences in three of the sectors are discussed next, involving retail sales, local equipment suppliers, and employment and unemployment [the original case study presented data for all the sectors].

Explanations for Changes in Three Illustrative Sectors

Retail Sales. The original fear of greatly reduced retail sales, loss of retail jobs, and declining tax revenues was not realized because much of the base's retail purchasing had been done at the base's commissaries, not the county's local outlets. Except for a number of outlets located near the base, such purchasing power, therefore, had not been part of the local economy in the first place. Moreover, a modestly sized population group associated with the base—military retirees—remained in the community after the base operations had transferred. These retirees then had to shift their purchasing from the (closed) commissaries to the local outlets, thereby creating a small positive impact on retail sales.

Local Equipment Suppliers. With regard to local equipment suppliers, the base had been undergoing a major construction project that had led to the Air Force's procuring of local equipment and equipment services. This activity did cease with the base closure, but instead of creating a total void, the remaining base operations involved the initiation of a new program, to clean up the toxic waste left behind by the closed base. Although the original suppliers might not have been involved in the new program, the overall economic effect was more balanced than had been expected.

Employment and Unemployment. The employment and unemployment trends for 1992 to 1997 are shown in Figure 10.1. The strong seasonal effects require that year-to-year comparisons be made by attending to the comparable months from one year to the next. Such comparisons for the month of April, for instance, indicate only a slight increase from 1994 (the year before the closure) to 1995, but in fact an overall decline in the unemployment rate by 1996 and 1997. Similar comparisons for October (1993–1996) or for January (1994–1997) result in similar patterns.

One potential difficulty in interpreting the employment and unemployment trends is that the county was in an economically growing state and region.

Figure 10.1   Employment and Unemployment Trends for 1992 to 1997

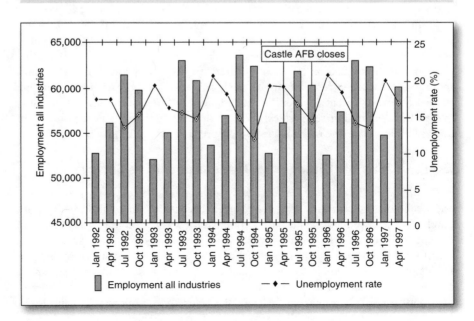

Therefore, a claim could be made that the employment-unemployment picture would have been rosier rather than roughly neutral had the base not been closed. Bradshaw explored this possibility by examining data from the neighboring counties. Although their trends were better, the differences were far from dramatic, much less catastrophic.

Conclusion

Bradshaw concludes that, although catastrophic effects had not occurred in this case, such effects still could occur in other cases. For instance, the consequences could differ if the military base involved a large manufacturing or research-and-development component that employed many civilian workers. Nevertheless, such conditions did not exist in the present case, and the case study aptly explained the reasons that the catastrophic effects predicted by Hypothesis 1 had not occurred.

AN EXAMPLE OF OVERLAPPING EXPLANATIONS IN A CASE STUDY

Illustrative Example No. 2 represents this more frequent manner of using rival explanations, which occurs when they are overlapping. Although helpful explanations and insights are produced, the rivals are not mutually exclusive.

Why a *Fortune 50* Company Went Out of Business After Only 40 Years

The Digital Equipment Corporation, known more popularly as DEC, successfully sold computer products during the latter part of the 20th century. Its volume of business was large enough that the company rose to be the No. 2 computer maker, with $14 billion in sales. This level of revenue, along with employing more than 100,000 people, put DEC in the *Fortune 50* as one of the top 50 U.S. corporations.

Nonetheless, after having established such a successful record, the company declined sharply in its later years and effectively went out of business when it was finally sold to another computer company in 1998. How and why the company suffered such a fate became the topic of a case study, appearing in a full-length book by Edgar Schein (2003).

The book is distinctive in at least one way. The main text permits Schein to develop and offer his own explanation for the company's demise. However, the end of the book also contains two independently written chapters. They provide two other persons, one of whom served as a high official at DEC, an opportunity to offer an alternative explanation.[2] The following text presents much-abbreviated versions of Schein's explanation as well as the alternative.

Clinging to a Corporate Culture

According to Schein, DEC had successfully developed and then totally internalized a unique corporate culture. In the short run, the culture was integral to DEC's success. But in the long run, the culture jeopardized the company's survival.

The culture had a threefold set of values: individualistic, technical, and family values. The individualistic value showed most prominently in the encouragement of innovation and entrepreneurism among individual staff. As one result of providing such freedom, DEC could and did attract extraordinarily talented engineers and other technical staff, because they could pursue more readily their own creative ideas within the company's mission.

The technical value was reflected by the quality of DEC's products. The computer market of the 1970s and 1980s tended to consist of "mainframe" computers (super-large sized), "minicomputers" (usually serving the needs of medium- to large-sized organizations), and "personal computers" (serving the needs of individual users). During these years, DEC dominated the minicomputer segment and the networking of such minicomputers. It was one of the first companies to be assigned a *dot-com* address by the U.S. government. From a commercial perspective, the company was able to develop "a series of highly successful products that virtually sold themselves" (Schein, 2003, p. 25).

The family value, beyond creating a supportive array of human resource policies and practices, found its main representation in the company's no-layoff policy, which changed only when DEC was in its final decline.

The entire company passionately embraced these values. They were a prominent part of DEC's internal documents, its training and orientation of new employees, and its daily operations. Employees and managers really liked the system and wanted to preserve it at all costs.

Equally important, the values became highly internalized. In this regard, Schein (2003) describes corporate culture as an "organization's accumulated learning that becomes so taken for granted that it drops out of awareness" (p. 20). He considered the driving force of the culture to be its shared tacit assumptions (p. 22).

Schein (2003) then drew an analogy between these tacit assumptions and the role of genes and DNA in biology: a powerfully internalized corporate culture acts like a gene in determining what an organization is destined to become, what it is capable and incapable of becoming, and what its immune system will reject (p. 22). Schein further noted that, in DEC's case, the employees' devotion to DEC's corporate culture was so strong that the employees continued to espouse DEC's values even after leaving the company.

Hardly incidental to the evolution of the corporate culture was that it represented the values of its founder. He not only had founded the company but continued as its CEO for nearly all of DEC's life. Schein discusses the conventional stereotype of founders who remain in place for too lengthy a tenure—that they can eventually lose their corporate vision, adhere to outmoded policies, and fail to take appropriate actions in the face of a changing marketplace. However, Schein rejects the idea that the stereotype accounted for DEC's decline.

Instead, Schein argues that DEC's corporate culture, rather than any executive shortcomings on the part of the founder, created DEC's problems. According to Schein, missing from the corporate culture was a business gene that could override the individual, technical, and family values when needed.

Although the company had been commercially successful, the absence of the business gene meant that DEC had not given either its marketing or finance operations sufficient internal prestige, in relation to its technical units. A strong business gene then might have led to earlier layoffs, the pruning of deadwood, and clearer priorities for choosing among technical projects. The business decisions also might have included the termination of obsolete products, making resources available for new development (Schein, 2003, p. 26). Altogether, Schein's explanation of DEC's decline leans heavily on the importance and potential dysfunction of its corporate culture.

An Absence of Strategic Planning and Thinking

The authors of the appended chapters offered a different explanation, acknowledging that it was not a true rival but could coexist with Schein's explanation. Thus, the second explanation claims that DEC's demise came from a strategic failure, in addition to being a cultural failure.

The strategic failure was reflected by the absence of strategic planning and strategic thinking at DEC. Such activity helps companies set clear goals and priorities. The activity typically forces company leaders to address such fundamental questions as, "What business are we in?" and "How are we to position ourselves for competitive success?" (Schein, 2003, p. 285). For example, in a product development world, the option of deciding whether to be a product leader, with a time-to-market imperative, differs from the option of not being the first to market but having a 100% quality product. The two options cannot both be pursued with sufficient excellence or in a competitive manner (p. 285).

This second explanation claimed that, in the absence of any strategic planning, DEC never addressed such key questions. The absence meant that, when the computer market shifted away from the mainframe-minicomputer-PC configuration to a much more highly differentiated configuration, DEC did not redefine its core identity, or its "brand." As a result, DEC no longer dominated any segment of the newly differentiated computer market (Schein, 2003, p. 288).

Because the second explanation was in part offered by someone who previously had been a high official at DEC, the appended material quotes text from the exchange of critical e-mails between this high official and DEC's founder (and CEO) regarding the key strategic planning questions. The e-mail documentation strongly suggests that the founder's replies were typically unresponsive to the issues being raised.

DEC's strategic floundering was reflected by some remarkable situations. As one example, with the initial emergence of the PC in the overall computer marketplace, DEC did not introduce one personal computer—it introduced three different ones that had considerably different capabilities (Schein, 2003, p. 187). The company also had become a "classic, well-run vertically integrated company" (i.e., operating or owning its own supply chain), when horizontal integration might have been more appropriate (p. 296). As one result, DEC's "per employee revenue was half that of its competitors in a horizontally integrated industry" (p. 298).

Through a series of reorganizations, DEC also lost sight of a key customer orientation by eliminating the part of the organization that acquired application software. Such a loss was crucial because customers conceive of themselves as buying solutions to their problems, not necessarily buying computer hardware (Schein, 2003, p. 297). These solutions are embodied in a computer's applications (which can then lead to the selling of the hardware), but with the change in organizational structure, these applications were now either less visible or absent (p. 297).

Finally, toward the end of its life cycle, DEC undertook a huge but flawed step. It hired nearly 27,000 new employees during a two-year period, hoping "to go head-to-head with IBM" (Schein, 2003, p. 290). The needed sales did not materialize, and the company was then saddled with the increased cost of these new employees—who could not easily have been let go because of the no-layoff policy.

Overall, the second explanation, while complementary to that of Schein, nevertheless leads to a more remediable situation. Whereas an ingrained corporate culture may not be easily altered, the practice of conducting strategic planning is common to businesses and could have led to better business decisions. In this sense, the two explanations differ in their implications.

Conclusion

Working through both explanations shows how they can create deeper insights into the case being studied. Each explanation not only has its own logic but also leads to the introduction of slightly different data by citing its own relevant set of events. The events differ, but they do not contradict each other (see **BOX 15**). Thus, the power of a single explanation can be augmented by alternative explanations, even if both are not directly competing rivals.

BOX 15

Explanation Building

The rival explanations presented in this summary of the DEC case study illustrate how case study analysis can involve an explanation-building process. The examination of each of the two rivals—a flawed corporate culture versus the absence of strategic planning and thinking—shows how plausible arguments can be weaved together by citing (and documenting) the conditions that were part of the firm's history. The credibility and trustworthiness of the procedure involves providing convincing evidence that these events and conditions have been fairly presented and discussed, not arbitrarily selected because they happened to support the explanation.

When doing a case study, you will need to go to considerable lengths, whether discussing your methodology or pursuing an explanation-building procedure, to establish the fairness of your efforts. Although no procedure is airtight (in doing case studies or doing other kinds of social science research), requesting that other participants and peers review a case study can be extremely helpful. In this sense, the presence of the appendices in the original book containing the DEC case study, showing how other authors constructed their own explanations, represents a significant step in the desired direction.

(For more information, see Yin, 2009a, Chapter 5, section on "Explanation Building.")

NOTES

1. All the information in this illustration comes from Bradshaw's article. A lengthier excerpt from the article itself appears in a case study anthology edited by the present author (Yin, 2004).

2. The two appendices are presented independently but speak to similar issues. Thus, for the purposes of the present chapter, the material from the two appendices has been cited together as if part of the same alternative explanation, even though neither of the two authors of these appendices referenced the other's explanation.

PART IV

CROSS-CASE SYNTHESES

All the applications previously presented in Parts II and III have represented *single-case* studies. Although the case study method typically has been associated with such a focus on single cases, a stronger and potentially more desirable use of the method is in conducting *multiple-case* studies—that is, a single empirical inquiry or study that contains two or more cases.

By definition, the multiple cases provide a broader array of evidence than do single cases. Depending on how the multiple cases have been chosen, the broadened array permits you to cover either the same issues more intensely or a wider range of issues. The result is a stronger case study. However, doing multiple-case studies takes more effort and may require a team of researchers rather than a solo investigator. Not surprisingly, the multiple-case studies often require external funds as a source of support. Though the efforts are more costly, sponsors benefit because they have greater confidence in findings that are not based solely on a single case.

The two chapters in Part IV both contain the cross-case synthesis stage of doing multiple-case studies, showing how the findings and conclusions from a multiple-case study can be developed. Absent from these chapters are the individual case studies that were part of the original research but that would have filled this entire book. However, one of the single cases for Chapter 12 previously has appeared in its complete form as a single case in Chapter 9.

In Chapter 11, the case study of university proposal processing was based on 17 cases. To reduce the burden of doing the study, and as a variant that you might consider in your own research, the data collection differed among the 17 cases. For all 17, the same documentation and archival evidence was collected, but the full fieldwork took place in only 7 of the cases. For the other 10 cases, telephone interviews substituted for on-site fieldwork. In Chapter 12, the case study of transformation in small manufacturing firms was based on 14 cases. In that study, the same kinds of data, including data from on-site fieldwork, were collected from all 14 cases.

The approach to cross-case synthesis differed in the two applications in Chapters 11 and 12. The cross-case synthesis in Chapter 11 was based on both quantitative and qualitative data, showing how they can be complementary parts of a case study.

In the study, the qualitative data were used to explain the pattern of quantitative data. In contrast, the cross-case synthesis in Chapter 12 was based entirely on a qualitative analysis, mainly taking the form of a pattern-matching procedure (comparing an *expected* pattern of transforming events with an *observed* pattern of actual events, within each of the 14 cases).

11

PROPOSAL PROCESSING BY PUBLIC AND PRIVATE UNIVERSITIES

Explaining how universities process their research proposals and at what cost were the main topics of a series of case studies of 17 individual universities (see **BOX 16**). The results from each university were compiled in a series of formal databases submitted as appendices to the final report. The cross-case synthesis was based on the information in these databases.

BOX 16

Importance of Multiple-Case Studies

Many of the applications in this book, whether presented as single- or multiple-case studies, were originally part of a multiple-case study. If given the choice and the resources, multiple-case designs may be preferred over single-case designs. In particular, if you can even do a two-case study, your chances of producing credible results will be better than using a single-case design. For instance, analytic conclusions independently arising from two cases, as with two experiments, will be more powerful than those coming from a single case (or a single experiment)

(Continued)

AUTHOR'S NOTE: This chapter presents excerpts from an original and fuller cross-case analysis that appeared in *The National Science Foundation's FastLane System Baseline Data Collection: Cross-Case Report*, COSMOS Corporation, Bethesda, Maryland, November 1996. Robert K. Yin was the main author of the original report. The excerpted text has been lightly edited for readability.

(Continued)

alone. You also can avoid a common criticism about single-case designs: that the choice of the single case reflected some unusual but artifactual condition about the case—for example, special access to a key informant or special data that unknowingly colored the findings—rather than any substantively compelling situation.

(For more information, see Yin, 2009a, Chapter 2, section on "Single- or Multiple-Case Designs?")

The participating universities deliberately represented a variety of research- to nonresearch-oriented universities, large and small, that were geographically distributed across the country. Data were collected either through site visits or through lengthy telephone interviews combined with additional documentation. Because proposal processing at a university can involve several different academic departments and administrative offices, data were collected from a large variety of sources, usually involving contacts and interviews with more than 15 key persons at a given university.

The research team also retrieved quantitative data from an archival source, estimating the universities' costs of processing the proposals. The resulting cross-case synthesis, therefore, not only illustrates the use of qualitative and quantitative data but also led to a surprising finding—that those universities producing larger numbers of proposals also had *higher costs per proposal*, a pattern contrary to the normal expectation based on any economies-of-scale logic. These quantitative results were subjected to statistical analysis, showing how such analysis is possible even with a modest number of cases.

The qualitative data had focused on describing how the proposal processes actually occurred at each university. Interestingly, these descriptions became the basis for explaining the unexpected finding regarding the costs per proposal. The entire experience, therefore, illustrates an explanatory, cross-case synthesis.

INTRODUCTION TO THE CASE STUDY

This cross-case synthesis is based on data collected from 17 universities about their research proposal processes. The study was supported by the National Science Foundation (NSF), a research-funding agency that was developing

FastLane, a then new electronic system for research investigators to submit their research proposals, proposal reviews, and grant reports.

The study team conducted site visits to 7 of the 17 universities. During these site visits, the team interviewed a variety of university staff, university officials, and faculty as well as reviewing relevant documents and archival records. For the remaining 10 universities, data were collected through telephone interviews with the same variety of persons as had been contacted during the site visits to the other universities. All 17 universities also made pertinent documents and records available to the case study team.

The data collection focused on each university's typical proposal processes, within which the experiences with three specific NSF proposals and one National Institutes of Health (NIH) proposal were examined in detail. The research administrators at each university had selected the specific NSF and NIH proposals, with the proposals to vary by discipline, college, and department, if possible. All proposals were intended to represent traditional principal investigator initiatives, not large institutional competitions.

Within each institution, the interview and archival data came from four organizational levels: the sponsored research office (SRO), the college (school), the department, and the principal investigator (PI). Upon completing the data collection, the case study team compiled individual databases for each university. Each database contained quantitative and qualitative information on five topics:

1. The general proposal processing procedures followed at each university, especially noting the respective functions at the four organizational levels

2. The proposal submission levels, amount of staff effort, and electronic (hardware and software) technology available to support the proposal process at the university

3. The proposal processing and submission procedures for the four specific proposals

4. The anecdotal perceptions and experiences of university personnel and NSF reviewers regarding the processing procedures

5. The administrative tasks related to monitoring proposals and receipt of grant awards (e.g., cash requests and reporting procedures)

Within each case study, three conditions received the highest priority: the time needed to process a proposal, the costs involved in that processing, and post-submission activities. These three were important because the *FastLane* developers wanted to make sure that the new system, when implemented, would improve (at least not worsen) these conditions.

The remainder of this chapter analyzes the data on the first two of these conditions.[1] To preserve the anonymity of the universities and ensure their confidentiality, dual coding schemes[2] were used in the data tables and flowcharts that appear in the two sections.

THE TIME NEEDED TO PROCESS AND SUBMIT PROPOSALS

Methodology

To understand the typical proposal preparation and submission process as it actually occurred, the study team assembled data for each university that identified the following: (1) the major tasks in the process; (2) the type of task (technical, administrative, or budget related); (3) the level at which the task was conducted (SRO, college, department, or PI); and (4) the amount of effort required for each task (calendar time and human level of effort). The data were based on interviews and records about the whole process as it had occurred during the preceding academic year. These were augmented by the specific experiences that had taken place for the three NSF proposals and one NIH proposal, deliberately selected to reflect the typical process within different colleges and departments within the university. The data then became part of the individual databases. From these data, the team developed a flow diagram to trace the process at each university (see **BOX 17**).

BOX 17

Process and Outcome Evaluations

Producing research proposals, as depicted in the present chapter, may be considered a *process*, which should then yield a sequence of *outcomes*: winning awards and then, ultimately, producing high-quality research. The proposal-producing process, nevertheless, also calls for a complex set of activities and may itself be worthy of study. Such a study would represent a *process evaluation*.

Processes occur over a period of time. Case studies also traditionally trace events over time. Therefore, the case study method initially was conceived as a strong method for doing process evaluations but not necessarily as useful for studying outcomes or process-outcome relationships. Traditionally, the conduct of a rigorous outcome evaluation was thought to need quantitative data not normally expected to be part of a case study.

The concepts espoused in this book are different. Case study evaluations can cover both processes and outcomes and can include both quantitative and qualitative data. The case study in this chapter tends to focus on processes. However, other applications in this book (e.g., see Chapters 8, 9, and 14) cover both processes and outcomes as well as their relationship.

(For more information, see Yin, 2009a, Chapter 5, sections on "Time-Series Analysis" and "Logic Models.")

Cross-Case Findings

In processing their proposals, the 17 universities appeared to fall into four different groups:

Group I: The SRO is actively involved early in the proposal preparation process (not just alerting investigators about the opportunity to submit proposals), engages throughout the process, and submits the proposal.

Group II: The SRO is actively involved early, but the PI submits the final proposal.

Group III: All levels (SRO through PI) are involved early, and the PI submits the proposal.

Group IV: The departments (but not the SRO) are involved early, and the PI submits the proposal.

The preceding groups have been arrayed hierarchically, with Groups I and II having the greater SRO involvement (and therefore being more centralized) and Groups III and IV having more departmental involvement (and therefore being more decentralized).

Figure 11.1 contains the flow diagrams for two contrasting university patterns—one from Group II (University E) and the other from Group IV (University G). In these diagrams, the horizontal axis represents the calendar time taken for the processing (note that the scales for the two universities differ), and the vertical axis represents the four organizational levels (from PI to SRO) doing the processing. The University E process is more complex than the University G process because of the increased interactions among the four levels. University E's process also consumes more calendar time.

The assessment of the time needed to process a proposal did not try to account for the time invested by principal investigators to develop their initial drafts (e.g., in Figure 11.1, the step represented by the "Prepares Proposal" box in the lower left corner of both illustrations might have consumed any length of time). Rather, the data collection mainly attended to tracking the time consumed by the administrative processes—for instance, reviews, editing, revisions, budget preparation, and sign-offs—once a reasonable draft existed. Furthermore, the study tried to establish the time needed for the average proposal at a university. Table 11.1 contains the results. It shows that, when the universities were grouped according to the four groups defined previously, the following pattern emerged: Shorter times were associated with universities in the more decentralized groups.

Figure 11.1   Proposal Processing at Two Illustrative Universities

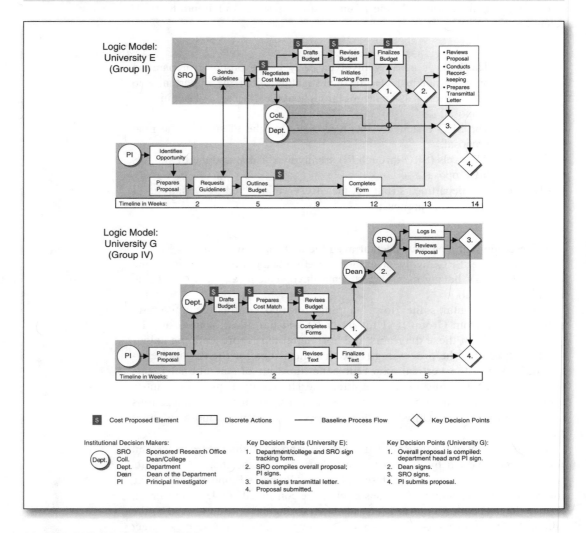

SOURCE: COSMOS Corporation (1996).

COSTS OF PREPARING PROPOSALS

Methodology

At each university, additional information had been collected about the proposal preparation process as it actually had been experienced during the preceding academic year, covering the following categories:

1. Number of proposals submitted

2. Dollar volume of proposals

3. Total university administrative costs, broken into two components (SRO and department—the latter including schools, colleges, and any other component beneath the SRO),[3] and the proportion of these costs estimated[4] for proposal development

4. SRO staff effort

5. Staff time spent on the proposal process

Table 11.1   Proposal Processing Time for Four Groups of Universities

Group Number and Characterization	University Code	Processing Time (Weeks)
Group I: SRO involved early and SRO submits proposals	D	17
Average Time		17
Group II: SRO involved early and PIs submit proposals	K	14
	E	14
	H	11
	F	10
	N	11
Average Time		12
Group III: All levels involved early and PIs submit proposals	B	11
	I	10
	O	7
	Q	9
	J	6
Average Time		9
Group IV: Department involved early and PIs submit proposals	M	5
	P	13
	C	7
	A	5
	G	5
	L	5
Average Time		7

Cross-Case Findings

For each university, the case study team calculated two cost indicators: the dollar cost per number of proposals submitted and the dollar cost per dollar value of proposals submitted. To estimate these indicators, the team used two variables as numerators—the total number of proposals and the total dollar volume of proposals submitted. For both indicators, the same denominator was used, derived from the administrative costs associated with the proposal process. Table 11.2 shows the results for each indicator and for each university (only 15 universities had sufficient data to calculate the indicators).

Table 11.2 Annual Unit Costs of Proposals, by Number and Dollar Value of Proposals Submitted

	Proposal Costs	Proposal Volume		Unit Cost	
University Code	Total (SRO and Department)	Number Submitted	$ Volume	Per No. of Proposals	Per $ Million Proposed
A	20,574,176	3,131	1,105,367,674	6,571	18,613
Q	12,870,000	4,250	582,146,000	3,028	22,108
M	5,945,500	3,054	983,874,839	1,947	6,043
N	4,576,300	2,566	105,570,071	1,783	43,348
H	3,957,500	2,028	297,191,823	1,951	13,316
G	3,148,060	1,184	400,071,787	2,659	7,869
F	2,312,900	2,101	402,900,000	1,101	5,741
O	1,933,350	2,224	1,224,004,668	869	1,580
D	1,640,000	3,235	732,636,790	507	2,238
K	947,550	1,277	112,408,806	742	7,741
B	608,476	436	81,341,805	1,396	7,480
J	489,000	1,339	134,176,180	365	3,644
I	200,000	318	44,983,744	629	4,446
C	135,000	635	137,698,881	213	980
P	30,580	96	13,579,628	319	2,252
E	–	2,850	461,639,989	–	–
L	–	2,097	270,107,629	–	–

Figure 11.2   Estimated Cost per Proposal, by Number of Proposals Submitted

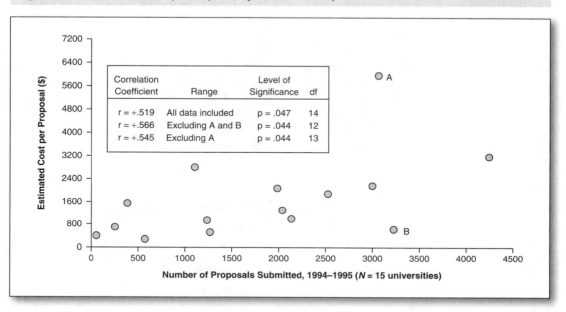

A natural assumption, based on a presumed economy-of-scale in dealing with higher volumes of proposals, was that the per-proposal costs would decline as the number of proposals submitted increased. Figure 11.2 tests this assumption by arraying the two variables in a scattergram. However, the scattergram showed just the reverse relationship: Universities with higher volumes of proposals also had higher unit costs (dollars per proposal). The relationship was statistically significant, even given the small number of universities (data points) in the estimate. (To ensure that the extreme outlying data points did not account for this relationship, the figure also shows the correlations when Points A and B were excluded from the analysis.)

Examination of these results on *proposal costs*—along with the earlier results regarding *proposal time* and the four groups of universities categorized by their centralized-decentralized hierarchy—showed that the most decentralized arrangements were associated with the higher unit costs and the shorter processing times, but also the higher proposal volumes.

The case study team offered a tentative explanation for the totality of these relationships, based on the qualitative data that had been collected: The higher unit costs (in the decentralized arrangements) appeared to result from having numerous departments participate in the proposal process. At the same time, the expanded participation also meant shorter processing times and higher proposal volume across the entire university. Under such circumstances, the high-volume conditions also mitigate against the more intense role of an SRO in a centralized arrangement: At high volumes, the SRO may become a bottleneck and also may not have the specialized staff skills to handle the increased diversity of proposal agencies and topics likely to accompany the high volume. Whether this scenario is correct, or whether mechanical artifacts in the data account for the results, needs to be the subject of future inquiries.

An important caveat to any interpretation based on proposal volume is that the present inquiry made no attempt to examine the eventual award sizes or frequency. The possibility exists that the high-proposal-volume universities have better "win" rates than the low-proposal-volume universities. If so, the unit costs per *award dollar* might very well be lower at the high-proposal-volume universities. Such a finding would modify the interpretation based solely on unit costs per proposals submitted.

INSIDE STORY FOR CHAPTER 11

Posing Questions for Further Research

One criticism of the present case study called attention to the fact that the universities' desired outcome is not necessarily a high volume of proposals but a high volume of dollars awarded. The analytic possibility is that the universities with higher costs per proposal might now appear in a more favorable light—because their proposals might have yielded a higher amount of dollar awards than the universities with lower costs.

Unfortunately, the present study was unable to examine this additional possibility because of a lack of data about the dollar amounts in the proposals, much less information about the award disposition of the proposals. (Proposals can be resubmitted a number of times, so tracking their eventual disposition would have extended the period of the study beyond the available time limits.) Nevertheless, the importance of one of the qualitative findings—that central units such as the sponsored research offices can become bottlenecks in high-volume situations—was still a valued finding. Exploring the additional possibility relating to the volume of dollars awarded now needs to be part of some later study. The extension would represent a common sequence in research, whereby the findings from one study can readily lead to new research questions and the need for new studies.

For Class Discussion or Written Assignment

The best research questions to be addressed in new studies often follow from the findings of earlier studies. Discuss a study (not necessarily a case study) that you might have completed and speculate on the new research questions emanating from the findings. Distinguish new questions that are methodological (e.g., the need to confirm the findings by refining some part of the research procedure) from those that penetrate the substance of the research. Was one type more prevalent in your speculation?

NOTES

1. The original text covering the third condition has been deleted, to streamline the current chapter.

2. Such a scheme means that a university designated as University A in one table or figure is not necessarily the same university as that designated University A in another table or figure.

3. Because not all universities were able to provide reliable budget information across all their organizational levels, the data used in the subsequent cost analyses were extracted from a federal data set of university administrative costs compiled annually based on university submissions. This data set gives each university's *total* administrative costs—with breakdowns including the distinction between SRO and departmental costs—to support its indirect rate agreement with the federal government.

4. Whereas the total university costs had been submitted by the universities to support their indirect rate agreements, the estimates of the proportion devoted to proposal development were made by the senior SRO official at each university during the interviews for the present study.

12

CASE STUDIES OF TRANSFORMED FIRMS

The cross-case synthesis in this chapter returns to a more traditional qualitative approach. Individual case studies had been conducted on 14 firms.[1] Each had been screened to satisfy two conditions: The firm had to have displayed exemplary bottom-line performance, and there had to be strong evidence that transformation of the entire firm—not just a change in one or a few of its operations—had occurred. The individual case studies then tried to explain the transformation process.

The screening of the candidate firms occurred prior to the conduct of the case studies. However, the subsequent case studies did not entirely corroborate the initial screening. The cases showed that all firms had indeed satisfied the first condition (easier for a screening process to establish), but several of the firms had not really been transformed (harder for a screening process to establish). The resulting cross-case synthesis serendipitously took advantage of the inadvertent outcomes of the screening in the following way: The original plan was to have a series of direct replications; however, the actual cross-case synthesis used the variations in transformation to pursue a design reflecting both *direct* and *theoretical replications* (see **BOX 18**).

AUTHOR'S NOTE: This cross-case synthesis, written by Robert K. Yin, appeared as an appendix to the report *More Transformed Firms Case Studies,* issued by the U.S. Department of Commerce, National Institute of Standards and Technology, Gaithersburg, Maryland, May 2000, pp. 109–123. The original work has been lightly edited for readability.

BOX 18

Direct and Theoretical Replications

This cross-case synthesis of manufacturing firms includes nine that were trans-formed (*direct* replications) and five that had not quite become transformed (*theoretical* replications). Chapter 2 discussed replication logic and its contrast to sampling logic; however, the chapter did not detail the distinction between direct and theoretical replications.

In a direct replication, two or more cases are predicted to follow courses of events similar enough that they repeat or replicate each other's experience—in a conceptual, not literal, sense. For example, in the present chapter, nine of the firms originally deemed to be transformed had evidence of the requisite changes listed in Exhibit 12.2. In a theoretical replication, two or more cases are predicted to have different experiences, but with conceptually consistent explanations. In the present chapter, the five additional firms fell into this category. As a result, the analysis of how transformation occurs drew from both groups' experiences.

(For more information, see Yin, 2009a, Chapter 2, section on "What Are the Potential Multiple-Case Designs?")

WHY STUDY TRANSFORMED FIRMS?

The Staying Power of Transformation

Analytic interest in successfully transformed firms (e.g., Garvin, 1993; Hayes & Pisano, 1994; Kotter, 1995; Pascale, Milleman, & Gioja, 1997; Raynor, 1992) derives from two motives: (1) that such firms can establish world-class perfor-mance levels and exemplary business outcomes and (2) that the firms also can maintain their world-class performance for an extended period of time, even as market, technological, and other conditions change.

Maintaining a competitive posture over time—in the face of changing market and technological conditions—drives interest in transformation because it calls for an adaptive or learning organization (Garvin, 1993). The desired transformation is intended to convey the expectation that a firm's corporate culture and internal sys-tems have not only changed markedly—that is, from one state to another—but also have become dynamic and can continually adapt to new conditions (Kotter, 1995).

Case Studies of Transformed Firms

To date, little empirical information has been available on the transformation process. How transformation occurs in small- to medium-sized manufacturing firms was, therefore, the subject of 14 case studies conducted for the National Institute of Standards and Technology, U.S. Department of Commerce, and its Manufacturing Extension Partnership (NIST-MEP). Each case covered the pertinent events and outcomes in a single firm. NIST-MEP nominated, screened, and selected these cases from field reports, strongly suggesting that each represented an instance of a transformed firm. Each firm was willing to serve as the subject of a case study.

Exhibit 12.1 summarizes the basic characteristics of the 14 case study firms: name, location, year started, size, and major product line. Notably, one of the firms (Texas Nameplate) had been the smallest company ever to win the Malcolm Baldrige National Quality Award, a major kudos in the commercial world. This firm has garnered numerous other awards as well.

The main purposes of the cross-case synthesis were as follows: (1) to summarize the extent and types of transformation in the individual cases—to aggregate knowledge about what constitutes transformation—and (2) to analyze the driving forces that produced transformation among the firms—to increase knowledge about how other firms might promote or facilitate transformation in the future (see **BOX 19**).

BOX 19

Common Preparation and Training When Doing a Multiple-Case Study

The 14 cases in the cross-case synthesis in the present chapter were conducted by *multiple investigators* serving on the same research team. Each investigator collected and analyzed the data from one or more of the firms. Under these circumstances, having a common case study protocol and common preparation were essential.

Unlike the situation where a *solo investigator* may be doing an entire case study, a team of investigators must ensure that it will use parallel procedures and methods. Otherwise, the resulting multiple-case study can produce uneven results, with the variations introduced by the multiplicity of team members wrongly being accepted as variations in the substance of the cases.

The role of protocols and formal preparation may be less important if you are a single investigator doing an entire case study. However, as a single investigator, you still must be concerned about unwanted variations in your data collection procedures, either from case to case (if you are doing a multiple-case study yourself) or from time period to time period (when doing a single-case study). Therefore, even for solo investigators, using a case study protocol still may be a desirable procedure.

(For more information, see Yin, 2009a, Chapter 3, section on "Preparation and Training for a Specific Case Study.")

Exhibit 12.1 Fourteen Case Study Firms: Year Started, Number of Employees, and Major Product Line

Firm	Year Started	Number of Employees	Products
Boozer Lumber, Columbia, SC	1946—established	145	Then: cabinets, windows, and doors Now: roof trusses and wall panels
Breeze-Eastern, Inc., Union, NJ	1926—incorporated under the name Breeze Corp. Early 1980s—purchased by Trans-Technology	173	Helicopter rescue hoists, external cargo hooks, and cargo winches
Dowcraft Division of the Dowcraft Corp., Falconer, NY	1934—purchased under the name Jamestown Steel Partition Company 1961—became Dowcraft Corp.	50	Movable steel walls
Dynagear Oil Pumps, Inc., Maquoketa, IA	Year unknown—Hoof Products established 1995—Dynagear, Inc., purchased Hoof 1997—Hoof name changed to Dynagear Oil Pumps, Inc.	137	Then: governors, timing devices, and oil pumps Now: oil pumps
Forming Technologies, Inc., * *Michigan*	Unknown	70	Stainless steel exhaust systems parts
Grand Rapids Spring and Stamping, Inc., Grand Rapids, MI	1960—incorporated as Grand Rapids Spring and Wire Products, Inc. 1985—purchased by Jim Zawacki and Ted Hohman Date unknown—name changed to Grand Rapids Spring and Stamping, Inc.	160	Then: springs and wire cable Now: springs and stampings
Jacquart, Fabric Products, Inc., Ironwood, MI	1958—created as a part-time business	52	Pet beds and other upholstered products

Firm	Year Started	Number of Employees	Products
KARLEE Company, Inc., Garland, TX	1974—established	400	Sheet metal fabricator
MPI,* main plant in Michigan	Founded approximately 80 years ago 1983—sold to conglomerate 1989—65% interest sold to Japanese companies	Fewer than 500	Auto parts (e.g., axles and control arms)
Rheaco, Inc., Grand Prairie, TX	Year unknown—Rheaco established	85	Full-service machining and metal fabricating
Texas Nameplate Company, Inc., Dallas, TX	1946—established	66	Metal identification and information labels
UCAR Composites, Inc., Irvine, CA	1988—established	70	Precision tooling for large composite parts
Venturo Manufacturing, Inc., Cincinnati, OH	Year unknown—Venturo established 1989—Collins Associates, Inc., purchased Venturo	40	Electric and hydraulic truck-mounted cranes
Williams-Pyro, Inc., Fort Worth, TX	1971—established	30	Stove-top fire extinguishers and connectors

*Fictitious name to protect confidentiality of information provided by company

WHAT IS A TRANSFORMED FIRM?

Contrasting Transformation With (Only) Manufacturing Process Improvements

For manufacturing firms, the transformation process contrasts with technical improvements in the manufacturing process alone (e.g., Upton, 1995). The latter improvements still can be significant, involving new capital investments, redesigned shop floors, transitions to just-in-time production processes, new plant facilities, and other important changes. The result may be a marked increase in productivity and profitability. However, despite their significance, such improvements alone may not necessarily involve a change in the firm's culture or produce the dynamic processes needed to sustain the longer-term competitiveness that characterizes transformed firms.

One major difference between transforming a firm and only making manufacturing process improvements may be the extent to which the changes involve employees in developing or sustaining the firm's infrastructure. Although both situations may involve skills training, transformation calls for a deeper empowerment of employees. Empowerment can occur through the following activities: co-ownership of firms under employee stock ownership plans; support for employees' education beyond manufacturing skills training (e.g., helping employees attain high school equivalency certificates); improvements in wages, fringe benefit packages, and other working conditions; or the sharing of a firm's management decision-making (not just manufacturing) processes.

As one example, the adoption of *cellular manufacturing* or other reorganizations of employees on the shop floor (often resulting in shared manufacturing decision making and significant productivity gains)—unaccompanied by other changes in human resource policies—still constitutes improvements in manufacturing processes only and does not alone result in transformation. Similarly, implementing improvements in human resource systems without making other structural changes in a firm also would be insufficient for achieving transformation.

The more distinguishing characteristics of transformation occur when changes affect a firm's strategic management, its marketing strategies or arrangements, or its use of new information technology—especially when requiring changes in key managerial procedures or norms. Again, the information technology changes should not be limited to the manufacturing process (e.g., implementing computer numerical control equipment) but should join manufacturing processes with business and management systems. The spirit of transformation, therefore, calls for change in the fundamental organization of the operations of a whole firm and not just its manufacturing process or even a combination of manufacturing and marketing changes, as might occur when product lines change.

The desired transforming changes need not occur all at once. The total package of changes over time, however, should be sufficiently strong and different from previous practices to signal a significant competitive repositioning of the firm. Symptomatically, a firm may reflect such repositioning by adopting a new name.

Toward an Operational Definition

Central to the case studies and to the present synthesis was the definition of transformed firms in operational terms. Through its literature review and consultation with experts, the case study team developed an overall framework and a list of the management, marketing, manufacturing, and business processes and policies that might signal genuine transformation. Figure 12.1 shows this framework, depicted as a logic model of sequential changes assumed to be causally related in a successful transformation process. Item 4 in this figure lists five domains (A-E) for the transforming events. These events, combined with an unspecified change process (see the empty square inside Item 4), are claimed to produce the improved business performance in Item 7.

Exhibit 12.2 fills in the empty square by listing the management, manufacturing, and business processes and policies expected to change in the transformation process. To become eligible as a case study, a firm had to demonstrate some change in at least four of the first five domains and had to provide evidence of significant improvement in the sixth domain: business results over the past five to seven years.[2] Furthermore, the business results were expected to be greater than mere improvements. The preferred goal was to demonstrate high performance, defined as productivity in the top 25% of firms within the same competitive market. This greater expectation, however, was not a mandatory requirement for a firm to become eligible as a case study.

WHAT KIND OF TRANSFORMATION DID THE FIRMS EXPERIENCE?

Compiling Data From Individual Case Studies

As an initial step, the cross-case synthesis called for a careful review of each individual case study. The synthesis involved compiling this information by organizing the key information about each firm's assumed transformation according to the six domains of interest (five organizational domains plus the business results domain).

The original compilation also paid close attention to the calendar year in which the transforming events occurred, addressing two concerns: (1) that the compilation represented data on the rapidity or lengthiness of the transformation process for each firm and (2) that the dates provided chronological benchmarks to help organize flow of events. Exhibit 12.3 presents highly abbreviated versions of these profiles, to facilitate a bird's-eye view of the entire cross-case pattern across the individual cases.

Figure 12.1 Transformed Firms Logic Model

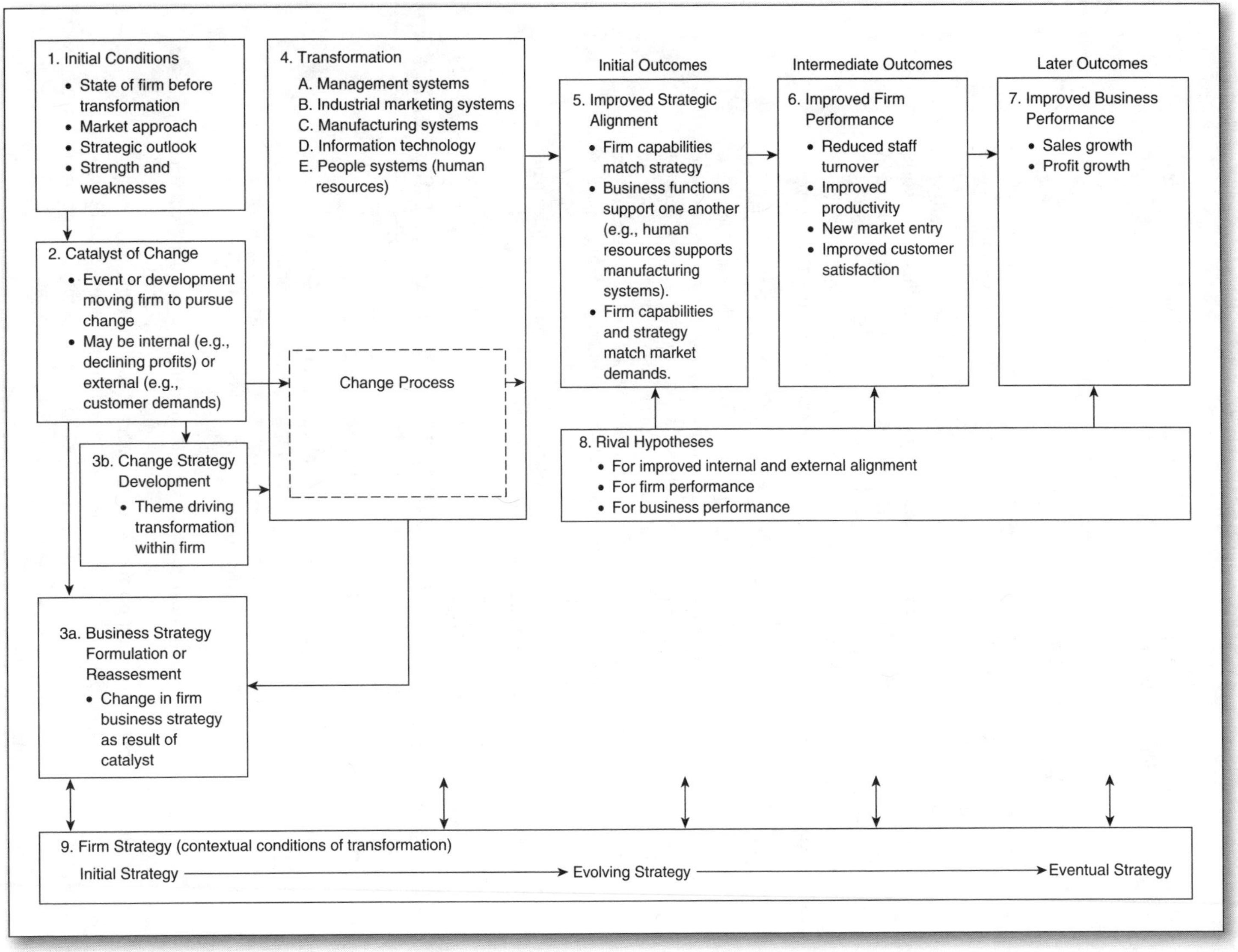

1. Initial Conditions
- State of firm before transformation
- Market approach
- Strategic outlook
- Strength and weaknesses

2. Catalyst of Change
- Event or development moving firm to pursue change
- May be internal (e.g., declining profits) or external (e.g., customer demands)

3b. Change Strategy Development
- Theme driving transformation within firm

3a. Business Strategy Formulation or Reassessment
- Change in firm business strategy as result of catalyst

4. Transformation
- A. Management systems
- B. Industrial marketing systems
- C. Manufacturing systems
- D. Information technology
- E. People systems (human resources)

Change Process

5. Improved Strategic Alignment
- Firm capabilities match strategy
- Business functions support one another (e.g., human resources supports manufacturing systems).
- Firm capabilities and strategy match market demands.

Initial Outcomes

6. Improved Firm Performance
- Reduced staff turnover
- Improved productivity
- New market entry
- Improved customer satisfaction

Intermediate Outcomes

7. Improved Business Performance
- Sales growth
- Profit growth

Later Outcomes

8. Rival Hypotheses
- For improved internal and external alignment
- For firm performance
- For business performance

9. Firm Strategy (contextual conditions of transformation)

Initial Strategy — Evolving Strategy — Eventual Strategy

152

Exhibit 12.2   Desired Areas of Change for Transformed Firms

The nomination process defined "transformed firms" as firms that have undergone broad-based change, affecting nearly all areas of the business and resulting in real improvements in business performance. Field manufacturing specialists nominated firms on the basis of being able to identify changes in at least four of the following six domains (the sixth domain was mandatory):

Domains of Change	Categories Within Domains
Management Systems	• Strategic planning processes • Business operations planning processes • Management information analysis and controls • Organizational culture • Financing processes • Administrative services processes
Industrial Marketing	• Market competitor analysis • Customer analysis • Product development processes • Sales and territory management • Selling strategies and channel management • Marketing planning process • Advertising and promotion practices
Manufacturing Systems	• Product or process design • Facility design • Planning and scheduling process • Procurement practices • Production control processes • Quality assurance processes • Maintenance practices • Environment, health, and safety practices • Distribution practices
Information Technology	• Communications infrastructure • Data management practices • Systems implementation • Process analysis and decision support processes • Firm's exposure to the Year 2000 (Y2K) problem
Human Resources	• Human resources strategy and management • Job design or analysis • Employee recruitment or selection processes • Compensation and benefits • Employee performance management • Training or employee development practices • Employee relations
Business Results (REQUIRED): Significant Improvement Over Past Five to Seven Years	• Customer satisfaction • Productivity (value-added per employee) • Sales • Sales to new customers • Profits

Exhibit 12.3 Brief Profiles of 14 Case Studies

Firm Name	Brief Summary of Transformation	Role of CEO in the Transformation Process
Transformed Firms:		
Dowcraft Division	Firm installs new CAD software, revamps sales and marketing network, and creates dynamic strategic plan; establishes ESOP program and starts new training opportunities; implements shop-floor work teams; and completes new manufacturing facility with new manufacturing control system.	President and five employees purchase control of firm; new CEO takes over and presses for changes; WNYTDC helps define and implement new manufacturing operations.
Dynagear Oil Pumps, Inc.	Firm drops two of three product lines, simultaneously investing in employees' working conditions, pay, and involvement in management; later upgrades information technology (computer systems), changes name of firm, and alters sales arrangements.	Acquisition of firm leads to new CEO, who is driving force for change; IMTC provides some assistance.
*Forming Technologies, Inc.**	Firm changes total operation because of shift in basic product material, requiring R&D to solve technical problems; increases employees' pay and benefits, training, and work conditions; and adopts continuous improvement philosophy.	CEO studies needed technical changes (due to shift in customer requirements) and is driving force for all changes.
Grand Rapids Spring and Stamping, Inc.	Firm refocuses product line; installs new manufacturing equipment, including PC access to all employees; reduces number of customers to work more closely with them; and expands employees' involvement in manufacturing and management practices and increases their training.	New owners purchase company, and one serves as new CEO and is driving force for change; MMTC assists in forming mini-companies and continuous improvement.
KARLEE Co., Inc.	Firm initiates leadership teams and strategic planning process, defines new relationships with customers, builds new manufacturing facility with cellular manufacturing, continues to expand facility, and implements new information system integrating business and manufacturing processes.	Spouse of original founder assumes majority ownership and becomes president and CEO and is committed to building a leadership culture.
*MPI**	Firm installs creative manufacturing cells, shifts product focus, improves marketing practices, makes working conditions more equitable, and implements participatory *kaizen* system.	Internal managers help get new CEO (who shakes up management ranks) appointed; CEO and new managers are driving forces for change.

Firm Name	Brief Summary of Transformation	Role of CEO in the Transformation Process
Rheaco, Inc.	Firm reorganizes production floor, focuses on smaller number of customers (the profitable ones), installs integrated information system, and invests in employee training and in-house capabilities.	Son of firm's founder becomes CEO, faces production problems. TMAC assists, but CEO is driving force for strategic planning and change.
Texas Nameplate Co., Inc.	Customer's mandated upgrade in production process leads firm to install new equipment, invest in total quality management training, and commit to zero defects; firm also invests in employee programs and completes strategic plan, starts new marketing practices, and upgrades computer system.	Son of owner takes over as president, commits to total quality management and to employees as a company's most important asset. Management sets successively higher standards.
Williams-Pyro, Inc.	Firm streamlines product design, implements cellular manufacturing, installs computerized and automated robotics system; also develops management team and creates participatory climate, along with strategic planning to develop single vision, as well as new marketing initiatives.	New CEO takes over upon death of former CEO, seeks to modernize manufacturing processes; CEO is driving force, but TMAC and senior managers also provide important assistance.
Not Quite Transformed:		
Boozer Lumber	Firm installs new assembly processes, later constructs new plant; plant workforce declines with combining of two shifts into one; plant productivity and capacity increase; new productivity increases now being sought in marketing area and in firm's other plant.	New person becomes president and CEO. SCMEP shares book with CEO, who engages SCMEP to do benchmarking and plan new plant.
Breeze-Eastern	Firm makes manufacturing changes to reduce lead time, production costs, and delinquency rates and to improve inventory turns and cash flow; implements paperless MIS system and performance measurement systems to focus departments on corporate, not just departmental, goals.	New CEO takes over struggling business, downsizes and streamlines operation, and rebuilds management team. Team engages external consultants, working with them for 14 months to clarify business strategy.
Jacquart Fabric Products, Inc.	Firm rearranges production process, changing to just-in-time delivery, using *kaizen* blitz to engage employees in improved communications, suggestions for new practices, and increased control over management procedures.	Owner (who also was CEO) wanted to improve production process asked MMTC to assist. It recommended *kaizen* blitz.

(Continued)

Exhibit 12.3 (Continued)

Firm Name	Brief Summary of Transformation	Role of CEO in the Transformation Process
UCAR Composites, Inc.	Firm claims to be constantly transforming, with no settled production process, stable markets, or even permanent location; internal culture retains features of a start-up company; major initiatives involve pushing new technologies (production and business functions) to their limits; employees typically work long hours and are expected to work better, faster, and cheaper.	Firm founded 11 years ago is constantly upgrading its machines and computers; parent company supplies funds after requesting that firm develop strategic plan (had assistance from CMTC).
Venturo Manufacturing, Inc.	Firm installs *kanban* just-in-time system, cutting production cycle time in half and giving employees increased responsibility for the flow of manufacturing; savings in space permit firm to consider strategic investments to grow production capability; new bar code technology now being considered to improve inventory control and production efficiency further.	New parent company purchases firm, relocates it, and streamlines operations. New production coordinator assists plant manager in implementing *kanban* system, with additional assistance from IAMS.

Glossary: of centers in NIST Manufacturing Extension Partnership (NIST MEP):

CMTC: California Manufacturing Technology Center—UCAR Composites

IAMS: Institute of Advanced Manufacturing Sciences, Inc.—Venturo Manufacturing, Breeze-Eastern

IMTC: Iowa Manufacturing Technology Center—Dynagear Oil Pumps

MMTC: Michigan Manufacturing Technology Center—Grand Rapids Spring and Stamping; Jacquart Fabric Products; MPI; Forming Technologies, Inc.

SCMEP: South Carolina Manufacturing Extension Partnership—Boozer Lumber

TMAC: Texas Manufacturing Assistance Center—Rheaco, Williams-Pyro

WNYTDC: Western New York Technology Development Center—Dowcraft

No centers mentioned: KARLEE, Texas Nameplate

*Fictitious name to protect confidentiality of information provided by company

Application of Operational Definition in the Cross-Case Synthesis

Examination of the completed case studies revealed that not all firms, in fact, turned out to have satisfied the needed criteria to be designated as a transformed firm. Such slippage can frequently occur and must always be tolerated in following the current type of case screening process, where eligibility to become a *case* depends on alleged organizational processes and not just (business) outcomes. In this design, a thorough and definitive screening process might have required a full case study just as part of the screening process, which is not a feasible expectation. At the same time, those firms that did not fulfill all the original criteria still provided useful information, as discussed next.

Firms Not Quite Transformed

Exhibit 12.3 shows that 5 of the 14 firms were not quite transformed because they did not show changes in five of the six domains in Exhibit 12.2. In four of the cases (Boozer, Breeze-Eastern, Jacquart, and Venturo), even though the firms had made substantial improvements in their manufacturing processes—including the installation of skills-based training and rearrangements of employees on the shop floor—the apparent transformations were, in fact, largely limited to these (manufacturing) processes.

Few other major changes, in human resource practices or in significant and broader strategic planning by the firms, were reported—although some changes were still in their planning stages at the time of the case study. For these cases, therefore, transformation still may be occurring, and the firms may meet the transformation criteria at some future date. However, for the present cross-case analysis, these firms were categorized as *not quite transformed.*

A fifth case (UCAR) was considered different for yet another reason: The firm appears still to be in the entrepreneurial phase of a young firm; for example, the case study suggests that the firm's internal culture still seems to reflect that of a start-up firm. Although the firm was 11 years old at the time of the case study and appeared to be in a continual state of change, the reported changes were not readily distinguishable from the transitions that might have been expected in a new firm during its early years. In this sense, the firm did not appear to have transformed from one state to another. Rather, the firm still seemed to be in its initial phase.

An important reason for distinguishing these five cases from the rest is that any examination of the organizational processes that might underlie transformation should not commingle information from these two groups of cases. In fact, the reverse may be true: The five cases may involve different underlying processes, to be contrasted with the remaining nine firms (see **BOX 20**).

BOX 20

Cross-Case Syntheses

Cross-case syntheses, such as those demonstrated in Chapters 11 and 12, bring together the findings from individual case studies and are the most critical parts of a multiple-case study. The desired synthesis will treat each individual case study as if it had been an independent study. The technique, therefore, does not differ from other research syntheses. If large numbers of case studies are part of the same multiple-case study, the synthesis can use quantitative techniques common to other research syntheses, including meta-analysis. However, in the more common situation, a multiple-case study will have only a small number of component case studies, requiring alternative analytic procedures. The assembling of word tables, displaying the data from the individual cases, and searching for patterns across them—as illustrated in both Chapters 11 and 12—represent such procedures.

(For more information, see Yin, 2009a, Chapter 5, section on "Cross-Case Synthesis.")

Transformed Firms

The remaining nine cases all did seem to satisfy the criteria for transformation, exhibiting important changes in at least four of the five domains and reporting impressive business results in the sixth domain. Their transformations reflected improvements in their manufacturing operations but also included shifts in organizational practices or norms such as the following:

- *Dowcraft:* Dynamic strategic plan and employee stock ownership program
- *Dynagear:* Open-book management and sharing of financial performance data
- *Forming Technologies:* Continuous improvement, covering broad variety of internal improvements
- *Grand Rapids:* Culture characterized by extensive employee involvement and quest for continuous improvement
- *KARLEE:* Team members taking ownership over corporate objectives
- *MPI:* Creative manufacturing cells
- *Rheaco:* New focus on customer-oriented manufacturing
- *Texas Nameplate:* Continuous improvement
- *Williams-Pyro:* Strategic planning emphasizing a single vision for the firm

For most of the firms, the transformations appeared to occur over a five-year period, with Dynagear, MPI, and Williams-Pyro seeming to have accomplished the change in two to three years.

DID THE TRANSFORMATIONS SHARE COMMON CONDITIONS?

Although the case studies were not intended to analyze the motives for the firms' transformations, the case studies did track some of the conditions underlying the transformation process. On this basis, the cross-case synthesis was able to examine whether the cases shared a more generic, common process. The analysis suggested that the nine transformed cases fell into two subgroups.

New Product Lines Can Drive Transformation

In the first subgroup are three firms (Dynagear, Forming Technologies, and Grand Rapids) whose transformations tie directly to substantial changes in either their product lines (Dynagear and Grand Rapids) or raw materials (Forming Technologies, from "mild" steels to stainless steel). In turn, these product-based changes accompanied or required widespread changes in the firms' manufacturing processes, marketing strategies, strategic planning, and relevant technological and human resource support. For Dynagear and Grand Rapids, the product lines changed so much that the firms eventually changed their names—an event not found in any of the other seven cases (though one firm had changed its name well before any transformation process started).

Desire for Productivity Gains
Also Can Drive Transformation

In the second subgroup are the other six firms, whose transformation occurred in the absence of major shifts in product lines or materials (although product mixes may have changed). These firms transformed to become more productive, through a broad array of changes in manufacturing processes, as well as in the organization of human and technological resources.

Distinguishing these two subgroups is valuable because, although many firms may want to make a successful transformation, not all firms will have the opportunity or need to change their product lines or materials substantially. The second group demonstrates that such changes are not necessary to the transformation process. The attractiveness of transformation, in fact, is understanding how to change an existing firm—making it more productive and changing its culture—even when its product lines remain unchanged.

Change in CEO as an Initiating Event

Across both subgroups, the transformation process appeared to emanate from an initial change in CEOs, which occurred in eight of the nine transformed cases (all but Forming Technologies, where the CEO's son drove the change process before buying out his father near the end of the firm's transformation). The CEOs were new for a variety of reasons. Some firms had been acquired by new owners (Dynagear and Grand Rapids). In others, sons had replaced fathers (Rheaco and Texas Nameplate), people had succeeded their spouses (KARLEE and Williams-Pyro), or a succession of CEOs had occurred (Dowcraft and MPI).

The events reported in the case studies suggest that the new CEOs appeared to have had the ambition, talent, and vision to initiate and sustain a transformation process. In the smaller firms, the CEO alone wielded a high degree of influence; in the somewhat larger firms (only two of the nine firms had more than 200 employees), the CEO worked with the top managers to influence change.

Among the not-quite-transformed firms, new CEOs or ownership were involved in two of the five cases. Therefore, an interesting possibility is that CEO turnover is a necessary but not sufficient condition for transformation, given the following additional observations.

CEOs' Visions and Subsequent Actions

First, improvements in the manufacturing process and productivity were a clear part of the CEOs' visions. Also important (in seven of the nine transformed cases) was the CEOs' ability to pursue or put into place a strategic planning or cultural change process that created broad goals for the entire company, such as environmental efficiency, continuous improvement, transition from production-driven to customer-oriented manufacturing, promotion of "business drivers," or development of a rallying theme and philosophy for the firm. In contrast, CEOs or new owners in the not-quite-transformed firms tended to define new needs in less global terms, often relying on a consultant or outside expert to define a more limited technical change.

Second, in eight of the nine cases, the nature of the manufacturing changes or the strategic planning (or both) meant decentralizing control and responsibilities on the shop floor, whether through the creation of manufacturing cells (a frequent change), shop-floor work teams, mini-companies, or employee committees. Such decentralization was not readily evident in the not-quite-transformed firms.

CEOs' Leadership Over External Technical Assistance

Third, another part of the scenario for the transformed firms had to do with the CEOs' use of external technical consultants or assistance. Such assistance occurred with some frequency, in both the transformed and the not-quite-transformed cases.[3]

A possibly subtle difference, however, is that in the transformed cases, the CEOs defined and directed such assistance more proactively; whereas in the not-quite-transformed cases, the external consultants exerted greater initiative. For instance, in at least four of these five latter cases, the consultants appeared to have provided the critical scope and operational definition of the needed changes—for example, a new plant, a SWOT (strengths, weaknesses, opportunities, and threats) analysis, a *kaizen* blitz training program, and a *kanban* just-in-time manufacturing strategy.

Issues to Be Addressed in the Future

Together, all 14 case studies suggest the beginnings of a common transformation scenario: A new CEO develops a strategic plan or unitary vision, implements improved manufacturing processes that decentralize control to the shop floor, and appears to influence rather than be influenced by external consulting assistance. Possible additions to this scenario, and further details, await more clues to the transformation process. The cases, for instance, did not systematically investigate the possible importance of such processes as manufacturing resource planning performance systems, ISO 9000 (manufacturing certification) or related registrations, clean plant and other environmental initiatives, employee incentive systems, turnover in other key personnel, or changes in other personnel or managerial policies. These topics require further investigation.

The evolving general scenario does suggest that a key ingredient for transforming a firm may be turnover in the CEO position rather than the transformation of an incumbent. The cross-case evidence also suggests that transformed firms may not be significantly different from "turnaround" or "turnover" firms. Whether this observation is true of most transformed firms also remains to be tested in future cases.

At the same time, the possibly critical vision and commitment of the CEO raises an important policy question for NIST-MEP in offering technical assistance to firms: How can one know beforehand if a new or incumbent CEO is capable and willing to lead a transformation process? Likewise, how might NIST-MEP or other consultants effectively engage and convince a CEO to undertake and lead a transformation process?

SUMMARY: GENERAL LESSONS ABOUT TRANSFORMED FIRMS

The current set of case studies has illustrated the transformation process, distinguishing it from other, more traditional technical improvements in manufacturing processes. Empirical evidence, based on a serendipitous cross-case design comparing nine of the firms with the other five, suggests the following conclusions.

Transformed firms successfully have made broad changes across their whole enterprise, thereby producing marked and discontinuous improvement in their business performance. Furthermore, transformation can be accomplished with or without major changes in a firm's product lines or basic product materials, although such changes could drive the transformation process.

Nine of the 14 cases met the criteria for transformation, with the other five being considered not quite transformed. The nine transformed firms had accomplished their transformations over roughly a five-year period. Two of these nine seemed to have completed the change in two to three years.

The typical scenario for transformation, derived from the nine cases, started with a change in the firm's CEO, followed by actions reflecting the ambition, talent, and vision of the new CEO. Such actions included important technical improvements in the manufacturing process but also put into place strategic planning, cultural change, or related processes.

Transformation also included decentralizing control and increasing responsibilities to the shop floor, if not throughout the entire firm. As noted, this scenario was not as readily identifiable in the five not-quite-transformed cases. Although those cases underwent substantial improvements in the manufacturing process—which included redesign of shop floors, implementation of just-in-time procedures, or installation of new technologies—these improvements alone did not translate into a strategic vision or decentralized control.

Implementing Exemplary Case Designs

The introduction to this chapter noted one of the unexpected circumstances that arose in doing the present case study: The initial screening of the candidate firms aimed to identify 14 exemplary cases of transformation and, therefore, to study the transformation process in 14 different settings. In fact, however, five of the firms were later found not to have been transformed. Given such a result, one possibility was to stick to the original (exemplary case) design and ignore the five firms that did not fit the design. However, the actual case study used the alternative design that has been presented in this chapter. The alternative design—besides offering a deeper understanding of the transformation process because contrasting and not just directly replicating cases were included in the synthesis—also had the benefit of using the data from all the firms rather than ignoring some of them on what might have seemed to be an arbitrary basis.

For Class Discussion or Written Assignment

Discuss the pros and cons of an exemplary case design. If only successful cases have been chosen for study, in what way might the findings appear to be biased or selective? How much of the bias or selectivity threat can be disregarded if the case study mainly focuses on unraveling how some process (e.g., transforming a firm) takes place, as opposed to trying to assess the effectiveness of the process?

NOTES

1. Chapter 9 of this book presents one of the individual case studies. The case studies involved field-based inquiries—with consultants or other experts making site visits to the firms—to analyze the firms' records, examine documents and related materials, interview key people, and observe manufacturing and business processes. Different case study consultants and experts participated, each authoring different case studies. Despite this diversity, all authors participated in an initial and intensive training workshop, shared a similar orientation toward the underlying conceptual framework, and agreed to follow similar case study and evidentiary procedures. As a result, the individual case studies represented a series of parallel inquiries.

2. The original pool of nominees came from consultants and staff associated with NIST-MEP Centers. The nominated firms, however, did not need to have had any prior affiliation or relationship with a NIST-MEP Center.

3. In many instances, the external assistance had been provided by NIST-MEP's manufacturing extension centers, although the cases were not selected because of this assistance.

PART V

CASE STUDY EVALUATIONS

As a methodology, case studies have become a popular choice for doing evaluations. What is being evaluated usually takes place in a real-world setting. Such settings may not provide a hospitable environment for using other methods or may pose insurmountable obstacles when other methods are tried (e.g., Streiner & Sidani, 2010). For instance, a common experience has been the difficulty of attaining an adequate response rate from particular kinds of community groups, when using the survey method (e.g., Watson, 2010), much less the difficulties encountered when implementing an evaluation using an experimental (or quasi-experimental) design.

You may find the case study method to be a useful way of evaluating some initiative of importance when it takes place in a real-world setting. Your case study may not address all the possible evaluation questions of interest, but you usually can complete case study evaluation successfully, and you may produce important as well as relevant findings.

Part V introduces you to case study evaluations and presents three applications. Chapter 13 describes the important phases of case study evaluations—their design, data collection, and analysis. Within each phase, the chapter differs from all those in the rest of this book: Each phase starts with a general discussion of the procedures and is then followed by the corresponding portion of a concrete case study. The concrete case study serves as the main application for Chapter 13 and covers the evaluation of a community coalition's efforts to prevent drug abuse.

The remaining chapters in Part V have two more applications. Chapter 14 contains a case study evaluation of a local law enforcement initiative that was implemented to reduce auto thefts. Chapter 15 presents the evaluation of a network of organizations deliberately created to prevent HIV/AIDS. The network was tasked to provide technical assistance to state and local public health agencies, and the evaluation focuses on the outcomes of this assistance as well as the lessons to be learned about making future assistance efforts more likely to succeed.

13

EVALUATION OF A COMMUNITY COALITION

Chapter 13 consists of four sections: introducing case study evaluations, designing a case study evaluation, collecting case study evaluation data, and analyzing case study evaluation data.

Unlike any of the other chapters in this book, each of the four sections in this chapter takes an iterative approach that works as follows: First, each section starts by reviewing the general case study procedures under the pertinent topic. Then, the section presents the related portion of a concrete application—the evaluation of a community coalition.

The iterative approach deliberately intersperses the desired procedures with the actual case study application. As a result, you can see how a concrete case actually works as it moves through the major phases of doing a case study evaluation. At the same time, the entire application is, therefore, not presented in one place. To gain a full appreciation of the evaluation of the community coalition, you would pull together all its subsections and separate them from the interspersed material.

I. INTRODUCTION TO CASE STUDY EVALUATIONS

The Challenge of Doing Evaluations

The case study method fills a distinctive niche as an evaluation tool. For many years now, the U.S. government's major evaluation agency—its Government

AUTHOR'S NOTE: This application was written expressly for the present book and is based on a more extensive and earlier case study that was part of an evaluation conducted by COSMOS Corporation for the U.S. Department of Health and Human Services. The entire evaluation was directed by Robert K. Yin, though individual case study evaluations were written by different staff persons at COSMOS.

Accountability Office—has included case study evaluations as part of its reper-toire of evaluation tools. In a seminal evaluation document, the Government Accountability Office (1990, p. 9) laid out six situations relevant to the use of a case study strategy: descriptive, exploratory, critical instance, program implemen-tation, or program effects evaluations; and cross-case syntheses (see **BOX 21**).

BOX 21

Guidelines for Case Study Evaluations

The U.S. Government Accountability Office (GAO) has been among the more frequent users of case studies as an evaluation tool. To help its own evaluators, the GAO (1990) published a comprehensive methodological report titled *Case Study Evaluations*. The report's usefulness and detailed operational advice make it an invaluable document for all others in the field (for example, studies evaluating interventions in such areas as justice, housing, welfare, environment, education, and foreign aid).

Throughout, the GAO report emphasizes quality control and rigor and, therefore, freely cites many of the procedures and concepts from the earlier editions of the companion text to this book (Yin, 2009a), such as the use of multiple sources of evi-dence, the establishment of a chain of evidence, and the reliance on pattern match-ing and explanation building as two major analytic strategies. However, the GAO report has the added virtue of citing case study evaluations that were completed by the GAO. Because of the age of the GAO report, you may want to scan the current GAO publications list to identify more recent evaluations.

(For more information, see Yin, 2009a, Chapter 1, section on "Variations Within Case Studies as a Research Method.")

Even though evaluations serve as a major application of the case study method, investigators may not be familiar with the basic procedures. This chapter, there-fore, reviews the main procedures, also presenting an abbreviated version of the evaluation of a community coalition as a concrete example. However, these clarifications must be preceded by a brief definition of *evaluation*.

What Are Evaluations?

Assessing Either Ongoing Operations or Innovative Changes. An evaluation is a study that seeks data to assess what some activity—a program, practice, project, or policy—has accomplished. The assessment may come at an earlier juncture and lead to recommendations for midstream improvements in what is being evaluated (*formative* evaluation) or at a later juncture when a more final judgment can be reached (*summative* evaluation). The activity being evaluated may be some ongoing operation in an organization or may have been deliberately started as an innovation, to test some new change.

Regarding ongoing operations, both public and private organizations commonly employ their own "in-house" or internal evaluation staffs to conduct continual evaluations of their operations. Regarding deliberately started innovations, a large majority of sponsored evaluations—those supported by federal, state, and local governments as well as by private foundations and other external funding sources—call for external evaluators to assess the innovations.

In either situation, the evaluation is intended to document and analyze the workability and outcomes of the activity being evaluated. The operations or innovations may involve many different kinds of activities, including the following:

- The use of new technological devices (e.g., an electronic blackboard for classrooms)
- Reconfigured service operations (e.g., different mixes of doctor-nurse teams)
- Neighborhood initiatives (e.g., residential crime prevention efforts)
- Newly installed policies (e.g., an increase in mass transit fares)

Real-World, Not Laboratory Conditions. Key to understanding the challenge of evaluating either the existing operations or the innovations is that both types of activities occur in real-world settings and not in the confines of research laboratories. As a result, evaluation studies have to forgo two advantages present in traditional laboratory projects.

First, a laboratory project needs to exert tight control over the desired experimental conditions—especially in comparing "treatment" versus "control" conditions. Second, the entirety of a laboratory project usually is managed by a research investigator in a university or a research organization, whereas the real-world activity being evaluated usually is directed by a project manager working for a service organization (and not a research organization) and trained to implement the activities (not organize them for the sake of an evaluation study).

Both of these typical conditions limit the types of research methods available for doing an evaluation study. In particular, evaluations will find it nearly impossible to pursue true experimental designs. As one result, a whole host of *quasi-experimental designs* have emerged (e.g., Campbell & Stanley, 1966; Cook & Campbell, 1979; Rosenbaum, 2002). They do not require the systematic manipulation of the activities being evaluated. These latter designs recognize the role of the real-world settings by referring to themselves as taking place in "field settings" or as "observational studies," although they do not use the case study method.

Case Study Evaluations. Case study evaluations also acknowledge the evaluator's inability to manipulate the activity being evaluated. However, the case study method may be better than quasi-experimental designs in dealing with the unexpected situations that may arise in real-world settings, such as the following:

- *Midstream changes* in the activity being evaluated, due to unpredictably changing external conditions—which, in contrast, might jeopardize even a quasi-experiment's original design and structure
- *Unacceptable attrition rates,* both of individual participants and of participating sites where an activity involves multiple sites, threatening a quasi-experiment's planned sampling or analysis strategies
- *Strained relationships* between the project managers of the activity and the researchers trying to conduct the evaluation, because of differences in priorities between implementation needs and evaluation needs

Case study evaluations can more readily accommodate any midstream shifts because a major premise of the method is the uncertain boundary between the phenomenon being studied and its context—thereby also tolerating changes in the boundary over time. Second, the case study's strong emphasis on using multiple sources of evidence can create alternatives that help offset the difficulties posed by high attrition rates. Third, the method's adaptiveness to these and other real-world conditions can ease the potential conflicts between project managers and evaluators.

To get an idea of how case study evaluations work, their procedures can be discussed in relation to the three main phases of conducting an evaluation study: study design, data collection, and data analysis. Within each phase, the discussion also tracks a concrete application—the case study evaluation of a community coalition.

Evaluation of a Community Coalition as a Concrete Application

At the time of the evaluation, the coalition was serving an extremely large urban area in Southern California. The area contained about 850,000 persons and had about 60 geographically identifiable neighborhoods. The coalition was an "umbrella organization," with a membership that largely consisted of other community organizations (e.g., houses of worship, service centers, tenant groups, parents associations) but that also had individual persons as members.

The community served by the coalition was predominantly African-American, with a 20% to 50% Hispanic population. Compared with the rest of the city and its surrounding county, the community suffered from the highest number of drug-related and juvenile drug-related arrests, and the highest rates of cocaine and heroin use, juveniles living in poverty, and housing vacancies.

Portions of the community had become a dumping ground for medical waste, and auto paint shops in alleys, recycling centers in the neighborhood, and blighted housing all had become breeding grounds for illicit behavior such as drug trafficking and prostitution. At one time, the local unemployment level was estimated at 47%. The area also was home to a large concentration of liquor stores, with 728 liquor licenses within a 40-square-mile area—a rate more than 10 times that of the rest of the county. Finally, a period of civil unrest had resulted in the destruction of housing and other property in the area, including more than 200 of the liquor stores. A preexisting community coalition took this as an opportunity to launch a formal campaign to rebuild the region without the same concentration of liquor stores.

II. DESIGNING A CASE STUDY EVALUATION

Virtually all evaluations will begin with a set of evaluation questions. These questions will set the priorities for designing the evaluation, collecting the needed data, and analyzing the data. The questions are relevant regardless of the evaluation methodology and, therefore, not discussed further. However, going beyond the questions are several considerations specific to designing case study evaluations, and these are the next focus of attention.

Defining the "Case"

The initial design of a case study evaluation must be based on a thorough understanding of the activity being evaluated, which may be considered the intended operations and outcomes of a "case," with explicit attention to contextual conditions.

For instance, in real-world settings, most activities do not start de novo but have some related predecessor activities. The definition of the "case" will have to establish the extent to which these predecessor activities are to be considered part of the "case" or part of the contextual conditions. Such a determination is made more complicated when the activity of interest occurs at multiple sites, as in the installation of the same curriculum at several schools. The experience at each school constitutes a separate "case," making the evaluation a *multiple-case study.*

In the illustrative application, the case consisted of the community coalition and its efforts to reduce illicit and unruly behavior in its constituent neighborhoods. Although the coalition had existed for some time, the case focused on a three-year period during which the coalition initiated a specific series of actions known as its Rebuild Campaign.

Theorizing About the Case: Activities and Their Outcomes

As a further part of the initial design work, a case study evaluation should involve explicit theorizing about the relationship between the processes and outcomes within the case as well as the role of contextual conditions. Most commonly, such theorizing will take the form of a *logic model,* which hypothesizes the potential causal links whereby an activity will produce (or not) its desired outcomes (e.g., Kellogg Foundation, 2004; Wholey, 1979). More complex cases will involve a multiple sequence—a repeated chain whereby one set of activities is said to lead to a more immediate set of outcomes that in turn become the stimulus for a later set of outcomes, and so on.

Especially for more complex cases, the articulation of a logic model can be a demanding but also rewarding procedure, in at least two respects. First, because the logic model calls for specifying concrete activities and outcomes, the articulation of the model can point to the relevant data that need to be collected during the case study. Second, the process of piecing a logic model together can be conducted as a joint effort—between evaluators and program managers working together. The collaboration can yield mutually beneficial insights and also reduce the tensions between the two parties.

The typical logic model follows a sequence of

- *inputs* (i.e., the monetary or staff resources used to conduct an activity);
- *activities* (i.e., the implemented actions believed to produce the outcomes of interest);
- *outputs* (i.e., the immediate results of the actions); and
- *outcomes* (i.e., the desired substantive benefits that ultimately justify the activity).

Theorizing in the Community Coalition Example

The initial logic model related to assessing the community coalition was straightforward. Resources (*inputs*) made available to the coalition enabled it to define actions (*activities*) to reduce illicit and unruly public behavior. In particular, the coalition had targeted drug-related behavior as its priority during the time of the evaluation.

In pursuing this priority, the reduction of opportunities for drug trafficking and other illicit behavior in the neighborhood environment served as the immediate benefit (*output*) being sought. Actual reduction in illicit drug use was the longer-term benefit (*outcome*) being sought. How the coalition undertook its drug prevention activities, and the outputs and outcomes that then followed, became the subject of the case study data collection.

III. COLLECTING CASE STUDY EVALUATION DATA

Data Collection Procedures

Case study evaluations likely will rely on multiple sources of field-based data. These sources include some combination of fieldwork and participant-observation, questionnaire-based surveys of such groups as service staffs or neighborhood residents, and social indicators. (Although the last category comes from archival sources, the indicators will have been based on some earlier fieldwork done by others, such as the data associated with census, neighborhood, housing, employment, education, and crime records.) You should use the data from the multiple sources in converging fashion, to determine the extent to which the data triangulate over the "facts" of the case. Quantitative and qualitative data both may be considered potentially important and relevant.

The actual types of data to be collected should try to capture the hypothesized understanding of the activity being evaluated. This orientation toward data collection, following the *input-activity-output-outcome* chain in the hypothesized logic model, will enable a case study evaluation to cover both the processes and outcomes of the activity being evaluated. Pilot testing and other preliminary probes can help assure that the data collection is well targeted and workable.

The use of a *case study protocol* to organize the data collection is now commonly accepted as the desired prelude to systematic data collection when doing case study evaluations. A protocol covers all the procedures and other instruments that may be part of the data collection, but the most important part of the protocol is a series of queries posed to the *evaluator, not any respondent.* The queries represent the evaluator's line of inquiry. The evaluator's later task is to assemble the collected data and compose the response to the protocol's questions.

The product from the preceding task is a *case study database,* which exists apart from and precedes the composing of the final evaluation report (see Yin, 2009a, pp. 118–122). The database may take both narrative and tabular form, a key feature being that the noted information contains explicit footnotes or references to the specific sources of evidence (thereby helping preserve a desired *chain of evidence*—see Yin, 2009a, pp. 122–124). The database, though not edited or intended for public presentation, nevertheless needs to be available for independent inspection by other researchers.

Data Collected About the Community Coalition

A Community Action Framework. To evaluate the community coalition, the main data came from fieldwork that included intensive interviews of the coalition's staff, careful review of the coalition's key documents and records, and observations at coalition-sponsored events.

The data collection revealed a distinctive set of *inputs* that involved the community coalition's resources and strategies. Unlike many other community organizations that provide an array of needed services (e.g., Boys & Girls Clubs and other community centers), the coalition being evaluated followed a *community organizing* model. According to this model, the goal is to mobilize residents so they can pressure known decision points in both political and policy arenas—for example, to voice support for (or opposition to)

- a political candidate,
- a legislative bill or proposal,
- a judicial case or ruling, or
- an intended regulation or initiative being adopted by the executive branch.

At the local level, the relevant venues include a city council (or local legislative body), a state or local court, and the mayor's or city manager's office, as well as local agencies. This manner of resident mobilization had been tested and documented many years earlier (e.g., Alinsky, 1946, 1971) and had been especially successful in supporting changes in the neighborhood politics in Chicago.

Using this strategy, an organization's objective is to design and conduct "issues campaigns." A single campaign may cover a series of events. Each event is intended to call attention to the issue and to strengthen the organization through the recruitment of additional human and financial resources. The organization also may seek media coverage for each event as well as for the issue campaign as a whole. Each event represents an opportunity for a positive result or "win," and the organization wants to cumulate "wins." Each "win" should further add to the reputation and strength of the organization. Over time, the organization can gain power in a number of arenas: political and legislative matters, consumer affairs, legal and regulatory rulings (including court rulings), and even the content of media coverage.

Contextually, the coalition took advantage of the period of social unrest during which the housing and other property had been destroyed, including the closure of about 200 of the large number of liquor stores that had populated the community. The coalition took this opportunity to launch a formal campaign to rebuild the region (the Rebuild Campaign), but without the same concentration of liquor stores.

In the target community, such liquor stores had contributed to community disorganization and disorder in at least two ways. First, the sale of beer, wine, and liquor had been accompanied by nuisance, disorderly, and other improper behavior in the area immediately surrounding the liquor store. Second, some of the liquor store sites also had become unwanted hangouts, fostering criminal activity by attracting drug dealers and hosting drug transactions.

The Coalition's Activities. The data collection showed that, a year following the social unrest, the coalition had launched its Rebuild Campaign with a series of community meetings, including a large conference addressing the problem of crack cocaine in the African-American community. The conference drew more than 250 attendees, many of whom represented other organizations and not just themselves as individuals.

As an integral part of the coalition's strategy of community organizing, the coalition then embarked on a series of events, extending over a period of time. The actions included specific efforts at rallying residents, by conducting door-to-door surveys and encouraging residents to attend public meetings related to the rebuilding of the community and the restoring of the liquor stores. For instance, the majority of the liquor stores had to have two or more hearings before they could have their licenses renewed and receive an approval to rebuild.

The coalition's leaders met with members of the mayor's office, the city planning commission, and the Alcohol Beverage Control (ABC) Board, discussing conditions for reissuing the liquor licenses. At the initial meetings, the coalition presented a petition with 25,000 signatures, calling for a moratorium on the rebuilding of liquor stores and the issuance of new licenses until new regulations could be put into place.

Some of the desired regulations—such as tightening the penalties (i.e., length of suspension of a license) if a store had been found to have sold its products to minors—required new local legislation. The legislation also was needed to require that the rebuilt stores improve their operations by having security guards, better lighting, and better control over nuisance and criminal activity. In addition, the new legislation would authorize the ABC Board to monitor these conditions and impose sanctions. Over the ensuing year, the coalition, therefore, trained residents to collect evidence, prepare briefings, and give public testimony in judicial and legislative hearings on these and related matters. Eventually, the city council passed the needed legislation.

The liquor store merchants questioned the city council's right to proceed on these matters, appealing to the local court to issue an injunction. The court denied the injunction. Later, the state appellate court had to deny a subsequent appeal to overturn the local court's ruling. In so doing, the appellate court added a strong statement in support of local government's right to deal with criminal nuisance problems. Other cities around the state subsequently used the local court's ruling to impose stricter conditions on the liquor stores in their own neighborhoods.

Throughout these events, the coalition urged residents to participate in all the associated hearings and to voice their support for the new regulations. By now, the coalition also had developed a strong relationship with the local media and with network and public television news reporters, leading to even broader public attention on the Rebuild Campaign.

As a separate but related activity, the coalition received a contract from the state department of health to support a related community action: identifying liquor stores that placed banners advertising the sale of tobacco products, potentially leading to the sale of such products to minors. The coalition organized meetings with the owners of such stores, calling attention to the owners' responsibilities and asking them to remove the banners from their storefronts and windows—especially those stores located near public schools or on students' routes walking to and from school.

IV. ANALYZING CASE STUDY EVALUATION DATA

Data Analysis Procedures

In case studies, data collection and analysis are likely to occur in an intermingled fashion. This is because newly collected field evidence may pose immediate challenges to any tentative interpretations made on the basis of earlier evidence. Throughout data collection, the case study evaluator must perform more as a detective than a research assistant—evaluating the adequacy and meaning of evidence as it is being collected. Thus, successful case study evaluators are likely to be diligent investigators who (a) understand the objectives of the inquiry and can identify relevant evidence even though specific sources may vary, and

(b) thoroughly document the methodological steps taken to assure an unbiased data collection procedure despite this variation.

For data analysis, several procedures can be followed, although none involve the formulaic solutions when entering numeric data into a computer and permitting a computer software package to calculate the needed statistics. Instead, case study analysis usually deals with narrative or alphabetic but not numeric data. Although useful computer software exists for coding and assembling such narrative data, the evaluator must instruct the software regarding the specific coding and assembling to be done (see Yin, 2011b, Chapter 8).

Once case study data have been organized or coded, a case study evaluator can follow any number of analytic strategies, such as explanation building, pattern matching, and time-series sequencing (Yin, 2009a, pp. 136–156). For instance, pattern matching calls for comparing the hypothesized and observed relationships among variables, whether they are process or outcome variables. If they are outcome variables, the pattern matching is not too different from one of the quasi-experimental designs and, in this respect, overlaps with this approach: the nonequivalent dependent variables design (Cook & Campbell, 1979, p. 118).

Analysis of the Community Coalition Data

Outputs. The immediate result (*output*) of the coalition's actions was to strengthen the ability of the ABC Board to impose new requirements when reissuing liquor store licenses. These conditions covered the tightened penalties discussed earlier but also included additional requirements. The other conditions included the need for the rebuilt liquor stores to have security guards (to reduce the undesirable behavior and potential criminal activities), improved lighting, and better control over their immediate premises. The ABC Board also now had strengthened powers to enforce the various requirements.

A subsequent but still early result (*output*) was the relicensing of a much smaller number of liquor stores. Because of the stringent requirements, only 56 of the original 200 stores were granted new licenses. Thus, the stores were not only presumed to be safer and less troublesome, but they also were fewer in number.

The analysis of the flow of events, from the initiation of the Rebuild Campaign to the turnouts at hearings and the heightened media attention, all supported the conclusion that the coalition had been among the primary actors—if not *the* primary actor—in reducing the number of liquor stores and improving their quality. Rival claims—that other parties were more instrumental in producing the observed results—did not exist. The centrality of the coalition's work was further recognized by requests for the coalition's guidance and assistance, coming from other communities, to pursue similar actions (see **BOX 22**).

BOX 22

Generalizing From a Case Study

One of the greatest challenges in doing case study research is understanding whether—and how—to generalize findings from a small number of case studies, much less from a single case study. The typical concern is that the "sample" of cases is too small for any generalizing to take place. However, any notion that the cases serve as a sample (of some known and larger universe) is the beginning of the wrong way to think about this challenge.

Instead, the findings from case studies can be generalized, but on *analytic* rather than *statistical* grounds. In the present chapter, the community coalition's strategy followed a *public health model* of drug prevention (though not explicitly labeled as such). Underlying the model is a theory stipulating that successful prevention can sometimes occur only when changes are made to a person's environment. The theory contrasts with individual-based theories that call for people to change their behavior, when in fact the individuals may be the victims rather than the perpetrators of public health problems.

The coalition's strategy (directed at reducing the overabundance of poorly monitored liquor stores) represents an instance of the application of the public health model. The findings can be used to generalize to other similar efforts—such as eradicating stagnant pools of water (to prevent the spread of mosquito-driven diseases), cleaning up tainted water supplies, eliminating cigarette vending machines in places easily accessible to underage youths, or even stopping the sales of cold beer at gas stations to reduce auto accidents. These analytic (rather than statistical) parallels all identify other situations to which the case study's findings might be generalized.

(For more information, see Yin, 2009a, Chapter 2, section on "Generalizing From Case Study to Theory.")

Longer-Term Outcomes. Finally, the case study evaluation checked a longer-term result (*outcome*) by surveying 8th- and 10th-grade students in nearby schools about their use of alcohol and other illicit drugs, before and after a two-year period (see **BOX 23**). Similar data were collected from comparable students in a comparison community. The comparison was located in a geographically proximal area with similar economic and demographic characteristics, but not any kind of community organization similar to the coalition being evaluated.

BOX 23

Qualitative and Quantitative Research

The dichotomy between qualitative and quantitative research has become a caricature in the social sciences. Qualitative research, including case studies, is characterized as being "soft" social science, dealing with inadequate evidence. Quantitative research is considered to be hard-nosed, data-driven, outcome-oriented, and truly scientific.

This book assumes that a case study can call on both qualitative and quantitative data (in this chapter, the fieldwork involving the coalition's community actions and the large-scale survey that tried to determine whether drug use rates had declined). The contrasting characteristics between what is *qualitative* (categorical data) and what is *quantitative* (numeric data), therefore, are not attributes of two competing types of research. Instead, they are attributes of two types of data.

Such a focus on the type of data also may minimize the unproductive debate between qualitative and quantitative research. Qualitative research also can be hard-nosed, data-driven, and outcome-oriented. Similarly, quantitative research can be soft because of inappropriate sample sizes or poorly specified variables. These are attributes of good and poor research and not of a dichotomy between two different types of research.

(For more information, see Yin, 2009a, Chapter 1, section on "Variations Within Case Studies as a Research Method.)"

Numerically, the comparison of reported drug use behavior, at both the 8th- and 10th-grade levels, showed no statistically significant changes in drug use between the youths in the coalition's community and the youths in the nearby community. Alcohol use had declined in the coalition's community, but the decline was not significantly different from that of the comparison community.

Conclusion

At the completion of all the data analysis, the evaluation's final conclusion was that the community coalition had successfully altered important neighborhood conditions related to drug-related behavior. However, at least during the period of the evaluation, these conditions did not yet connect to changes in the reported drug use behavior by students. The evaluation ended by noting that the final conclusion could, therefore, still be affected by further follow-up surveys of later 8th- and 10th-grade students, though such surveys were beyond the scope of the evaluation.

Media Reports as Evidence

In some case studies, the "case"—as in the community coalition in the present chapter—may have been associated with a large amount of media coverage. Local as well as community newspapers and the television media then can become valuable sources of information in doing the case study. Thoroughly reviewing these sources can be of great use. For instance, at a minimum, they usually provide key dates and the properly spelled names and titles of relevant individuals and organizations. The journalistic and media accounts also can help fill in key details about the case, as long as you are aware that these sources may have their own slant on events—such as what they choose to report and not report.

When nationally recognized newspapers and television media are the source, you may have some confidence in the accuracy of their information. However, your vigilance needs to increase if you use other materials that are frequently available these days—mainly the electronic information available on various websites. When using websites, you need to be extremely wary of how the nature of those sources might influence the accuracy and trustworthiness of the information.

For Class Discussion or Written Assignment

Identify a highly public but controversial event that might have occurred recently in your community. Collect two or three renditions of this event from news, Internet, or similar sources. Compare the renditions for possible differences in their coverage of the event, editorial slant and content, information presented about the event, or persons and other sources cited in the rendition. Draw a conclusion about whether and why the two or three renditions all need to be cited, to provide a fair account of the event, or whether the renditions are so similar that only one of them needs to be cited.

14

SHERIFF'S COMBINED
AUTO THEFT TASK FORCE

Law enforcement services also have been the subject of case study evaluations. A common evaluation question has been the extent to which (a) external funding (e.g., an award from the federal government to a local police department) might lead to (b) an innovative practice that in turn produces (c) desirable and documentable outcomes. Case studies can be one way of tracking such a presumed sequence of events.

The present case study focuses on the creation of a 14-county auto theft task force that provided cross-jurisdictional authority to the deputies in all 14 counties. One claim is that federal funds helped create this unprecedented, multicounty law enforcement collaboration. A second claim is that the collaboration's activities reduced the auto thefts in the area. The chapter shows how a case study of modest length can address such claims.

Critical to the line of evidence is acknowledging the complexity of real-world conditions. For instance, regarding the first claim, state-level funds were available and being used earlier than the federal funds. However, the state funds were not associated with the formation of the multicounty task force or with the needed equipment purchases. Although the state funds did augment the local budget by supporting additional officers to work on the task force, the federal funds appear to have served in the more catalytic role. Similarly, the entire effort might not have taken place without a newly elected sheriff who saw the need for the multicounty effort and led to its creation.

AUTHOR'S NOTE: This is a revised version of 1 of 18 case studies that were part of an evaluation report titled *National Evaluation of the Local Law Enforcement Block Grant Program: Final Report for Phase I*, COSMOS Corporation, Bethesda, Maryland, March 2001, whose main author was Robert K. Yin.

CONTEXTUAL CONDITIONS

Four major highways intersect the central Texas region, providing thoroughfares for offenders engaged in interstate and international auto theft. For example, automobiles stolen in Travis County (which includes the city of Austin) can be transferred to surrounding rural counties, where their vehicle identification numbers are altered to facilitate resale; the vehicles are "chopped" (dismantled for sale of parts, which are often more valuable in the illegal market than the total vehicle); and the parts are consolidated for transshipment. Rural areas (especially those with little auto theft activity and limited law enforcement coverage) provide excellent locations for "chop shops" that support organized auto theft from neighboring counties and cities. The rural counties cover a broad expanse—averaging more than 700 square miles and with population densities reaching as low as fewer than 10 persons per square mile.

Earlier, Single-Jurisdiction Efforts

A few years earlier, the Texas Auto Theft Prevention Authority (ATPA), supported by a $1.00 premium per insured automobile per year assessed to all Texas vehicle insurance companies, had funded several projects in a statewide attempt to reduce vehicle-related criminal activity. Projects eligible for ATPA funds included activities such as law enforcement/apprehension, prosecution/adjudication, public education, prevention of sale of stolen auto parts, and reduction of stolen vehicles moved across the Mexican border (see **BOX 24**).

BOX 24

Multiple Sources of Evidence

In this chapter, the data about the ATPA funds come from an archival source. The source of evidence is but one of several used in the case study. Other sources included direct field observations, interviews of task force members, and reviews of key documents, such as the Interlocal Assistance Agreement cited later in the case study.

Using such multiple sources can strengthen the evidence for case studies, and nearly all the case studies in the present book involve data collected from multiple sources. In principle, evidence can come from at least six sources: documentation, archival records (e.g., computerized records of clients in a service delivery system), interviews, direct observations, participant-observation, and physical artifacts (e.g., the actual condition of actual houses in a housing study). When findings, interpretations, and conclusions are based on such multiple sources, the case study data will be less prone to the quirks from any single source, such as an inaccurate interviewee or a biased document.

(For more information, see Yin, 2009a, Chapter 4, section on "Principle 1: Use Multiple Sources of Evidence.")

ATPA made state funding available to single jurisdictions (cities or counties), even though auto theft crime networks operated across jurisdictional boundaries and transported stolen vehicles from populous areas into rural locations, decreasing the likelihood of being detected. Furthermore, funds could be used only for personnel salaries and not for equipment. The allocation of funds was formula driven, based on the UCR (Uniform Crime Reporting) auto theft reports by each location. Theft of farm or industrial equipment was not considered, nor was the location of recovered vehicles. To a great extent, ATPA funding supported prevention programs and targeted criminals who could be caught in the act. However, it did not provide for multijurisdictional approaches that would identify chop jobs and consolidation areas in isolated, nonpopulous regions favored by organized crime.

Formation of a Multijurisdictional Task Force

Recognizing the need for a multicounty cooperative effort to reduce auto-related criminal activity in central Texas, the Travis County Sheriff's Office took the initiative in 1997 and expanded its auto theft unit to create the Sheriff's Combined Automobile Theft-Prevention Task Force (SCATT). The regional task force united the 14 law enforcement agencies in the counties of Bastrop, Bell, Blanco, Burnet, Caldwell, Colorado, Comal, Fayette, Hays, Lee, Llano, Milam, Travis, and Williamson. The initiative was facilitated by the availability of federal funds administered under its Local Law Enforcement Block Grant (LLEBG) program.

SCATT has been one of the few multicounty law enforcement task forces in the state. Because of the independent nature of Texas's counties and sheriffs, some have even conjectured that it might be the first such collaboration in state history. Before the formation of SCATT, car-theft–related law enforcement was reactive and essentially driven by the need to satisfy the Uniform Crime Reporting system. Available data showed that the vast majority of automobile thefts occurred in the high-population areas of Travis County (population 710,000), with some occurrences in Bell (223,000) and Williamson (224,000). The remaining 11 counties have a combined population of less than 400,000 and lacked both the incidence rates to generate citizen concern and the resources to respond effectively, even if auto theft were a problem.

A Complementary Initiative

Help End Auto Theft (HEAT), a statewide vehicle registration program, was implemented in 1993 to assist law enforcement officers in identifying stolen vehicles throughout Travis and surrounding counties. Participating vehicle owners sign an agreement stating that their vehicles may be stopped between the hours of 1 a.m. and 5 a.m. or when crossing the border into Mexico. An identifying decal in the rear window enables Texas law enforcement officers to observe and stop vehicles to verify ownership. HEAT is a primary prevention program for SCATT, using officers to support a public education and awareness campaign throughout the 14-county region. This effort recognizes that 94% of all recovered vehicles are related to amateur, joy-rider outings, whereas the remaining 6% constitute the work of professional thieves who feed organized criminal networks—the primary interest of SCATT.

IMPLEMENTATION OF THE PRACTICE

In 1996, the newly elected Travis County Sheriff recognized that, although auto theft was increasing in the county, the number of recovered vehicles was not matching the increase. The sheriff observed that crackdowns on chop shops located in Travis County had only driven such operations to barns and isolated buildings outside the county—beyond the reach of the Travis County Sheriff's auto theft unit.

Despite the lack of any history of cross-jurisdictional cooperation, the sheriff emphasized the need for improved law enforcement communication across county boundaries, because such boundaries were not observed by the region's organized-crime–supported auto theft network. However, the budgets of the surrounding county sheriffs' offices were unable to support a compatible radio system to patch into the Travis County system. The issuance of cell phones to deputies was the most reasonable alternative. Even this outlay, nevertheless, was impossible to make because the surrounding counties—most with populations less than 30,000—had no equipment budgets, and the Travis County budget authority was not likely to approve using its sheriff's budget to fund another county's operation, no matter how small.

LLEBG funding, having supported the formation of SCATT, provided additional flexibility by allowing the local determination of expenditures, including the purchase of the equipment needed to strengthen communications between Travis and the surrounding counties. Travis County then augmented the LLEBG funds by applying for and receiving funds from ATPA to provide salaries for additional officers who were to be assigned to the participating counties. Together, the LLEBG and ATPA funds led to an expansion of the original auto theft budget from $160,000 in 1996 to $350,000 in 1997, $400,000 in 1998, and $497,000 in 1999.

The LLEBG funds awarded to the Travis County Sheriff's Office provided support and flexibility at an especially opportune time. Having spent the previous six months developing interest in a multicounty task force, "talking the talk," the Travis County Sheriff "walked the walk" by sharing the LLEBG funds with the 13 surrounding counties, to purchase the equipment needed to coordinate services.

SCATT began in September 1997. The 14 sheriffs selected the Travis County Sheriff to be the standing chair of a board of governors that included a representative from every county. The SCATT team was provided with "the power to conduct investigations, make arrests without a warrant, execute search warrants, and make other reasonable and necessary law enforcement actions for the purpose of and in pursuit of achieving Task Force objectives *outside the jurisdiction from which the officer is assigned* and within the territory of a specific Task Force operation."

To support SCATT's structure, all 14 sheriffs formally signed an Interlocal Assistance Agreement,[1] and SCATT provided the smaller counties with the equipment and manpower needed to identify vehicle-related criminal activity (i.e., chop shops). In the past, the less populous counties had insufficient resources to conduct surveillance or investigate potential stolen vehicle trafficking. Many could not provide basic patrol during the late-night and early-morning hours and were not inclined to devote scarce resources to a crime that, because of its rarity in rural counties, was perceived as a Travis County or Austin problem. As SCATT became operational, rural counties recognized their role and responsibility in combating a larger organized crime network. They also began to focus on thefts of farm vehicles and construction equipment that often went unreported and usually were not missed by owners for days or weeks after the theft.

This comprehensive network continued to encourage communication between the county sheriffs and provided prevention, detection, and interdiction related to vehicular theft. Each county was covered by additional officers placed in adjoining jurisdictions as needed by the Travis County Sheriff's Office. Because the additional sheriff's deputies were recruited from and resided in the counties in which they were stationed, they not only brought local knowledge but also created a trusting and cooperative atmosphere across county lines.

The task force's initial focus on stolen vehicles later paved the way for cooperation on other law enforcement matters (e.g., revenues from vehicle thefts were found to support the purchase of illegal drugs for distribution) and also led to additional collaboration with the U.S. Drug Enforcement Agency (DEA); U.S. Bureau of Alcohol, Tobacco, and Firearms (ATF); and related state agencies. Furthermore, Travis County began to use its crime lab to support investigations by SCATT sheriffs for crimes other than car theft.

As of the time of the case study, SCATT had been holding formal monthly meetings to prioritize activities and plan coordinated operations. As needed, other law enforcement entities (such as the U.S. Attorney's Office, ATF, DEA, Texas Rangers, and Customs) participate in the meetings. SCATT officers, as part of their routine investigative duties, also are authorized to interface with their counterparts in these agencies between meetings.

The original cooperative effort would not have been possible without the LLEBG funding. Now, SCATT has been institutionalized in all 14 counties with local and state support and will no longer require LLEBG funding.

OUTCOMES TO DATE

SCATT is a fully operational unit providing services in interdiction, field training, salvage yard inspections,[2] covert interdiction, overt interdiction, and public awareness.

From September 1997 to April 1999, SCATT trained 665 officers—many from counties outside the SCATT area—in 31 classes, uncovered 18 chop shops, recovered vehicles valued at more than $7.5 million, and recovered $550,000 in property. Typical of the effect of task force collaboration was an operation described in the *Austin American-Statesman* ("Theft ring targeting building work sites") on June 17, 1999:

> Authorities (officers from the Travis County Combined Auto Theft Task Force, working with a U.S. Drug Enforcement Agency task force from the Waco area) have arrested at least two people suspected of being part of a ring of thieves who have stolen $400,000 in trailers, loaders, and a backhoe from construction sites in Travis and Williamson counties during the past six months. . . . The suspects in the thefts are also suspected of trafficking in methamphetamines.

The following figures summarize SCATT's progress during 1998 to 1999, also demonstrating how its original goals were exceeded:

• *Training:* 23 classes taught, with 383 officers participating. Originally stated goal: Members of the task force will conduct a total of 18 training classes for the law enforcement agencies within the 14-county area, to educate the officers on how to locate, detect, and recover stolen vehicles.

• *Public awareness:* 38 demonstrations performed. Originally stated goal: Agents of the task force and its participating agencies will conduct a total of 24 public awareness services to the public within the 14-county area by promoting auto theft prevention and the HEAT program through task force agents, crime prevention officers, community policing officers, and the use of several forms of media.

• *Salvage inspections:* 117 inspections performed. Originally stated goal: Agents will conduct a total of 80 inspections of the following auto-related businesses:

   A. Unlicensed salvage yards
   B. Licensed salvage yards
   C. Auto body and repair shops
   D. Wrecker/storage yards

   E. Garage and mechanic shops
   F. Auto auctions
   G. Inspections for the public
   H. Used car lots
   I. Auto crushers

- *Checkpoints:* 45 performed. Originally stated goal: Agents of the task force will conduct 12 auto theft checkpoints; due to the laws and legalities of surrounding checkpoints, the following operations will be utilized to conduct these checkpoints:

   A. Working with license and weight officers at weigh stations
   B. Working "Operation Gate"
   C. Making stationary parking lot checks
   D. Checking boat ramps
   E. Marking checkpoints by using signs stating "Checkpoint Ahead"
   F. Highway interdiction

- *Chop shops:* Nine uncovered. Originally stated goal: Agents of the task force will search out and locate five chop shops within the 14-county area.

- *Intelligence information:* Nine submitted. Stated goal: The task force will distribute auto theft intelligence information to all agencies within the 14-county region via the *Travis County Intelligence Bulletin.*

- *Decrease in auto theft:* During the first year of the grant, field agents had tremendous success identifying stolen vehicles. Auto-related arrests made by unit investigators increased from 6 in the first quarter to 18 in the second. The task force made 4 seizures and inspected 69 salvage yards in the first two quarters, recovering 232 stolen vehicles. The vehicles represented a value of approximately $2.4 million. By mid-1999, the year-to-date auto thefts had declined by 25% (from 368 per 100,000 residents the previous year to 276 per 100,000 residents). Originally stated goal: Decrease the overall auto thefts in the 14-county area.

CHRONOLOGY

1991: Establishment of the ATPA by the 72nd Texas Legislature, to create a statewide effort to reduce vehicle theft. (Statewide, 164,000 auto thefts were reported in 1991, with an average loss per vehicle of more than $5,000.)

1992: Travis County receives first funds from ATPA to support its auto theft unit.

1993: ATPA funds the "Watch Your Car HEAT" program. Window decals authorize officers to apprehend a vehicle between the hours of 1 a.m. and 5 a.m.

1996: The new Travis County Sheriff explores the creation of a multi-county regional task force to combat auto theft.

1997: Travis County's LLEBG funds are used to purchase cell phones and other equipment. SCATT is established. Fourteen county sheriffs are represented on the board of governors, headed by the Travis County Sheriff. LLEBG funds support two additional deputies assigned to SCATT.

1997: An Interlocal Assistance Agreement provides cross-jurisdictional authority to SCATT deputies.

1997: Auto theft budget increases from $160,000 to $350,000, for expanded multicounty activities.

1998: ATPA award increases the budget to $400,000.

1999: SCATT budget increases to $497,000, supporting eight deputies and a public information specialist.

2000: LLEBG funds no longer required for SCATT, which now has expanded its role into other multicounty functions besides auto theft.

INSIDE STORY FOR CHAPTER 14

Studying Innovations

Case study evaluations offer the opportunity to study different innovative practices—in this case, the formation of an auto theft task force to cover a multicounty area in the state of Texas.

The sponsor of the case study reported in the present chapter recognized that a case study method was more likely to capture the (process *as well as* outcome) experiences with these innovative practices, because their innovativeness implies a newness and even uniqueness of situations that cannot be readily captured by using other methods—such as surveys, much less experiments.

Surveys make less sense because the innovative practices might not have enough participants to warrant a survey. Experiments make less sense because the design of an experiment might take an excessive amount of time, while also requiring the implementers to adapt their practices to satisfy the needs of an experimental design. In contrast, the case study method may be well suited to the study of innovations, whether they are innovative practices, innovative policies, or other kinds of innovative changes.

For Class Discussion or Written Assignment

Assume a hypothetical innovative practice, such as a new way of teaching, a new community initiative, or a new change in a business firm. Assume further that the new practice is totally unique—that is, never been tried before in any setting. Discuss the pros and cons of how such an innovation might be studied by using any of three different methods: a case study, a survey, or an experiment (or quasi-experiment).

NOTES

1. The Interlocal Assistance Agreement, Regional Auto Theft Enforcement Task Force, was entered into pursuant to Chapter 791 of the Texas Government Code, concerning interlocal cooperation contracts, and Chapter 362 of the Texas Local Government Code.

2. SCATT conducted extensive salvage yard inspections throughout the 14 counties. Each inspection ensures that persons involved in the business of salvaging and repairing vehicles conduct their business in accordance with the laws of the state of Texas.

TECHNICAL ASSISTANCE
FOR HIV/AIDS
COMMUNITY PLANNING

This cross-case synthesis covers the findings from eight explanatory case studies. Each case study evaluated the provision of technical assistance (TA), covering a single TA *engagement* as the unit of analysis. In these engagements, a *TA provider* (one or a combination of organizations that the U.S. Centers for Disease Control and Prevention—CDC—had supported as part of a network known as the TA Network) assisted a *TA recipient* (a state-level community planning group—CPG). The TA was intended to assist the CPG in developing its own annual community plan for allocating funds for HIV/AIDS prevention services.

A single engagement could take place over a period of months and over multiple occasions. The TA could include any combination of workshops, consultations, hands-on assistance, or provision of relevant materials.

The cross-case synthesis starts by clarifying the theoretical framework underlying the eight cases, especially clarifying the expected outcomes from the TA engagements. The synthesis then presents the data from the eight case studies, using a replication logic—the overall evaluation question having to deal with explaining the performance of the TA Network as a whole, not the results from any single TA engagement. Also distinctive about the cross-case synthesis is the explicit identification of rival explanations that might have been alternative reasons for the observed outcomes.

AUTHOR'S NOTE: The original cross-case analysis appears in the *Final Report for the Evaluation of the CDC-Supported Technical Assistance Network for Community Planning*, Vol. I, COSMOS Corporation, Bethesda, Maryland, July 1999, whose lead author was Robert K. Yin. The original text has been lightly edited for readability.

The cross-case analysis concludes by reviewing the strength of the evidence for eight hypotheses that had been defined at the outset of the evaluation, before any of the individual case studies had been conducted. The purpose of the hypotheses was to address issues that could improve the future operations of the TA Network and not just to arrive at a summary judgment about its work.

INTRODUCTION: A FRAMEWORK FOR ASSESSING THE EFFECTIVENESS OF TECHNICAL ASSISTANCE (TA)

Defining Relevant Outcomes

The desired and meaningful outcomes of any HIV prevention effort normally might be expected to be assessed in relation to *reductions in the incidence of HIV/AIDS*. To this extent, the work of the technical assistance (TA) Network should be evaluated simply in terms of this outcome.

However, such a straightforward expectation is not reasonable (and may not be possible), because the TA Network's assistance is not aimed directly at reducing HIV/AIDS incidence. In fact, the assistance occurs, logically, at a much earlier step in a much elongated process. The array of steps in the full process might be considered as follows:

1. The U.S. Centers for Disease Control and Prevention (CDC) mandates that each state create a community planning group (CPG) to implement a *community planning process*. The TA Network is mainly formed to assist CPGs in carrying out this planning process.

2. One outcome of the planning process is a *comprehensive prevention plan,* reviewed annually by CDC. The plan indicates how the state will allocate prevention resources among a variety of HIV prevention services, based on the CPG's analysis of its communities' existing needs and services.

3. The state or local health department associated with the CPG then allocates *prevention resources* according to the plan, and the resources are used to support HIV prevention services.

4. *HIV prevention services* are implemented. In order to be effective, the services must (a) follow an appropriate design, properly targeting a priority population; (b) be implemented well; and (c) overcome other conditions in order to reduce HIV/AIDS incidence.

5. Only if all the preceding steps have occurred properly might the desired ultimate outcome—a *reduction in HIV/AIDS incidence*—occur.

Figure 15.1 depicts these steps in the form of a logic model. The TA Network's assistance mainly occurs early in the sequential process (see "HIV Prevention Community Planning" box in Figure 15.1), whereas the ultimate desired outcome

Figure 15.1 Relationship Between TA Network and Desired Outcomes

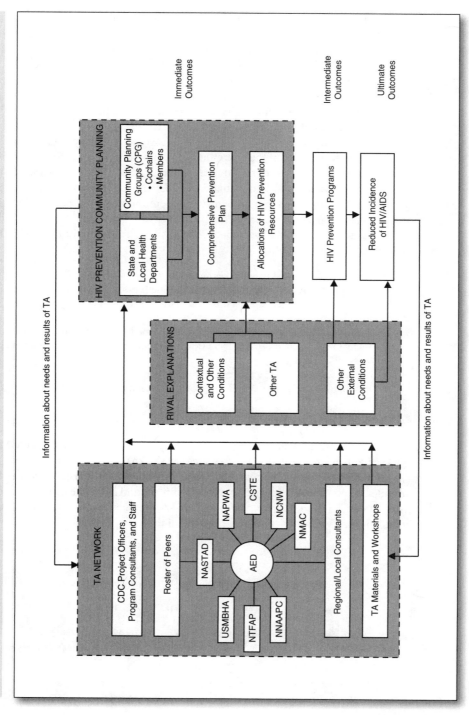

AED = Academy for Educational Development; CDC = Centers for Disease Control and Prevention; CSTE = Council of State and Territorial Epidemiologists; NAPWA = National Association of People With AIDS; NASTAD = National Alliance of State and Territorial AIDS Directors; NCNW = National Council of Negro Women; NMAC = National Minority AIDS Council; NNAAPC = National Native American AIDS Prevention Center; NTFAP = National Task Force on AIDS Prevention; USMBHA = U.S.-Mexico Border Health Association of prevention occurs at the fifth step (see bottom of third column). Such a relationship means that the TA Network's work is *distal* with regard to the ultimately desired HIV prevention outcome. In other words, any reduction or change in HIV/AIDS incidence in a community is likely to be affected only indirectly by the work of the TA Network. The outcome is more likely to be affected by many other conditions, including the manner in which the intervening steps are followed. Reduction in HIV/AIDS incidence, therefore, is not a good benchmark for judging the TA Network's effectiveness.

Given this framework, the TA Network was assumed to be more fairly assessed in relation to the success of the community planning process as an outcome. Such a process was assumed to consist of three functions that became the subject of the case study evaluation: (1) better-functioning CPGs, (2) improved planning processes, and (3) improved comprehensive prevention plans and better allocations of HIV prevention resources.

The desired positive changes could have resulted from the following kinds of TA offered by the TA Network:

- Conducting a formal needs assessment
- Setting explicit priorities for HIV/AIDS initiatives
- Fostering parity, inclusion, and representation (PIR) in the planning process, for all at-risk groups
- Developing a sound epidemiologic profile of the local population
- Using the planning process to increase cooperation and reduce conflicts among local HIV/AIDS groups
- Complying with CDC's formal community planning guidelines
- Responding appropriately to CDC's annual reviews of a CPG's plan

Selecting the Cases

To evaluate the TA Network, eight cases were selected. Each case covered a TA engagement as the unit of analysis (see **BOX 25**). In each engagement, the TA Network was known beforehand to have produced desirable outcomes as a TA provider. In other words, the cases were exemplary and not representative, chosen from about 25 nominations. Although all were exemplary, the cases were intended to reflect a variety of TA modes and topics.[1]

BOX 25

The "Case" as the Unit of Analysis

The eight case studies in this chapter are about organizations providing technical assistance to public health agencies in eight states. However, the unit of analysis for the cases was neither the organizations nor the agencies. Rather, each case focused on a technical assistance *engagement,* which was the actual unit of analysis.

Careful definition of the case(s) in a case study will help establish the priorities for collecting and analyzing data. For instance, in the present case study of technical assistance (TA), the relevant data were about the TA engagements, with data about the organizations and agencies serving more of a background role. Similarly, the findings from the case study were intended to pertain to related kinds of TA engagements (note that the hypotheses at the end of the case study are about the engagements, not about the organizations and agencies). In this sense, the case(s) in a case study fulfill the same function as the unit of analysis in non-case study research.

(For more information, see Yin, 2009a, Chapter 2, section on "Unit of Analysis.")

The inquiry also sought to examine *how* the TA Network had produced any desirable outcomes and, thus, to *explain* the work of the TA Network. In conducting the inquiry, the evaluation team, therefore, also developed a series of hypotheses regarding the conditions that were believed to be important in producing the desired outcomes (see **BOX 26**).

BOX 26

Replication, Not Sampling, for Multiple-Case Studies

The selection of the eight case studies in the present chapter followed a replication, not sampling logic. This means that all eight cases were chosen because they were claimed beforehand to have had positive outcomes, and the initial screening data used to select the cases supported this claim. The ensuing evaluation then predicted that similar processes would be found to account for these outcomes (*direct replications*). Such replications, if found, can produce greater confidence than if results have been derived from only a single case or two.

The replication logic for case studies borrows directly from the same logic in doing experiments. The number of cases or experiments is not likely to be large, but if the cases (or experiments) corroborate one another, the findings can be considered to be more robust. In contrast, a sampling logic is used when a study is mainly interested in having its findings pertain to a larger universe. The sample is chosen according to pre-identified representational criteria—and the sample must be sufficiently large (usually more than a few data points) to satisfy a statistical power analysis.

(For more information, see Yin, 2009a, Chapter 2, section on "Replication, Not Sampling Logic, for Multiple-Case Studies.")

Collecting Data

For each case, the evaluation team conducted a site visit to the CPG that had received the TA. Discussions also were held with the CDC staff person who was the project officer at the time the TA was provided. The site visits called for interviews with the key participants in the TA, as well as the collection of relevant documents and archival materials. As a result, the cases attempted to track the actual course of events, going beyond those field studies that largely focus on open-ended interviews and, hence, are limited to self-reports by participants.

Upon completing the site visits, the materials for each case were compiled into a formal database (a collection of narrative and numeric evidence organized according to the topics in a case study protocol). The eight databases also included individual logic models, showing the claimed flow of events in each case—from the conditions that existed prior to the TA engagement to the outcomes of the TA. These logic models represented the confirmed events of the cases and, therefore, their presumed logical flow. Drafts of the databases were shared with the participants at the original sites, for review and comment, and corrections and comments were incorporated into the final versions. The remainder of this chapter discusses the outcomes and varieties of TA that were studied, an examination of rivals, and the findings for each hypothesis.

DOCUMENTED OUTCOMES, VARIETIES OF TA STUDIED, AND POSSIBLE RIVAL EXPLANATIONS FOR THE OUTCOMES

Outcomes Associated With the TA by the TA Network

Exhibit 15.1 summarizes the outcomes from the eight case studies. Originally, the summaries were to emphasize the community planning process outcomes. However, an unexpected finding was that the outcomes of the TA appear to have gone beyond the planning process and influenced the next phase of the prevention process—HIV/AIDS prevention service delivery.

Exhibit 15.1 (Column 1) shows that in seven of the eight cases, the TA did affect the community planning process. For instance, nearly every case demonstrated the TA's influence on better-functioning CPGs. The specific outcomes were substantiated by both interviews and documentary evidence in the case studies.

Also shown in Exhibit 15.1 (see Column 2) is that the TA influence went beyond the planning process in all but the two Florida cases, by assisting in the following steps: designing requests for proposal (RFPs) used to solicit service-delivery proposals from local agencies and organizations (Mississippi, North Carolina); reaching out to minority and ethnic groups (Idaho, Montana, Utah); and supporting efforts to improve or strengthen the prevention programs of community-based organizations (CBOs) (Montana, Nebraska).

The fact that the outcomes included not only the community planning process but extended into HIV/AIDS prevention service delivery had not been anticipated

Exhibit 15.1 Outcomes Associated With TA by the TA Network

	Effect on Community Planning Process (1)			Effect on Service Delivery (2)	
State	Better-Functioning CPGs	Improved Planning	Better Comprehensive Plan	Allocation of HIV Prevention Resources	Implementation of HIV Prevention Services
Florida (Statewide)	CPG members have enhanced appreciation of epidemiologic profile as driver of further planning steps.	Completed epidemiologic profile for the entire state.	—	—	—
Florida (Miami-Dade)	Groups with history of hostile relationships reach consensus on the consolidation process.	New (county) ordinance enacted, creating consolidated planning organization; new (city) ordinance still being sought.	—	—	
Idaho	Formation of statewide CPG and seven regional CPGs; statewide CPG develops bylaws.	Priority populations are identified using epidemiologic data.	CDC judges application, previously out of compliance, to be in compliance in 1996 and 1997.	Program funding is established for a number of priority populations.	—
Mississippi	Four African-American women join the CPG.	Health department designs additional forums targeting other at-risk groups.	—	CPG issues RFP shortly after forum and makes multiple awards, including cultural pride program with HIV education as main focus.	—

(Continued)

Exhibit 15.1 (Continued)

	Effect on Community Planning Process (1)			Effect on Service Delivery (2)	
State	Better-Functioning CPGs	Improved Planning	Better Comprehensive Plan	Allocation of HIV Prevention Resources	Implementation of HIV Prevention Services
Montana	Improved relationship between statewide CPG and Native American Advisory Committee (NAAC); NAAC more involved in community planning process.	Statewide planning group selects research-based HIV prevention interventions; the group bases priority setting on data in the epidemiologic profile.	CDC finds 1996 plan in compliance with community planning guidelines.	Seven Native American tribes receive contracts for the first time to provide HIV prevention services; 14 county health departments and a CBO also receive contracts.	Prevention services are research-based.
Nebraska	Participants gain better understanding of community planning and of role as CPG members; statewide and six regional CPGs operate more efficiently; members share ideas more comfortably.	—	—	—	Some CBOs improve or revamp programs around effective interventions.
North Carolina	—	—	CDC accepts revised plan in September 1998 (original priority setting had failed to weed anything out).	CPG issues new RFP to solicit proposals reflecting new priorities.	—
Utah	CPG develops better screening process for membership; African-American participation has increased.	Conference participants help CPG identify ways of reaching ethnic and minority populations.	—	Two CBOs serving ethnic communities apply to health department for funding after conference; CDC provides additional funding for CBOs.	—

at the outset of the evaluation and may be considered a positive outcome. Again, because of the way the eight cases had been selected and screened, the frequency of similar experiences in other TA engagements is unknown.

How TA Might Have Worked to Produce the TA Outcomes

Across the eight cases were patterns of TA activity potentially explaining how these outcomes had been produced. Examined were the mode of TA delivery, the topics covered by the TA, the identity of the TA recipient(s), and the role of the organizations in the TA network (see the four columns in Exhibit 15.2).

Regarding the mode of TA delivery, of the eight cases, seven involved "on-site" assistance, which may have a greater impact than other modes of TA delivery (e.g., the provision of materials only or telephonic consultation only). Therefore, the possibility exists that the outcomes might not have occurred had only "off-site" or other modes of TA delivery been used.

Exhibit 15.2 itemizes the characteristics of the TA for each of the eight case studies. The first column in the table shows that not only did seven of the eight involve on-site TA, but in most cases the TA occurred over an extended period of time, involved multiple on-site events, or both. These cases, therefore, represent instances of long-term TA, the implication being that the observed outcomes might not have occurred if the TA had been only short term.[2]

Regarding the TA topics covered by the eight cases (see the second column of Exhibit 15.2), a diversity of topics was found, partially as a result of the case selection process, which had deliberately sought such diversity. The main objective in so doing was to see whether desirable outcomes tend to be limited to one or a small set of TA topics, and the observed diversity suggested no such limitation.

The pattern of the TA recipients and the presumed role of the various organizations in the TA Network in arranging and supporting the TA engagement (the third and fourth columns in Exhibit 15.2) also yielded no surprises: The recipients most often included a public health department and the CPGs, and the TA Network's involvement ranged from situations in which a single TA organization made the entire arrangement and provided the entire support (Florida—statewide, Miami-Dade, Montana, and Nebraska) to those where multiple organizations were involved (Idaho, Mississippi, North Carolina, and Utah).

As an additional note, the case studies had difficulty defining the TA recipients because most TA providers believe that they are delivering TA to an organizational unit (e.g., the CPG), whereas the specific knowledge imparted by a TA provider appears mainly to be imparted on a small group of individuals. No data were collected, however, to confirm which individuals actually benefited from a TA engagement, or even to test whether the CPG as an organization had been affected.

Exhibit 15.2 Varieties of TA Found in the Eight Cases

	TA Characteristic			
State	**Mode (1)**	**Topic (2)**	**Recipient (3)**	**Role of the TA Network (4)**
Florida (Statewide)	Two months on-site TA, with follow-up visit; off-site TA for following year, including additional on-site TA at two training workshops	Development of epidemiologic profile for whole state and for two local examples	Mainly the Division of Sexually Transmitted Diseases/HIV/Tuberculosis in health department	CSTE fully arranges and supports this TA, involving one of its staff. The engagement would not necessarily have been recorded or tracked as part of AED's coordinating role.
Florida (Miami-Dade)	On-site TA, with multiple TA consultants participating in several meetings and public forums during a single event	Development of partnership model for streamlining HIV prevention planning across four federal programs	Steering committee, local health department, and other local (not state) participants	TA is provided by one external consultant and two external peers, all arranged and supported by AED.
Idaho	Extensive on-site TA at conference and off-site TA following conference, combined with TA provided by a regional (non-TA Network) provider	Community planning process, development of epidemiologic profile, and development of comprehensive plan	The health department, as well as participants who would become part of the statewide or seven regional CPGs	AED, CSTE, and NASTAD staff and consultants all participate, each organization covering its own costs but with AED coordinating the on-site TA and continuing to arrange needed follow-up TA.
Mississippi	On-site TA involving presentations and facilitation at a single forum	PIR and outreach to African-American women	Health department, as well as a CBO selected to target services to African-American women	AED arranges and supports TA by NAPWA and NCNW staff persons, selected in conjunction with request by health department.

TA Characteristic

State	Mode (1)	Topic (2)	Recipient (3)	Role of the TA Network (4)
Montana	On-site TA involving three separate events, each several months apart	Priority setting, assesment, and behavioral science	Mainly CPG and health department	AED arranges and supports TA by its staff and by consultants.
Nebraska	On-site TA involving multiple statewide and regional events occurring over a nine-month period	PIR, community planning, harm reduction, evaluation, "AIDS 101," and social marketing	Mainly CPG and health department	AED arranges and supports TA by its staff and by consultants.
North Carolina	Off-site TA involving materials and information provided over a period of several months	Priority setting and epidemiologic profile	Two local TA consultants (immediate recipients); CPG (indirect recipient)	NASTAD and CSTE provide information at the request of two local TA consultants. The local consultants, in turn, do on-site work with the CPG and health department (paid by the health department).
Utah	Multiple on-site TA at different annual events	PIR and outreach to ethnic minorities	Health department and the CPG	USMBHA staff person presents and facilitates at annual meeting, arranged directly with health department. AED arranges and supports outside consultant and own staff at later annual meeting.

Rival Explanations for the Observed Outcomes

The preceding analysis indicates how an array of desirable outcomes may have been produced by the TA provided by the TA Network. To test this claim further, the case studies deliberately sought data regarding rival explanations for the same outcomes. Four types of rivals were considered across the eight cases, and Exhibit 15.3 lists these and the evidence collected about them.

Exhibit 15.3   Rival Explanations for Outcomes Found in Eight Cases

---

RIVAL 1: CPGs will achieve the same goals, just not as quickly and not necessarily to the same extent, without the TA Network's assistance. Examples partially supporting Rival 1:

- The CPG already had been updating its epidemiologic profile, even though the eventual TA product represented innovative ways of presenting and interpreting data. (Florida—statewide)

- Staff of the health department already had made a concerted effort to fund ethnic and minority groups. (Utah)

RIVAL 2: The important TA was provided by other federal sources, not just the TA Network. Only one relevant example was found, and it did not support Rival 2, as follows:

- Additional assistance was provided by another federal program. However, this assistance occurred later and did not affect the plan for streamlining prevention planning across four federal programs. (Miami-Dade)

RIVAL 3: The important TA was provided by local groups, consultants, or health department staff, not just the TA Network. Examples partially supporting Rival 3:

- At the same time that the TA Network was providing TA, the health department and CPG also had been engaging a regional TA group to assist with meeting facilitation, community organizing, and meeting planning. However, although the presence of the regional TA group contributed to the improvement of the state's community planning process, it is doubtful that the regional TA group could have provided the type and level of TA that came from the TA Network. (Idaho, Montana)

- The TA Network assisted two local TA providers; the providers themselves brought their own expertise, on complementary topics, that helped produce the outcomes. (North Carolina)

- Efforts by the health department staff, not just the TA Network, contributed to greater participation of minority groups in community planning and greater targeting of services to minority populations. (Utah)

RIVAL 4: CPG membership is enhanced by conditions other than parity, inclusion, and representation (PIR) and the outreach facilitated by the TA Network. The only example partially supporting Rival 4:

- Four African-American women joined the CPG; however, only two joined after participating in an outreach forum assisted by the TA Network, as the other two had not even attended the forum. (Mississippi)

The data show some support for three of four rivals (Rivals 1, 3, and 4 in Exhibit 15.3). For instance, Rival 3 shows that complementary conditions, such as the provision of TA by those not in the TA Network (e.g., local TA providers, or consultants to or staff of the health department) existed in four cases (Idaho, Montana, North Carolina, and Utah). However, no support was found for Rival 2, as only one instance of TA by another federal program was encountered, and this TA occurred later and appears to have been irrelevant to the observed outcomes.

At the same time, none of the rivals was supported to the extent of completely undoing the claimed connection between the TA Network's work and the observed outcomes. Rather, the examination of these rival explanations supports the basic conclusion that the work of the TA Network appears to have played a prominent role in producing the observed outcomes, in spite of a coexistence with other relevant conditions.

INDIVIDUAL HYPOTHESES REGARDING SUCCESSFUL TA DELIVERY: FINDINGS AND FUTURE IMPLICATIONS

Beyond the documentation of the observed outcomes and support for their claimed link to the work of the TA Network, an examination of specific hypotheses developed at the outset of the evaluation was intended to produce other lessons about the TA Network. The main findings and implications to be drawn from each hypothesis are discussed next.

H_1: Joint Definition of TA Needs

Successful TA will result when TA needs are jointly defined by TA recipients and TA providers (e.g., by a CPG and the providers in the TA Network).

Findings. At least two steps need to be taken to define any TA assignment. The first is to determine the need for TA. Once such a determination has been made, the second is to produce a refined definition of the TA to be provided. When first stipulated, H_1 did not distinguish between these two steps. The eight cases helped clarify the steps as well as the role of the TA recipients and TA providers in both of them.

With regard to the first step, nearly all organizations in the TA Network affirmed that the CPG or the CDC project officer had been the dominant definer of the initial need for TA. The TA providers were not usually involved in this process, so there was little, if any, joint definition of the TA need.

In the second step, the specific TA providers did become involved in refining the understanding of needed TA. For instance, TA providers held repeated conference calls or other discussions to define the specific TA services to be supplied (e.g., Nebraska, Idaho). However, situations also arose where the TA provider worked with a CPG representative who was not fully knowledgeable about the TA needed by the CPG. As a result, the ensuing TA was not as well defined as it could have been, as occurred in one of the eight cases (North Carolina). For this second step, therefore, a critical question may be the identity and knowledge of the CPG representatives who act as the TA recipients in defining the needed TA.

Possible Implications. The findings suggest that to strengthen the TA Network, more attention should be given to the identity of the specific person(s) in the CPG (and his or her professional expertise) who represent(s) the CPG in defining the needed TA. To the extent that a CPG contains subgroups with uneven technical skills, any TA provider who follows the advice of one or a small number of CPG representatives in defining the needed TA risks the possibility of defining TA that will not meet the CPG's genuine needs.

An institutional remedy would be to have all CPGs appoint a TA subcommittee charged with covering both steps and then also evaluating the TA. This TA subcommittee would then be the main point of contact between any TA provider and the CPG. The subcommittee would be charged with engaging all the TA on behalf of the CPG, including local and regional providers engaged directly by the CPG and not through the TA Network. Such an oversight subcommittee would then be more likely to represent multiple views and also cumulate the benefits of the TA over time.

H_2: Externally Defined TA Objectives

The community planning process is improved and plans are found to be more comprehensive when TA objectives are externally defined, as a result of a peer or CDC review of comprehensive plans or through CDC project consultants' monitoring activities.

Findings. TA engagements were defined not only by TA recipients and TA providers but also as a result of CDC's external reviews, which occurred annually and covered the adequacy of a CPG's comprehensive plan as well as the health department's official application for the upcoming year of prevention (not just planning) funding. TA needs most often arose when an external review judged a state's submission to be out of compliance (e.g., Idaho, Montana, Utah) or a specific component of the plan, such as priority setting, to be unsatisfactory (e.g., Montana, North Carolina).

When TA needs were externally defined in this manner, the subsequent comprehensive plans usually were found to be more compliant with CDC's requirements. The cases also showed that the community planning process was improved and the plans were better targeted for prevention initiatives. The first column of Exhibit 15.4 lists the experiences in the eight cases, indicating that external reviews initially played a role in defining the TA needs for half of them (Florida—statewide, Idaho, North Carolina, and Utah).

Over the course of the first four years, nearly all the CPGs' comprehensive plans have come to meet CDC requirements, reflecting CDC's five core objectives (CDC, 1998). Furthermore, CDC has indicated a continuing desire to "raise the bar" by adding new issues to be addressed over and above its five core objectives (CDC,

Exhibit 15.4 TA Features Related to Three Specific Hypotheses Discussed in the Text

State	H_2: Extent of External Definition of TA Objectives From CDC's External Reviews (1)	H_3: Extent That TA Providers Are From Multiple TA Organizations (2)	H_4: Extent That TA Engagement Consists of Multiple TA Events (3)
Florida *(Statewide)*	External review identified four limitations with state's epidemiologic profile.	All TA is provided by staff from one TA organization, CSTE.	CSTE staff person provided TA over an extended period of time, covering two months on site and later followed by two other on-site visits, including training workshops (hence, multiple TA events).
Florida *(Miami-Dade)*	CDC's external reviews played no role.	All TA was provided by one TA organization, AED. The individual TA providers were a TA consultant and two peer representatives, all arranged and supported by AED.	There were several TA activities (an open committee meeting, a public meeting, and a local summit). However, all occurred as part of the same event.
Idaho	External review found plan to be out of compliance with community planning guidelines.	TA involved staff or consultants from three different national TA organizations (AED, CSTE, and NASTAD), as well as a regional TA organization.	Major TA event was a conference; however, continued TA was arranged by AED for the following two years.
Mississippi	CDC provided supplemental funds to health department to support outreach to minorities.	TA involved staff from two TA organizations, NCNW and NAPWA, both selected by the TA recipient.	TA consisted of a single TA event—a forum.

(Continued)

Exhibit 15.4 (Continued)

State	H₂: Extent of External Definition of TA Objectives From CDC's External Reviews (1)	H₃: Extent That TA Providers Are From Multiple TA Organizations (2)	H₄: Extent That TA Engagement Consists of Multiple TA Events (3)
Montana	External review found state to be out of compliance with CDC's community planning guidance.	TA is provided by one TA organization and by state health department staff.	TA consisted of three events occurring over a year-long period.
Nebraska	CDC's external reviews played no role.	All TA was provided by one TA organization, AED. The individual TA providers were both AED staff and consultants.	TA was provided at multiple events over about a six-month period.
North Carolina	CDC's external review rejected the state's plan for 1996–1999, taking issue especially with the priority-setting effort, which in CDC's view "failed to weed anything out."	All TA was provided by two local TA providers. They worked together and received off-site TA from two national TA organizations (CSTE and NASTAD).	Two local TA providers delivered a series of TA events over a multimonth period; CPG pondered how to produce updated plan to cover next three-year period.
Utah	CDC's external review found the plan to be out of compliance in 1996.	TA was delivered by staff from USMBHA as well as consultants and staff from AED.	TA was provided at multiple events over a period of about 12 months.

1998). Over time, as CDC continues to expect more from the community planning process, the process is likely to improve and the plans to become increasingly comprehensive.

Possible Implications. Continuation of the direct links among the external reviews, the availability of TA, and the compliance requirements is likely to lead to continued improvements in the planning process. Furthermore, CDC should emphasize giving early signals to the TA providers regarding emerging requirements. Such early signals are needed so that the TA providers have time to assemble the needed expertise, anticipate the likely calls for new TA, and prepare high-quality responses.

H_3: Collaboration Among TA Providers

When TA providers are from multiple TA organizations, TA is more successful when the TA providers try to collaborate.

Findings. Collaboration among TA providers was defined as an occasion when persons representing two or more TA Network organizations provided joint TA. (The two persons might have been staff or consultants.) The overall frequency of such occasions is not clear, although the likelihood is that such TA is only a low proportion of all the TA. For instance, the tracking of all TA engagements by the Academy for Educational Development (AED) showed that most of the engagements involved AED staff or consultants. Among the eight cases, the proportion of joint TA was much higher (see Column 2 in Exhibit 15.4, which shows four of the eight having involved joint TA—Idaho, Mississippi, North Carolina, and Utah), but the eight cases are not claimed to be representative of the entire universe of TA provided by the TA Network.

The TA providers reported that collaborative TA, especially when involving on-site TA, did not occur more often because of its high cost, as well as the increased difficulty of scheduling such events to suit the TA providers and maximizing local participation. Thus, one TA provider noted that such a collaboration would be likely only when a CPG was in need of TA on multiple topics. This type of situation appeared in at least one of the eight case studies (Idaho), in which a broad variety of TA was provided to address the CPG's multiple needs.

At the same time, all TA providers expressed satisfaction with those occasions when collaborative TA had been provided, because the individual providers saw how their own special topics fit better with the other topics, and the CPG benefited from the explicit cross-linkages that had been created. Some of the TA organizations, however, only rarely collaborated with others.

Possible Implications. The high cost of collaborative TA efforts means that a joint TA engagement is likely to displace several single TA engagements (given the costs of arranging and scheduling, not just delivering the TA). The results are nevertheless beneficial, especially if a CPG has a complex or broad array of needs.

As a result, one possibility is for the organizations in the TA Network to budget, at the outset of any given year, a small and explicit number of joint TA engagements, apart from the single TA engagements. The TA Network would then set priorities for using these resources devoted to joint TA, separate from the resources devoted to single TA. Such a division of resources might increase the effective use of the limited TA resources.

The resources for joint TA should be used on those occasions when two or more different skills and issues are at stake—for example, PIR and epidemiologic profiles, or competition among two different minority groups. Such situations would appear to make the best use of this more costly type of TA.

H_4: Series of TA Events

Successful TA experiences involve a series of TA events that build on and support one another.

Findings. The notion of a series of TA events overlaps with the TA Network's definition of long-term TA. For instance, AED's TA briefing book for CPGs (AED, 1995, p. 7) defines short-term TA as limited phone consultation, one-time visits, and nonrecurring consultation with local, regional, or national TA providers. Long-term TA is defined as more than one site visit, or coordination among local, regional, or national providers over a period of time. At the same time, most of the TA providers did not distinguish between short- and long-term TA and could not provide information on the advantages of one over the other.

Column 3 of Exhibit 15.4 shows the distribution among the eight cases. Six of the eight cases involved multiple events, or long-term TA (Florida—statewide, Idaho, Montana, Nebraska, North Carolina, and Utah). Such long-term TA could include one or more on-site visits, spread apart and interspersed with phone TA (Florida—statewide). Some long-term TA extended over a period of a year or more (Idaho, Utah). Other long-term TA needs followed the annual cycles imposed by CDC, with a priority-setting plan, for instance, in need of being updated with the onset of the new planning cycle for the coming year(s) (North Carolina).

Possible Implications. The TA Network should continue to provide both single-event and series TA, not favoring one over the other. The TA Network might also consider routine follow-up assessments of the effectiveness of on-site TA, one to two months following an event, and holding a conference call with CPG representatives, the CDC project officer, and the TA providers to discuss follow-up or additional TA needs. AED currently follows this procedure, but the others in the TA Network do not. The objective would be to provide ongoing support to CPGs and to continually reinforce the importance of the community planning process and a responsive comprehensive plan. Follow-up TA could involve providers from the TA Network or from local TA providers.

H_5: Coordination With Other Federal Agencies

Successful TA provided by the TA Network is coordinated with HIV prevention and community planning TA provided by other federal agencies.

Findings. Few instances of coordination of the community planning process for HIV/AIDS prevention with community planning and prevention programs of other federal agencies were uncovered by the case studies or mentioned by the providers in the TA Network. In one case (Miami-Dade), the potential benefits from such coordination were considered sufficiently high that a local ordinance was enacted to create a single planning body to deal with four federal programs, including the CDC program.

CPGs and TA providers believe that the federal agencies themselves need to collaborate first, before encouraging any coordination at the CPG level. The requirements of the various federal programs have not been especially coordinated to date, and the fear is that the CPGs will get stuck with an entirely new set of problems that could have been averted had the federal agencies first taken care of matters properly.

Possible Implications. Any intention or plan to have the TA Network emphasize greater coordination across federal programs needs to be approached cautiously. Until it is evident that the requirements and procedures are more compatible, attempts at starting coordination at the local level might be difficult.

H_6: Informing National TA Providers of TA Network Activities

The TA Network is more effective when national TA providers are informed of the activities of the overall TA Network.

Findings. TA assignments generally focused on a single specialty such as needs assessment, epidemiologic profiles, PIR, or conflict resolution. Some TA providers were not necessarily knowledgeable about the other specialties in the process and especially about whether TA had previously been provided to a CPG with regard to the other specialties. For instance, there was no formal procedure in place, reported by the TA providers, whereby part of the preparation for a new TA engagement included retrieving information on any previous TA to either the same CPG or on the same topic (nor was there any database that included all previous TA done by all the TA organizations).

Over time, all members of the TA Network had become better informed about specialties besides their own, with at least two positive effects. First, diagnostic capabilities—and, therefore, the precision of referrals—had increased, potentially leading to better TA outcomes. Second, at least one individual TA organization noted that when pursuing its own specialty, knowledge or awareness of other specialties was useful in linking the TA to the other specialties. In this case, assistance on epidemiologic profiles was considered more useful when the TA provider was aware of the latest needs assessment and priority-setting practices being promoted so that the epidemiologic profile could be better connected to the needs assessment and priority-setting procedures.

Possible Implications. The TA Network has relied mainly on informal procedures to share information about its own activities and specialties, although more formal sharing has begun to occur. Examples of a more formal procedure are monthly conference calls among the TA providers and face-to-face meetings deliberately planned to occur in conjunction with other professional meetings. In this manner, the TA providers are using conferences and annual meetings as the occasion for holding working sessions among themselves. These and other modes of sharing should continue to be encouraged.

H_7: Reactive and Proactive TA

Both reactive and proactive TA need to be available.

Findings. The TA providers traditionally have assumed a reactive posture, at least with regard to on-site TA, and they made no claims to being proactive. In other words, although the availability of TA had been made known through general channels (including the distribution of pamphlets as well as communication through CDC project officers and other word-of-mouth techniques), the TA providers made no offers to specific CPGs regarding possible new TA assignments.

The most proactive TA occurred when a CPG had been found to be out of compliance with CDC's guidelines by CDC's external review. In those situations, the CDC project officer alerted the CPG to the need for TA and, in this sense, served as the proactive agent (e.g., Idaho, Utah). Thus, in this sense, proactive TA has been available.

Possible Implications. Unless CDC establishes a further rationale for proactive TA, the availability of proactive TA is likely to be limited to compliance situations.

H_8: Long-Range TA Planning

The planning process is more successful when CPGs engage in long-range TA planning in addition to serving other needs.

Findings. None of the cases showed strong evidence of long-range planning for TA on the part of the CPGs. Some TA engagements, such as assistance in establishing a single planning body to deal with the possible coordination of four federal programs (Miami-Dade), involved issues that would have potential long-range implications. However, the TA itself was not long-range. Evidence of the need for long-range planning arose in at least one case (North Carolina), where CPG members were concerned over their ability to update upcoming prevention plans, having benefited from TA on earlier plans. However, no mechanism had been put into place to anticipate the specific TA needs that could arise.

Possible Implications. A standing TA subcommittee or task force as part of every CPG—previously discussed under H_1, above—could serve as a coordinating body to increase consistency across TA episodes. This same subcommittee could define and plan for long-range TA, which might be to the benefit of many if not all CPGs.

INSIDE STORY FOR CHAPTER 15

Collecting Data From Social Networks

Studying formal networks of people or organizations can create additional barriers for you to overcome. In particular, although your case study may be aimed at differentiating the various roles in the network, the network members may prefer to present a more united front.

For instance, the present chapter deals with a network in which some organizations provide assistance to others. However, the service providers and service recipients may not have wanted to reveal all the actual difficulties in their transactions, fearing that a case study evaluation may then have concluded that their network needed to be altered in some manner. Despite some troublesome transactions, the providers and recipients might have become comfortable with each other and, hence, perceived any alteration as a threat to their network.

If you directly confront these matters as part of your fieldwork, you risk the possibility that the whole network will react negatively and jeopardize your entire study. Instead, your main alternative is to spend more time in the field than you might have planned and to pursue your inquiries in a patient and gentle manner. Your fieldwork demeanor and forthrightness will count a lot.

For Class Discussion or Written Assignment

Discuss the ways of gaining trust when studying networks of formal groups of people, including staff that may be part of the same organization. Having a key informant assist you in establishing your credibility with the group has been a frequent strategy of some well-known case studies. Discuss the possible challenges in managing a relationship with a key informant, and also suggest other ways of dealing with networks and formal groups.

NOTES

1. A separate methodology section in the original report describes the entire process for nominating, screening, and selecting the eight cases. In addition, the original cross-case synthesis contained numerous citations, not duplicated in the present chapter, referring to individual interviews, documents, or other sources of evidence that supported the specific assertions made in the text and especially the conditions described in the eight hypotheses.

2. The possibility exists that the nominating process was biased in favor of long-term TA engagements. Short-term TA engagements (involving only a single on-site event) may not have been sufficiently memorable (or might have been viewed as being too common or producing effects that were too transient) to be recognized during the nomination process.

REFERENCES

Academy for Educational Development. (1995). *Technical assistance briefing book for community planning groups.* Washington, DC: Author.

Alinsky, Saul D. (1946). *Reveille for radicals.* Chicago, IL: University of Chicago Press.

Alinsky, Saul D. (1971). *Rules for radicals: A practical primer for realistic radicals.* New York, NY: Random House.

Allison, Graham T. (1971). *Essence of decision: Explaining the Cuban missile crisis.* Boston, MA: Little, Brown.

Allison, Graham T., & Zelikow, Philip. (1999). *Essence of decision: Explaining the Cuban missile crisis* (2nd ed.). New York, NY: Addison-Wesley Longman.

Bradshaw, Ted K. (1999). Communities not fazed: Why military base closures may not be catastrophic. *Journal of American Planning Association, 65,* 193–206. [An abridged version of this article appears in Robert K. Yin, Ed., 2004, pp. 233–249.]

Bromley, D. B. (1986). *The case-study method in psychology and related disciplines.* Chichester, Great Britain: Wiley.

Buraway, Michael. (1991). The extended case method. In Michael Buraway et al. (Eds.), *Ethnography unbound: Power and resistance in the modern metropolis* (pp. 271–287). Berkeley, CA: University of California Press.

Campbell, Donald T., & Stanley, Julian. (1966). *Experimental and quasi-experimental designs for research.* Chicago, IL: Rand McNally.

Centers for Disease Control and Prevention. (1998, February). *External review of FY9H HIV prevention cooperative agreement applications: Summary of process and findings.* Atlanta, GA: Author.

Chen, Huey-tsyh. (1990). *Theory-driven evaluations.* Newbury Park, CA: Sage.

Chen, Huey-tsyh, & Rossi, Peter H. (1989). Issues in the theory-driven perspective. *Evaluation and Program Planning, 12*(4), 299–306.

Cook, Thomas D., & Campbell, Donald T. (1979). *Quasi-experimentation: Design and analysis issues for field settings.* Chicago, IL: Rand McNally.

Corbin, Juliet, & Strauss, Anselm. (2007). *Basics of qualitative research: Techniques and procedures for developing grounded theory* (3rd ed.). Thousand Oaks, CA: Sage.

COSMOS Corporation. (1985, December). *Attracting high-technology firms to local areas: Lessons from nine high-technology and industrial parks.* Bethesda, MD: Author.

COSMOS Corporation. (1989, September). *Interorganizational partnerships in local job creation and job training efforts.* Bethesda, MD: Author.

Creswell, John W. (2007). *Qualitative inquiry and research design: Choosing among five approaches* (2nd ed.). Thousand Oaks, CA: Sage.

Cronbach, Lee J. (1975). Beyond the two disciplines of scientific psychology. *American Psychologist, 30,* 116–127.

Downs, George W., Jr., & Mohr, Lawrence. (1976, December). Conceptual issues in the study of innovation. *Administrative Science Quarterly, 21,* 700–714.

Duneier, Mitchell. (1999). *Sidewalk.* New York, NY: Farrar, Straus, & Giroux.

Garvin, D. A. (1993, July/August). Building a learning organization. *Harvard Business Review,* 78–91.

Ginsburg, Alan L. (1989, December). Revitalizing program evaluation: The U.S. Department of Education experience. *Evaluation Review, 13,* 579–597.

Glaser, Barney G., & Strauss, Anselm L. (1967). *The discovery of grounded theory: Strategies for qualitative research.* Chicago, IL: Aldine.

Hayes, R. H., & Pisano, G. P. (1994, January/February). Beyond world class: The new manufacturing strategy. *Harvard Business Review,* 77–86.

Henrich, Joseph, Heine, Steven J., & Norenzayan, Ara. (2010). The weirdest people in the world? *Behavioral and Brain Sciences, 33,* 61–83.

Hersen, Michel, & Barlow, David H. (1976). *Single-case experimental designs: Strategies for studying behavior.* New York, NY: Pergamon.

Hooks, Gregory. (1990). The rise of the Pentagon and U.S. state building: The defense program as industrial policy. *American Journal of Sociology, 96,* 358–404. [An abridged version of this article appears in Robert K. Yin, Ed., 2004, pp. 69–83.]

Jacobs, Ronald N. (1996). Civil society and crisis: Culture, discourse, and the Rodney King beating. *American Journal of Sociology, 101,* 1238–1272. [An abridged version of this article appears in Robert K. Yin, Ed., 2004, pp. 155–178.]

Kellogg Foundation. (2004). *Using logic models to bring together planning, evaluation, and action: Logic model development guide.* Battle Creek, MI: Author.

Kelly, Anthony E., & Yin, Robert K. (2007). Strengthening structured abstracts for education research: The need for claim-based structured abstracts. *Educational Researcher, 36,* 133–138.

Kotter, J. P. (1995, March/April). Leading change: Why transformation efforts fail. *Harvard Business Review, 59–67.*

Lincoln, Yvonna S., & Guba, Egon G. (1985). *Naturalistic inquiry.* Thousand Oaks, CA: Sage.

Marwell, Nicole P. (2004). Privatizing the welfare state: Nonprofit community-based organizations as political actors. *American Sociological Review, 69,* 265–291.

Maxwell, Joseph A. (1996). *Qualitative research design: An interactive approach.* Thousand Oaks, CA: Sage.

Miles, Matthew B., & Huberman, A. Michael. (1994). *Qualitative data analysis* (2nd ed.). Thousand Oaks, CA: Sage.

Mohr, Lawrence. (1978, July). Process theory and variance theory in innovation research. In Michael Radnor et al. (Eds.), *The diffusion of innovations: An assessment.* Evanston, IL: Northwestern University.

Pascale, R., Milleman, M., & Gioja, L. (1997, December). Changing the way we change. *Harvard Business Review,* 127–139.

Patton, Michael Quinn. (2002). Two decades of developments in qualitative inquiry. *Qualitative Social Work, 1,* 261–283.

Pyecha, John N., et al. (1988). *A case study of the application of noncategorical special education in two states.* Research Triangle Park, NC: Research Triangle Institute. (Robert K. Yin collaborated in the design, conduct, and analysis of the research.)

Raynor, B. (1992, May/June). Trial-by-fire transformation: An interview with Globe Metallurgical's Arden C. Sims. *Harvard Business Review,* 117–129.

Reichardt, Charles S., & Mark, Melvin M. (1998). Quasi-experimentation. In Leonard Bickman & Debra J. Rog (Eds.), *Handbook of applied social research methods* (pp. 193–228). Thousand Oaks, CA: Sage.

Rosenbaum, Paul R. (2002). *Observational studies* (2nd ed.). New York, NY: Springer.

Rosenthal, Robert. (1966). *Experimenter effects in behavioral research.* New York, NY: Appleton-Century-Crofts.

Schein, Edgar. (2003). *DEC is dead, long live DEC: Lessons on innovation, technology, and the business gene.* San Francisco, CA: Berrett-Koehler.

Shavelson, Richard, & Towne, Lisa. (2002). *Scientific research in education.* Washington, DC: National Academy Press.

Small, Mario L. (2006). Neighborhood institutions as resource brokers: Childcare centers, inter-organizational ties, and resource access among the poor. *Social Problems, 53,* 274–292.

Small, Mario L. (2009). How many cases do I need? On science and the logic of case selection in field-based research. *Ethnography, 10,* 5–38.

Streiner, David L., & Sidani, Souraya (Eds.). (2010). *When research goes off the rails: What happens and what you can do about it.* New York, NY: Guilford.

Supovitz, J. A., & Taylor, B. S. (2005). Systemic education evaluation: Evaluating the impact of systemwide reform in education. *American Journal of Education, 26,* 204–230.

Sutton, R. I., & Staw, B. M. (1995). What theory is *not. Administrative Science Quarterly, 40,* 371–384.

Teske, Paul, Schneider, Mark, Roch, Christine, & Marschall, Melissa. (2000). Public school choice: A status report. In Diane Ravitch & Joseph P. Viteritti (Eds.), *Lessons from New York City schools* (pp. 313–338). Baltimore, MD: Johns Hopkins University Press. [An abridged version of this article appears in Robert K. Yin, Ed., 2005, pp. 177–204.]

Trochim, William M. K. (1989). Outcome pattern matching and program theory. *Evaluation and Program Planning, 12*(4), 355–366.

Upton, D. M. (1995, July/August). What really makes factories flexible. *Harvard Business Review,* 74–84.

U.S. Government Accountability Office. (1990). *Case study evaluations.* Washington, DC: Government Printing Office.

Van Maanen, John. (1988). *Tales of the field: On writing ethnography.* Chicago, IL: University of Chicago Press.

Walker, Edward T., & McCarthy, John D. (2010). Legitimacy, strategy, and resources in the survival of community-based organizations. *Social Problems, 57,* 315–340.

Watson, Dennis. (2010). Community-based participatory research: A lesson in humility. In David L. Streiner & Souraya Sidani (Eds.), *When research goes off the rails: What happens and what you can do about it* (pp. 254–262). New York, NY: Guilford.

Wholey, Joseph. (1979). *Evaluation: Performance and promise.* Washington, DC: The Urban Institute.

Yin, Robert K. (1981, January/February). Life histories of innovations: How new practices become routinized. *Public Administration Review, 41,* 21–28.

Yin, Robert K. (1982, September/October). Studying phenomenon and context across sites. *American Behavioral Scientist, 26,* 84–100.

Yin, Robert K. (1992). The case study method as a tool for doing evaluation. *Current Sociology, 40,* 121–137.

Yin, Robert K. (1994). Discovering the future of the case study method in evaluation research. *Evaluation Practice, 15,* 283–290.

Yin, Robert K. (1997). Case study evaluations: A decade of progress? *New Directions for Evaluation, 76,* 69–78.

Yin, Robert K. (2000). Rival explanations as an alternative to "reforms as experiments." In Leonard Bickman (Ed.), *Validity and social experimentation: Donald Campbell's legacy* (pp. 239–266). Thousand Oaks, CA: Sage.

Yin, Robert K. (Ed.). (2004). *The case study anthology.* Thousand Oaks, CA: Sage.

Yin, Robert K. (Ed.). (2005). *Introducing the world of education: A case study reader.* Thousand Oaks, CA: Sage.

Yin, Robert K. (2006). Case study methods. In Judith L. Greene, Gregory Camilli, & Patricia Elmore (Eds.), *Handbook of complementary methods in education research* (3rd ed., pp. 111–122). Washington, DC: American Educational Research Association.

Yin, Robert K. (2009a). *Case study research: Design and methods* (4th ed.). Thousand Oaks, CA: Sage.

Yin, Robert K. (2009b). How to do better case studies. In Leonard Bickman & Debra J. Rog (Eds.), *The SAGE handbook of applied social research methods* (2nd ed., pp. 254–282). Thousand Oaks, CA: Sage.

Yin, Robert K. (2011a). Case study methods. In Harris Cooper (Ed.), *APA handbook of research methods in psychology* (pp. xxx-xxx). Washington, DC: American Psychological Association.

Yin, Robert K. (2011b). *Qualitative research from start to finish.* New York, NY: Guilford.

Yin, Robert K., & Davis, Darnella. (2007). Adding new dimensions to case study evaluations: The case of evaluating comprehensive reforms. In George Julnes & Debra J. Rog (Eds.), *Informing federal policies on evaluation methodology* (New Directions in Program Evaluation No. 113, pp. 75–93). San Francisco, CA: Jossey-Bass.

Yin, Robert K., & Gwaltney, Margaret K. (1981, June). Knowledge utilization as a networking process. *Knowledge: Creation, Diffusion, Utilization, 2,* 555–580.

Yin, Robert K., & Moore, Gwendolyn B. (1988, Fall). Lessons on the utilization of research from nine case experiences in the natural hazards field. *Knowledge in Society: The International Journal of Knowledge Transfer, 1,* 25–44.

INDEX

SAGE Research Methods Online

The essential tool for researchers

Sign up now at www.sagepub.com/srmo for more information.

An expert research tool

- An **expertly designed taxonomy** with more than 1,400 unique terms for social and behavioral science research methods

- **Visual and hierarchical search tools** to help you discover material and link to related methods

- Easy-to-use navigation tools
- Content organized by complexity
- Tools for citing, printing, and downloading content with ease
- Regularly updated content and features

A wealth of essential content

- The most comprehensive picture of quantitative, qualitative, and mixed methods available today

- More than **100,000 pages of SAGE book and reference material** on research methods as well as editorially selected material from SAGE journals

- More than **600 books** available in their entirety online

Launching 2011!

$SAGE research methods online